The Power Of:™

RUNNING PC-DOS 3.3

Second Edition

**COMPLETE USER'S GUIDE
PLUS DOS UTILITIES
AND APPLICATIONS**

Carl Siechart and Chris Wood

MIS: PRESS

MANAGEMENT INFORMATION SOURCE, INC.

COPYRIGHT

Copyright © 1987, 1986 by Management Information Source, Inc.
1107 N.W. 14th Avenue
Portland, Oregon 97209
(503) 222-2399

Second Edition
First Printing

ISBN 0-943518-47-4

Library of Congress Catalog Card Number:87-24410

All rights reserved. Reproduction or use, without express permission of editorial or pictorial content, in any manner is prohibited. No patent liability is assumed with respect to the use of the information contained herein. While every precaution has been taken in the preparation of this book, the publisher assumes no responsibility for errors or omissions. Neither is any liability assumed for damages resulting from the use of the information contained herein.

The Power Of: is a registered trademark of Management Information Source, Inc.

IBM, IBM PC, IBM-AT, IBM PC-XT, PC Convertible, PC-DOS, and Personal System/2 are trademarks of IBM.
Intel 8088/8086 is a trademark of Intel Corporation
Lotus 1-2-3 is a trademark of Lotus Development Corporation.
EDLIN, MS-DOS, Microsoft, and Microsoft Word are trademarks of Microsoft.
Norton Utilities is a trademark of Peter Norton Computing, Inc.
Sidekick is a trademark of Borland International.
SuperCalc4 is a trademark of Sorcim Corporation.
WordStar is a trademark of MicroPro International Corporation.

DEDICATION

This book is dedicated to all those who have struggled with the DOS manual and to Barbara and Jan, who give us incentive (and encouragement) not to sit in front of our computers *all* the time.

ACKNOWLEDGMENTS

There are only two people's names on the cover, but there are others who contributed greatly to this book.

Most importantly, our associate and ghostwriter extraordinaire, Jim Law, deserves credit and thanks for his many contributions to this tome.

We would like to thank our friend and advisor Zach Bovinette for getting us into this business. His advice is good, and he has always been generous with his time, even when his own business keeps him working fourteen-hour days.

And we would be remiss if we did not thank our publisher, Bob Williams, for taking on this project, putting up with our whims, and still getting the first book about PC-DOS on the shelves, as well as this timely second edition.

TABLE OF CONTENTS

Introduction vii
   How to Use This Book vii
   Key Notations viii

SECTION I: INTRODUCTION TO PC-DOS 1

Chapter 1: Introduction to PC-DOS 3
   What DOS Can Do for You 5
   Version of DOS 5
      Is MS-DOS the Same as PC-DOS? 5
      Evolution of PC-DOS 6
      DOS 1.0 6
      DOS 1.1 6
      DOS 2.0/DOS 2.1 7
      DOS 3.0 7
      DOS 3.1 7
      DOS 3.2 7
      DOS 3.3 8
   Which Version to Use 8

Chapter 2: Fundamentals of DOS 11
   Disks and Disk Drives 12
      Types of 5-1/4" Diskettes 12
      3-1/2" Diskettes 14
      Types of Diskette Drives 15
      Compatibility of Drives and Diskettes 15
      Preparing Disks for Use 18
   Device Names 19
      One-drive Systems 21
   The Default Drive 21
   What is a File? 22
      Naming Files 22

Chapter 3: Directory Structures 25
   Tree-structured Directories 27
   Organizing your Disk 29
   Creating Directories 33
   Accessing Subdirectories 33
      Changing the Current Directory 34
      Specifying a Path to a File 35
      Using the PATH Command 36

    Displaying Directory Structures 37
    Removing Directories 38

Chapter 4: Redirection and Piping 41
    Redirection 42
        Redirecting Output 43
        Redirecting Input 45
        Combining Input and Output Redirection 47
        Standard Error 47
    Piping 48
    Combining Redirection and Piping 49

SECTION II: HOW TO USE THE DOS COMMANDS 51

Chapter 5: How to Use the DOS Commands 53
    Conventions Used in this Book 54
        Command Name and Version Number 54
        Internal and External Commands 54
        Functions 55
        Command Format 55
        Variables 56
        Options 56
        Comments 57
        Exit Codes 57
        Messages 57
        Examples 58
    How to Enter and Use the Commands 58
        DOS Editing Keys 58
    Wild Cards in File Specifications 60
    General DOS Messages 62

Chapter 6: DOS Commands 71
    APPEND 72
    ASSIGN 76
    ATTRIB 78
    BACKUP 82
    BREAK 90
    CHDIR or CD 92
    CHKDSK 96
    CLS 104
    COMMAND 105
    COMP 110
    COPY 114

CTTY	119
DATE	121
DEL	123
DIR	127
DISKCOMP	130
DISKCOPY	138
ERASE	146
FASTOPEN	147
FIND	149
FORMAT	154
GRAFTABL	167
GRAPHICS	169
JOIN	171
LABEL	173
MKDIR or MD	176
MODE (Redirect printer output)	179
MODE (Set asynchronous communications options)	181
MODE (Set color/graphics options)	184
MODE (Set printer options)	187
MORE	190
PATH	192
PRINT	195
PROMPT	202
RECOVER	207
RENAME	209
REPLACE	211
RESTORE	216
RMDIR or RD	224
SET	226
SHARE	228
SORT	230
SUBST	235
SYS	238
TIME	241
TREE	243
TYPE	245
VER	247
VERIFY	248
VOL	250
XCOPY	251

Chapter 7: Batch File Commands 257
    BATCH 258
    CALL 266
    ECHO 268
    FOR..IN..DO 271
    GOTO 273
    IF 275
    PAUSE 281
    REM 283
    SHIFT 285

Chapter 8: Configuration Commands 287
    Configuring Your System with CONFIG.SYS 288
    BREAK 289
    BUFFERS 290
    DEVICE 291
    ANSI.SYS 292
    VDISK.SYS 294
    DRIVER.SYS 296
    FCBS 300
    FILES 301
    LASTDRIVE 302
    SHELL 303

SECTION III: SUPPLEMENTAL PROGRAMS 305

Chapter 9: DOS' Word Processor: EDLIN 307
    Starting EDLIN 308
    Entering EDLIN Commands 309
    Entering Control Characters 311
    Displaying Text 312
        L Command 312
        P Command 314
    Editing Text 315
        I Command 315
        Edit Line Command 316
        D Command 316
        M Command 317
        C Command 317
    Automatic Search and Replace 318
        S Command 318
        R Command 320
    Ending an EDLIN Session 321

       E Command 321
       Q Command 322
    Other Features 322
    EDLIN Messages 323

SECTION IV: APPLICATIONS 325

Chapter 10: Setting Up a Diskette System 327
    Creating a Startup Diskette 328
       Configuring Your Startup Disk 330
       The STARTUP.BAT File 332
       Checking the Startup Disk 334
    Creating a Program Diskette 335
       Checking Your Disk 337
    Modifying START.BAT 339
    Creating Data Disks..340
    Organizing Your Files 341
    Protecting Your Data 341

Chapter 11: Setting Up a Fixed Disk System 343
    Starting Out With a New Fixed Disk 344
       Creating a DOS Partition 344
       Formatting the Fixed Disk 346
       Loading DOS onto the Fixed Disk 348
    Creating an Organized File Structure 350
       Naming Your Directories 351
       Creating a Startup Batch File 352
       Making a Configuration File..354
    A Menu System 356
    Starting a New Project 360

Chapter 12: Applications for Fixed Disk Users..363
    Moving Files Between Directories 365
    Making a Directory of Your Entire Disk 366
    Locating Files on a Fixed Disk 368
    Backing Up Your Fixed Disk 370
       Limitations of this Backup System 371
       Making Full Backups 371
       Daily Backups 372
    Duplicating Diskettes..374
    Returning to a Previous Directory 376

Chapter 13: Useful DOS Applications **377**
    A Time Log 378
        How to Use the Time Log 378
        The LOG.BAT File 380
        How LG.BAT Works 383
        For Diskette Users 385
    A Batch File Data Base 385
        How to Use the Phone List 385
        The PHONE.BAT File 389
        How PHONE.BAT Works 393
    A Simple Note Filer 395
        How to Use the Note Filer 395
        The NOTE.BAT File 397
        How NOTE.BAT Works 399
    A Printer Setup Command 400
        How to Use the PRINTER Command 401
        The PRINTER.BAT File 402
        How the PRINTER.BAT File Works 404
    Turning Your Printer into a Copier 404
        How to Use MPRINT 405
        The MPRINT.BAT File 405
        How the MPRINT.BAT File Works 407

Chapter 14: DOS Utilities **409**
    The Sorted Directory Command 410
        The DIRSORT.BAT File 411
        How DIRSORT.BAT Works 412
    Automatically Deleting Backup Files 413
        How to Use DELBAK 413
        The DELBAK.BAT File 414
        How DELBAK.BAT Works 415
    Adding Wild Card Capabilities to TYPE 416
        Using the TYP Command 416
        The TYP.BAT and TY.BAT Files 417
    Preventing Accidental Formatting 418
    A Low-cost Security System 418
    Using a Serial Printer 420
    Using Programs That Don't Understand Paths 421
        Using Old Programs with DOS Version 2 422

Index **423**

INTRODUCTION

If you use PC-DOS on an IBM Personal System/2, IBM-PC, PC-XT, PC-AT, or PCjr, or if you use MS-DOS on a compatible computer, then this book is for you. PC-DOS and MS-DOS are virtually identical, and this book covers the use of all versions of DOS from 1.0 through 3.3.

This book is not a beginning tutorial on how to use your computer; you should be familiar with how to turn it on, insert diskettes, and press keys on the keyboard. Beyond those simple prerequisites (which you can glean from your computer's guide to operations), this book will teach you the basics of DOS, provide a complete command reference, and show you how to use the power of DOS to create useful applications.

How to Use This Book

Section I of this book is an introduction to DOS, which will be most useful for the new user. If you've been using your computer for a while, you may want to skim through the chapters on versions of DOS and types of diskettes. Even experienced users, however, should find the information about tree-structured directories and redirection interesting. These concepts provide tremendous power and flexibility to those in the know, and they are often overlooked or misunderstood.

Section II provides a complete command reference to all of the useful DOS commands. While it may not read like a spy thriller, it is recommended that you skim through this section first, and then refer to it often as you use DOS. It is a more complete reference than that provided in the DOS manual, yet it is also more accessible. Explanations, recommendations, and examples show how and when to use each of the commands. And side tabs make it easy to find commands for later reference.

In an effort to keep the book from becoming too unwieldy, a few special-purpose commands have not been included. DOS includes several commands for programmers: BASIC, BASICA, DEBUG, EXE2BIN, and LINK; their use is beyond the scope of this book. And there are several commands that are used to change the characters that are displayed and printed (CHCP, KEYB, NLSFUNC, SELECT). Because these commands are not needed by most American users, they have been omitted from this manual to make it easier to find references to those commands that you will use frequently.

Section III explains a supplementary program provided with DOS, called EDLIN. It is a simple text editor that is ideal for creating and editing **batch files**, which are programs made up of DOS commands. Unless you already have another text editor with which you are familiar, read this section before you start into Section IV.

Section IV is where your accumulated knowledge of DOS is put to use. Chapter 10 describes how to set up a flexible and useful system if your computer uses floppy diskettes. Chapter 11 shows how best to organize a fixed disk system. The rest of the section contains useful utility and application programs for many purposes. The programs are ready to use, and they are fully explained so that you can use similar methods to create your own applications.

By the time you reach the comprehensive index, you too should understand the power of DOS.

Key Notations

Unless otherwise noted, information listed after the instruction "enter" indicates a command to be typed in from the keyboard. Each command is executed by pressing the **Return** key, which is noted as ⏎ after each command. The **Return** key is synonymous with the **Enter** Key. For example,

format ⏎

means to type in "format" and press the **Return** key.

Parenthetical expressions to the right of command entries are instructions to the reader and are *not* to be entered as text. For example,

^Z   (use the **F6** key)

represents an instruction to use the **F6** key to create the ^Z command.

SECTION I

INTRODUCTION TO PC-DOS

CHAPTER 1

INTRODUCTION TO PC-DOS

A logical place to begin a description of DOS and its applications is a definition. **DOS** (which most users pronounce as a word that rhymes with "boss" instead of enunciating each of the letters separately) stands for **Disk Operating System**.

To understand DOS, it is helpful to have a basic knowledge of the components involved. When you think of your computer system, you probably think first of its hardware: the system unit, which does all of the processing, the keyboard, through which you enter your commands, the display screen, through which the computer (and your programs) communicates with you, the printer, which provides printed output, and the disk drives. Whether you have floppy diskette drives or hard disk drives, they are a very important part of your system, for the disks are used to store programs and information (such as a word processing document or the numbers on a spreadsheet).

The hardware can't do anything without **software**. Software provides the instructions that tell the hardware exactly what to do. Programs you purchase or write for a certain function (such as accounting or word processing) are called **applications software**. A program like DOS is called **systems software**.

In general, an operating system is a program that provides an interface between the user, application programs (such as WordStar or Lotus 1-2-3), and the computer. It controls input to the computer (from the keyboard or disk files, for example) and output from the computer (such as to the display screen, a printer, or disk files).

More specifically, a disk operating system is designed to provide an easy way to use disks (either floppy diskettes or hard disks) for storage. DOS provides a method for organizing and using the information stored on disks that is (hopefully) understandable to you, your application programs, and the computer itself.

DOS tells the computer how to read the information you have stored on the disk by telling it exactly where the information is located on the disk surface. And it tells you (and your programs) how to save and retrieve information on the disk by giving you a directory of the files on that disk. You never need to know the physical location of the data on the disk (that is between DOS and the computer).

WHAT DOS CAN DO FOR YOU

To many users, DOS is a program that allows them to use other programs, nothing more. Each time they start up the computer, they load DOS (probably unknowingly, for it happens automatically) and then start an application program. Meanwhile, the DOS manual sits up on the shelf.

If you've gotten this far, you are one of those users who realizes there's more to this thing called DOS. By necessity (so you can run applications programs), it is always there, so you may as well use some of its features. Basically, DOS allows you to keep track of the information you store on disks. But through the use of its commands, you can keep records of your computer usage for tax or billing purposes or create a menu system for making your computer easier for casual users to operate (or more secure to keep out snoops). You can also automate tasks such as backing up files; you can print files making full use of your printer's features, and more.

VERSIONS OF DOS

MS-DOS (which stands for Microsoft DOS) was originally developed in 1980 for personal computers using Intel's 8088/8086 family of central processor chips. The most widely known computer in this category is the IBM Personal Computer. Following its huge commercial success was a swarm of "IBM compatibles" or clones from other manufacturers. The same processor chip and the same operating system (MS-DOS) give these clones the ability to use programs written for the IBM PC.

Is MS-DOS the Same as PC-DOS?

In this book, PC-DOS will be discussed, which is a version of DOS published by IBM for their PC and Personal System/2 families of computers. Like MS-DOS, it was developed by Microsoft Corporation, and there are, in fact, very few differences between the two. Nearly all of the information in this book applies to users of MS-DOS on "PC clones" as well as to users of the "true blue" IBM PC. The only difference you're likely to encounter will be in the discussion of some of the more obscure external commands in the reference section of this book. Some versions of MS-DOS do not include all of these commands.

Evolution of PC-DOS

More important than the distinction between MS-DOS and PC-DOS is the version number (for example, DOS 2.1). The needs of users, the requirements of application programs, and hardware capability have all changed radically since the first release of DOS. And sometimes bugs (errors) are discovered. To maintain DOS as a viable operating system, new releases are periodically made.

Major revisions are signified by the number before the decimal point (DOS 2.0, which supported the use of hard disks and added many new commands, replaced DOS 1.1). Minor changes are signified by increasing the number after the decimal point (DOS 2.0 was followed by DOS 2.1, which offered compatibility with the IBM PCjr but no significant improvements). For the most part, these minor changes are not noticeable, so this book will not distinguish between DOS 2.0 and DOS 2.1, for example. Instead, they will be referred to collectively as DOS 2 except when there is a functional difference.

DOS 1.0

PC-DOS Version 1.0 was released with the original IBM PC in August, 1981. Like the computer it was sold with, DOS 1.0 was a small, unsophisticated operating system by today's standards. It could only handle single-sided diskettes (with a storage capacity of 163,840 characters of information on each disk). Most personal computers sold then were equipped with 16K to 64K of random access memory, and DOS 1.0 worked well in this environment.

DOS 1.1

A short time after the release of DOS 1.0, double-sided diskette drives (with a storage capacity of 327,680 characters per disk) were introduced. DOS 1.1 made it possible to use these drives; in addition, printers with a serial interface were supported by an improved MODE command.

DOS 2.0/DOS 2.1

In 1983 IBM introduced the IBM PC-XT, which sported a hard disk drive. This computer prompted the release of DOS 2.0, which was able to organize and use files on a disk drive with more than thirty times the capacity of its earlier diskettes. To make it easy for the user to deal with the larger number of files on a disk, DOS 2.0 introduced tree-structured directories and volume labels for each disk. In addition, diskette capacity was increased, and 26 new DOS commands were added.

All the additional capabilities of the new DOS came at a price: not only did the more powerful programs require more storage space on disks, but they needed more main memory. IBM recommended that DOS 2 be used only in floppy-based systems with at least 64K of main memory or hard disk systems with at least 128K of main memory.

DOS 3.0

The release of DOS 3.0 coincided with the release of the IBM PC-AT. DOS 3.0 not only supports the faster processor speeds of the AT, but its high-capacity diskettes (1,228,800 characters—that's over 600 typed pages) as well. PC-DOS 3.0 also offered keyboard layouts for several languages.

DOS 3.1

IBM's next version of DOS added support for networking (a **network** consists of several computers wired together to share common peripherals and files). This support allows the use of DOS commands on a network disk, directory, or printer.

DOS 3.2

The next DOS release, announced in March, 1986, added support for its token ring network and the newest disk format: 3-1/2" diskettes. Like each release of DOS before it, a few new commands were added and several old commands were improved.

DOS 3.3

In April, 1987 IBM unveiled its Personal System/2 series of computers. Although their full potential may not be realized without Operating System/2, IBM chose instead to sell these computers with a new version of DOS (3.3). Compatibility with the PS/2 computers is DOS 3.3's most important new feature, although it added some new commands and made minor enhancements to several others. In addition, DOS 3.3 is the first version of DOS sold with both 5-1/4 and 3-1/2 inch diskettes.

WHICH VERSION TO USE

If you are using DOS now, and you are unsure which version you have, take a look at the screen when you start DOS by turning on the computer with a DOS disk in drive A (drive A is the disk drive that lights up when you turn on the computer—normally the one on the left or the bottom), or by "re-booting" when you simultaneously press the Ctrl, Alt, and Del keys with a DOS disk in drive A. After you enter the date and time, a copyright notice and the version number will appear as part of the startup display. An easier way to determine which version you are presently using is with the DOS VER (Version) command. At the A> prompt (the **prompt** is DOS' on-screen signal to you that it is ready to receive a command; to get to the prompt, place a DOS diskette in drive A and turn on your computer), type

ver ⏎

The screen will display the following response:

```
IBM Personal Computer DOS Version   3.3
```

Be sure to execute the command by pressing the **Return** key (noted throughout the book as ⏎) after typing the command line. The use of DOS commands is more fully explained in Chapter 5.

Many application programs are considered obsolete the moment a new release is announced; sales of the old version are discontinued and users are offered an upgrade to the newest version (often at a hefty fee). This obsolescence is not necessarily true with systems programs such as DOS, however. In fact, earlier releases are often sold and supported for some time after the newest version is introduced because the earlier version still has all the capabilities required by some users.

So which version should you use? The choice is dictated, in part, by your hardware. If you use a hard disk for storage, you must use DOS 2 or higher. If you use an IBM PC-AT (or compatible) with high capacity diskettes, you must use DOS 3 or higher. If your computer is part of a network, you should use DOS 3.1. If, on the other hand, you have a floppy diskette system with a small amount of memory (64K or less), you are better off with DOS 1 (a better alternative would be to add some more memory; DOS 2 added many useful features).

The applications software you use will also be a factor. Some programs require the use of a certain version (or higher) of DOS; many of the newer programs available require at least DOS 2 (this requirement is usually stated on the outside of the package). In general, DOS is "upward compatible"; that is, anything that was written for DOS 1 will work on DOS 1, DOS 2, or DOS 3; any program that requires DOS 2 will work with DOS 2 or DOS 3; and so on. (Unfortunately, there are a few programs that violate this convention. They might, for instance, use the space reserved for a future DOS function at a time when that function didn't exist as a part of DOS. When a later release of DOS does claim that space, there is a conflict. If you should find a program that works with an earlier version of DOS, but not the latest release, contact the program publisher.)

CHAPTER 2

FUNDAMENTALS OF DOS

In the first chapter, several types of diskettes were mentioned on which you could store information. This chapter covers the various diskette formats in more detail. More importantly, you'll learn how to start using those diskettes: what a file is and how it's put on a diskette. To get the most out of this chapter, get your DOS diskette, a blank diskette or two, and have a seat in front of your computer; you'll have a chance to use them shortly.

DISKS AND DISK DRIVES

DOS allows you to store information on a variety of media, including fixed disks, 3-1/2" disks, and 5-1/4" floppy diskettes. Throughout the brief history of IBM PCs and PC-DOS, 5-1/4" disks have changed considerably, resulting in a variety of (sometimes incompatible) disk formats (a **format** defines the physical layout of the information on a disk). At the risk of getting too mixed up with bytes and sectors, you should understand the various disk formats in order to avoid any compatibility problems.

Types of 5¼" Diskettes

Through the evolution of disk drive technology and DOS, several diskette formats have been developed. The diskettes themselves haven't changed: they are all 5-1/4" floppy diskettes. What has changed as disk drives have improved is the way information is stored on the disk, which is determined by DOS (within the limitations of the disk drive). To understand the differences among the various diskette types, you might find it helpful to know about the physical structure of the disk, which is shown in Figure 2.1.

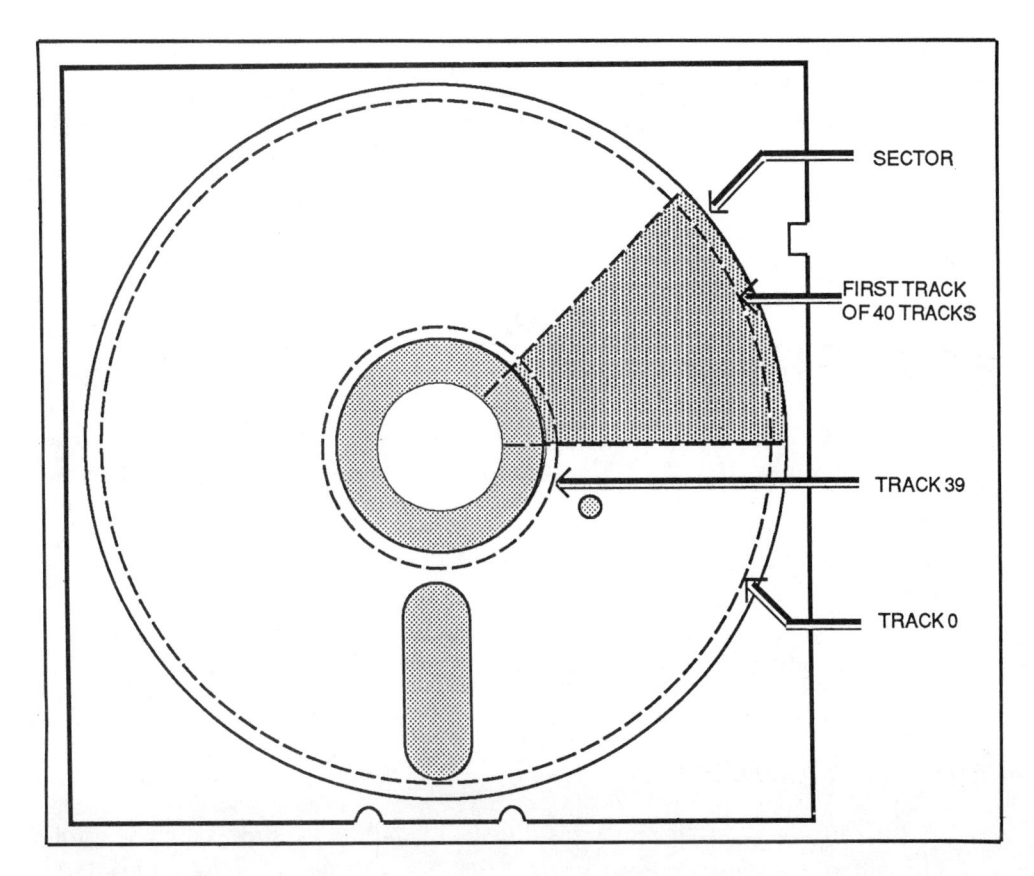

*Figure 2.1 Information on a diskette is written along concentric circles, which are called **tracks**. Each track is divided into sections called **sectors**.*

The capacity of a diskette is measured in **bytes**. A byte is a single character: a letter, a number, or a special symbol. Information is stored in blocks of 512 bytes; each block is called a **sector**. The different disk capacities are determined by the number of sectors in each **track** (tracks form a series of concentric circles on the diskette), the number of tracks on each side of the disk, and the number of sides in use. Table 2.1 summarizes the various 5-1/4" diskette formats used by DOS.

13

Type	Sides/disk	× Tracks/side	× Sectors/track	× Bytes/sector =	Bytes/disk	
Single-sided	1	40	8	512	163,840	160KB
Single-sided	1	40	9	512	184,320	180KB
Double-sided	2	40	8	512	327,680	320KB
Double-sided	2	40	9	512	368,640	360KB
High-capacity	2	80	15	512	1,228,800	1.2MB

**Table 2.1
Types of Diskettes**

In the interest of brevity when the various disk types are discussed, the capacity is usually stated in **kilobytes** (abbreviated as **KB**) or **megabytes** (**MB**). A kilobyte is 1,024 bytes (if you're wondering why kilo doesn't mean 1,000 in this context, as it usually does, it's because nearly everything computer scientists do is based on binary arithmetic; 1,024 is equal to 2^{10}). A megabyte is 1,024 kilobytes (or 1,048,576 bytes or 2^{20} bytes). So the disk types described in Table 2.1 are commonly referred to as 160KB, 180KB, 320KB, 360KB, and 1.2MB respectively.

3½" Disks

With the introduction of the IBM PC Convertible in 1986 came a completely new type of disk for PC-DOS users: the 3-1/2" disk. This type of disk differs from the old 5-1/4" diskettes not only in size, but also in construction with its hard plastic case.

There are presently two types of 3-1/2" disks recognized by DOS. Double-sided disks with a capacity of 737,280 bytes (720KB) can be used on any PC with a 3-1/2" drive running DOS 3.2 or higher. The 3-1/2" drives available with the PS/2 computers can format disks with 1,474,560 bytes (1.44MB). These drives require the use of DOS 3.3 or higher.

Types of Diskette Drives

Diskette drives come in a variety of sizes (one-third height, half-height, and full-height), colors, and door configurations. These differences are merely superficial; the real differences can't be seen from the outside, but they are crucial in determining which types of diskettes the drive can read from and write to (getting information from a disk is called **reading**; saving information on a disk is called **writing**).

To date, there are three types of 5-1/4" disk drives used in IBM PCs and compatibles. The first type is **single-sided**; it has only one read/write head and can use only one side of the disk. It wasn't long until **double-sided** drives were introduced. They have a read/write head on each side of the disk, doubling the amount of usable disk storage. The IBM PC-AT came with **high-capacity** drives. The read/write heads are more sensitive, and they move from track to track in smaller steps, allowing nearly four times the storage capacity of double-sided drives.

IBM (and the clone makers) offer two types of 3-1/2" disk drives. The first type, introduced with the PC Convertible, is known as a 720KB double-sided drive. These drives can read from or write to 720KB disks. The Personal System/2 computers come with the second type: 1.44MB double-sided drives. These drives can read from and write to both 3-1/2" disk formats (720KB and 1.44MB).

Compatibility of Drives and Diskettes

So why are the different types of 5-1/4" drives and diskettes important? As long as you are using one version of DOS on a single computer with your own diskettes, it doesn't really make much difference. But if you have a computer at home and one at work with different disk drives, or you ever exchange disks with another user, or you ever purchase programs on disk, it is important to understand the differences. Not every version of DOS will read every type of disk on every type of disk drive.

If you know which type of disk drives you have, Table 2.2 will show you which version of DOS you must use and which types of disk formats your drive can read from and write to.

If you are unsure which drive type you have, the DOS FORMAT command can be used to tell you. This command will prepare a new disk for use by DOS and is described later in this chapter.

5-1/4"

If you have this drive type	and you use one of these DOS versions	you can read/write these disk formats
Single-sided	All	160KB
Single-sided	2.0 and above	160KB, 180KB
Double-sided	1.1 and above	160KB, 320KB
Double-sided	2.0 and above	160KB, 180KB, 320KB, 360KB
High-capacity	3.0 and above	All*

*High-capacity drives can read and write all five disk formats; however, a disk written by a high-capacity drive in one of the lower capacity formats may not be readable on a single- or double-sided drive due to alignment differences.

3-1/2"

If you have this drive type	and you use one of these DOS versions	you can read/write these disk formats
720KB double-sided	3.2 and above	720KB
1.44mb	3.3 and above	All

**Table 2.2
Disk drive compatibility**

If you have a disk with a known format, use Table 2.3 to see on which types of systems the disk can be used.

If you are unsure of how a particular disk is formatted, DOS has a command that can tell you: CHKDSK (which is short for Check Disk). It will display several facts about the disk, including its total capacity. To try the command, place your DOS disk in drive A, and at the A> prompt, enter

chkdsk ⏎

The screen will display the following information:

```
362496 bytes total disk space
 38912 bytes in 3 hidden files
320512 bytes in 39 user files
  3072 bytes available on disk

524288 bytes total memory
317408 bytes free
```

Remember to execute the command by pressing the **Return** key. In this example, CHKDSK reports 362496 bytes of total disk space, so it is a 360KB disk.

5-1/4"

With this disk capacity	you must use one of these DOS versions	on one of these drive types
160KB	All	All
180KB	2.0 and above	All
320KB	1.1 and above	Double-sided or high-capacity
360KB	2.0 and above	Double-sided or high-capacity
1.2MB	3.0 and above	High-capacity

3-1/2"

With this disk capacity	you must use one of these DOS versions	on one of these drive types
720KB	3.2 and above	All
1.44MB	3.3 and above	1.44MB double-sided

**Table 2.3
Disk type compatibility**

Preparing Disks for Use

Throughout this chapter, the term "format" has been used and various formats, or disk layouts, used by DOS have been described. But how does a particular format get on a disk? The DOS FORMAT command prepares the disk for use by creating an empty directory of the contents of the disk, as well as defining the physical layout of the information that will be placed on it. All disks must be formatted before they can be used by DOS.

Caution is necessary when using FORMAT, since it *deletes all the information* from a disk. If you are not careful, the command could just as easily "prepare" a disk that is not new and has valuable information on it.

Fortunately, there is an easy way to protect disks from accidental erasure. On 5-1/4 inch diskettes (except some on which you purchased programs, including, possibly, PC-DOS), there is a notch in the upper right corner of the disk jacket called the **write-protect notch**. If you cover it with a silver self-adhesive tab (which comes with diskettes), information (including format information) cannot be written to the disk. If you are using 3-1/2 inch disks, then you'll notice a small sliding tab in the upper right corner. To write-protect a 3-1/2 inch disk (i.e., prevent erasure), slide the tab so that you can see through the little window.

To use the FORMAT command, you'll need your DOS disk and a blank, unused disk. Put the DOS disk in drive A, and at the A> prompt, enter

format a:⏎

The screen will display the following message:

```
Insert new diskette for drive A:
and strike ENTER when ready
```

At this point, put the diskette that you want to prepare in drive A and then press the **Return** key (with DOS versions earlier than 3.0, you can press any key to start the process). It will take a few seconds for the program to do its work, but soon you'll see this message displayed:

```
Formatting...Format complete
362496 bytes total disk space
362496 bytes available on disk

Format another (Y/N)?n
```

Be sure to put in the blank disk when prompted by the system; this command will destroy any information that was previously placed on that disk.

When you issue this command as shown, it will format the diskette to the maximum capacity of the disk drive. (In the previous example, the program shows that the disk has 362496 bytes of total disk space, so the drive must be double-sided.)

Now that you have safely created a new disk, you can remove the write-protect tab (or close the window on a 3-1/2 inch disk) on your original disk. If you don't remove the tab, you won't be able to save any more information on the disk.

There are many more options to the FORMAT command; they are discussed in detail in Chapter 5.

DEVICE NAMES

Several references to drive A have been made. "A" is the name DOS uses when referring to a particular disk drive. A disk drive is one example of a **device**, which is really just a fancy term for a place to send or receive information. But disk drives are not the only places where DOS sends and receives information. Other devices include the keyboard, the display screen, and the printer.

So that DOS knows with which device it is supposed to be communicating at any given time, each device is given a name. Disk drives are given one-letter names: the first floppy disk drive is drive A; the second is drive B, and the first fixed (or hard) disk drive is called C. If you have more disk drives, they are lettered alphabetically, right through Z. Table 2.4 shows the other device names used by DOS; you'll need these names if, for instance, you want to print a file.

In DOS commands, disk drive names are followed by a colon (for example, when you refer to drive A you type "A:"). The colon reduces confusion (on DOS' part as well as yours) between device names and file names or commands. This convention holds true in most application programs as well, except for a few which, when specifically asking for a drive name, save you the extra keystroke.

The other DOS device names shown in Table 2.4 are **reserved**; you cannot use them as file names. If DOS allowed you to use these words as file names, it would not be able to tell when you are referring to a file and when you are referring to the device.

DOS name	Description
A:	First diskette drive
B:	Second diskette drive
C:	First fixed disk drive
D: - Z:	Additional disk drives
CON	Console (which includes keyboard and screen)
COM1	First serial (also known as asynchronous) port
COM2	Second serial port
COM3	Third serial port
COM4	Fourth serial port
AUX	Same as COM1
LPT1	First parallel printer
LPT2	Second parallel printer
LPT3	Third parallel printer
PRN	Same as LPT1
NUL	Null (dummy) device, used for testing applications

**Table 2.4
Device names used by DOS**

One-drive Systems

If you have only one floppy disk drive (even if you also have a fixed disk drive, as on an IBM PC-XT), DOS refers to it as both drive A and B. But, in this instance, A and B represent diskettes instead of physical disk drives. DOS will tell you which disk to insert (A or B) when it is necessary. This feature allows you to copy a file from one disk to another with just one disk drive, for example.

THE DEFAULT DRIVE

Several times in this chapter the A> prompt has been mentioned. This signal from DOS contains an important piece of information: the fact that drive A is the **default drive**, which means that when you give DOS a command, if you don't specify a disk drive, it will assume that you mean drive A. This feature saves some keystrokes when you enter commands.

For example, earlier in this chapter you entered the following command:

chkdsk ⏎

Without the default drive feature, this command would have to be entered as

a:chkdsk a: ⏎

The first "a:" tells DOS where to look for the CHKDSK command; the second "a:" tells DOS which disk to check. Even with DOS' default drive feature, this is a perfectly acceptable way to enter the command; it is just more work than necessary.

If you want to change the default drive so that DOS assumes you are referring to drive B except when you specifically mention another drive by name, at the prompt, type

b: ⏎

The screen will display the following:

    B>

Note how the prompt changes to let you know the default drive. (If you have a one-diskette drive system, DOS will ask you to insert a disk for drive B; you remove the first disk and replace it with another one.)

WHAT IS A FILE?

As previously mentioned a high-capacity disk can hold more than 600 typed pages of information. Without some sort of organization, that information would be practically useless; that's where **files** come in. A file consists of related information on a disk (much like a file folder in a filing cabinet). Each file has a unique name so that when you want DOS to find information, you tell it the name of the file to look in.

Naming Files

You can store hundreds of files on a disk, depending on the capacity of the disk and the size of the files. To distinguish among them, each file must have a unique name.

The name of a file consists of two parts: a **file name** and a suffix called an **extension**. The file name can be up to eight characters long, and the extension can be up to three characters. The file name is separated from the extension by a period, for example,

income86.cal

"Income86" is the file name; "cal" is the extension.

File names can be from one to eight characters long, and you can use letters, numbers, and most of the special characters available on the IBM PC. In fact, you can use any character except the following:

(space) " * + , . / : ; < = > ? [\ ] |

Extensions can be from one to three characters long. The same character restrictions exist for file names and extensions. File extensions are optional; when you name a file, you do not have to use an extension. But the extension is an important part of the file name; it provides enough information for DOS to distinguish between different files. For example, DOS will recognize SALES.JAN and SALES.FEB as two different files.

Typically, extensions are used to describe the type of file. Some commonly used file extensions are shown in Table 2.5. The first four extensions in the table are recognized by DOS as containing the type of information indicated in the table. The others are examples of extensions automatically added by application programs.

Extension	Usage
.BAT	Batch files (see Chapter 7)
.COM	Command (program) file
.EXE	Executable program file
.SYS	DOS system information
.BAK	Backup file
.BAS	BASIC programs
.CAL	Spreadsheet files
.DBF	Data base files
.DOC	Word processing documents
.WKS	Lotus 1-2-3 worksheets

**Table 2.5
Common file extensions**

In naming files, you should be as descriptive as possible. While it may be convenient for you to use a very short name, when a disk directory becomes full it may be difficult to remember just what each file contains.

In the next chapter, you will see how to organize your disks so that directories don't become large and unmanageable.

CHAPTER 3

DIRECTORY STRUCTURES

In the last chapter, files and file names were discussed. So that DOS can find your files, it maintains a **directory**. The directory is essentially a list of the files on a disk and their locations, but it contains some other key information, such as the size of each file and the date and time the file was created or last modified.

You can look at a disk's directory with the DIR command. Its use is fully explained in Chapter 6, but you can try it in its simplest form to see a disk directory. At the system prompt, enter

dir ⏎

The screen will display the following information:

```
Volume in drive A is PC-TALK
Directory of A:\

TALK128    BAT        10    4-24-83
TALK64     BAT        23    4-24-83
PC-TALK    EXE     82048    9-08-83    10:01P
PC-TALK    BAS     34449    9-08-83     9:48P
PCTKREM    MRG      3584    4-24-83
COPYTALK   BAT      1152    4-24-83
README     DOC       384    4-24-83
PC-TALK    DEF       640    5-01-84     7:08A
PC-TALK    KEY      5248    5-01-84     7:08A
PCT        BAS     45326    9-06-84     6:00A
       10 File(s)    82272 bytes free
```

The disk directory shown here is fairly small since the disk contains only 10 files. The techniques described in this chapter apply mainly to fixed disk users since those directories can be very large. Even diskette users may want to use tree-structured directories, however. With ever-increasing disk capacities, directory management could be very difficult if all the files were kept in one directory. Can you imagine trying to find a file in a directory of a full hard disk as hundreds of file names scroll by? Naturally, DOS has a way to manage directories easily.

TREE-STRUCTURED DIRECTORIES

Instead of storing the names of all files in one large directory, DOS allows you to create several directories, with each one containing related files. Because these directories are organized as a series of subdirectories, if they are diagramed, the structure consists of a series of branches extending from a root—hence the name **tree-structured directories**. The result is a directory system that prevents overcrowding in any particular directory. A typical directory structure is shown in Figure 3.1.

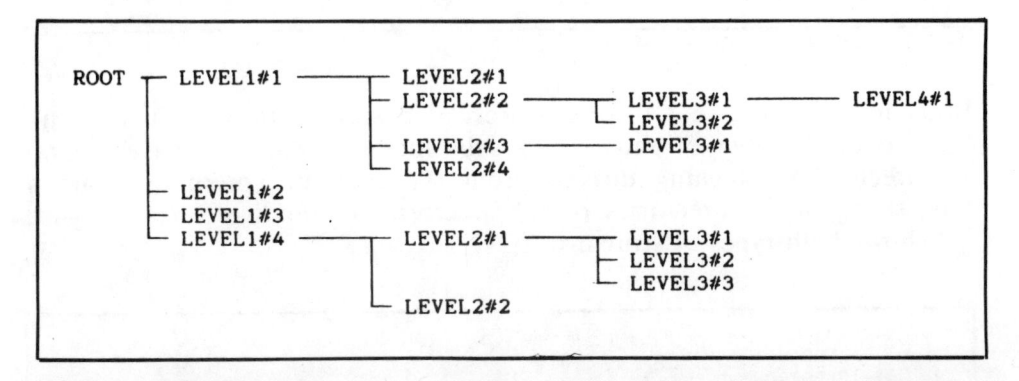

```
ROOT ─┬─ LEVEL1#1 ─┬─ LEVEL2#1
      │            ├─ LEVEL2#2 ─┬─ LEVEL3#1 ──── LEVEL4#1
      │            │            └─ LEVEL3#2
      │            ├─ LEVEL2#3 ──── LEVEL3#1
      │            └─ LEVEL2#4
      ├─ LEVEL1#2
      ├─ LEVEL1#3
      └─ LEVEL1#4 ─┬─ LEVEL2#1 ─┬─ LEVEL3#1
                   │            ├─ LEVEL3#2
                   │            └─ LEVEL3#3
                   └─ LEVEL2#2
```

Figure 3.1 DOS' directory structure starts at the root, with subdirectories branching from there.

Every disk has a **root directory**, which is created by DOS when the disk is formatted. If no subdirectories are created, the root will be the only directory. When you start DOS, you will be in the root directory. The root directory of a disk can hold a fixed number of entries—an **entry** is either a file name, a subdirectory name, or a volume label. The maximum number of directory entries for each type of disk is shown in Table 3.1.

Disk type	Maximum directory entries
160KB/180KB 5-1/4"	64
320KB/360KB 5-1/4"	112
720KB 3-1/2 inch"	112
1.2MB 5-1/4 inch"	224
1.44MB 3-1/2"	224
Fixed disk	512

**Table 3.1
Maximum entries in root directory**

Branches from the root directory are called **subdirectories**. There is no limit to the number of entries in a subdirectory. You may have several subdirectories branching directly from the root, or you may create a long string of subdirectories of subdirectories of subdirectories. Figure 3.2 shows both types of structure.

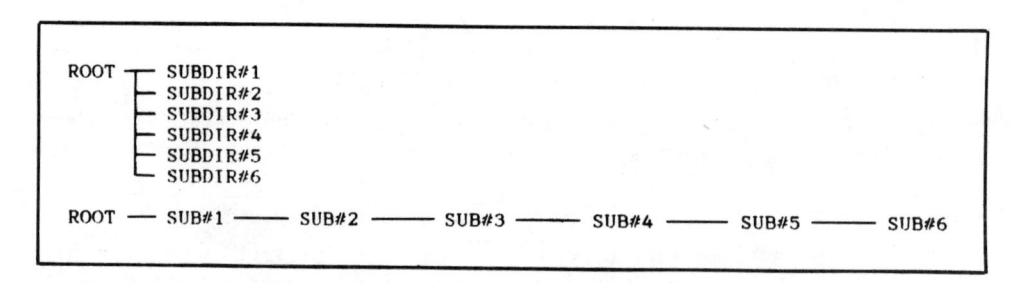

```
ROOT ─┬─ SUBDIR#1
      ├─ SUBDIR#2
      ├─ SUBDIR#3
      ├─ SUBDIR#4
      ├─ SUBDIR#5
      └─ SUBDIR#6

ROOT ── SUB#1 ── SUB#2 ── SUB#3 ── SUB#4 ── SUB#5 ── SUB#6
```

Figure 3.2 Subdirectories can be created directly from the root or created as subdirectories of subdirectories.

ORGANIZING YOUR DISK

There are advantages to each approach shown in Figure 3.2. By creating many subdirectories as branches directly out of the root (the first approach shown in Figure 3.2), you can switch quickly from one subdirectory to another without a lot of keystrokes. (To change directories, you must specify its name and the path DOS must follow to find it, which normally consists of the names of all the subdirectories along that branch.) However, if you create many directories as branches from the root, you'll end up with a crowded root directory where it may be difficult to find the particular file or subdirectory you are looking for. And preventing crowded directories is the primary reason for having tree-structured directories. You might conclude that a long series of subdirectories in one branch (like the second structure in Figure 3.2) is best. It would certainly keep any single directory from becoming too crowded with subdirectory names. Alas, this strategy too has its drawbacks. Specifying the path to a subdirectory way down the line would be time-consuming (and you would need to remember the proper order). Also, most DOS commands and many application packages don't allow a path specification longer than 63 characters.

So the best method lies somewhere in between. You will want to create a few "major" subdirectories from the root, with each of those containing a few subdirectories. As a general rule, don't go more than three levels deep. Making subdirectories at greater depths not only requires typing longer path names, but such an approach slows down the computer when it must look through many directories to find a file.

To determine what your overall structure should be like, you'll need to consider how your computer and its disk files are used. For example, if you have a fixed disk that is used by several people, you may want to create a subdirectory for each person's files, as shown in Figure 3.3. When Paula wants to write a letter, she merely changes to the directory \PAULA\LETTERS (a complete subdirectory name consists of the names of each subdirectory along the branch, separated by backslashes). In a company with several departments sharing a computer, the structure could be divided by function, as shown in Figure 3.4.

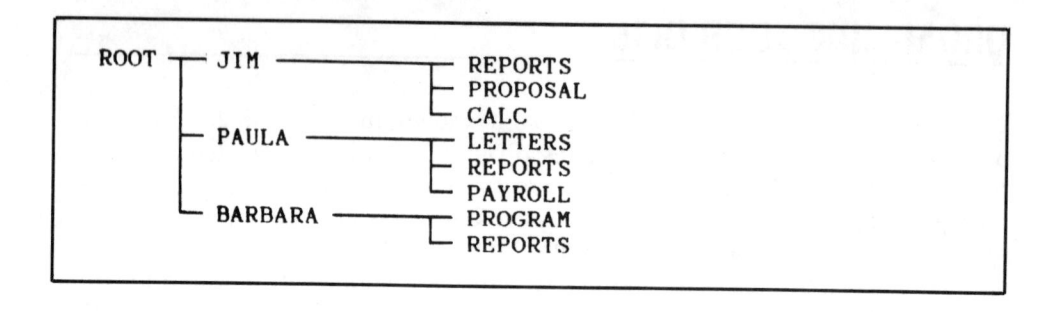

```
ROOT ─┬─ JIM ──────────┬─ REPORTS
      │                ├─ PROPOSAL
      │                └─ CALC
      ├─ PAULA ────────┬─ LETTERS
      │                ├─ REPORTS
      │                └─ PAYROLL
      └─ BARBARA ──────┬─ PROGRAM
                       └─ REPORTS
```

Figure 3.3 This directory structure would be useful for several people sharing one computer.

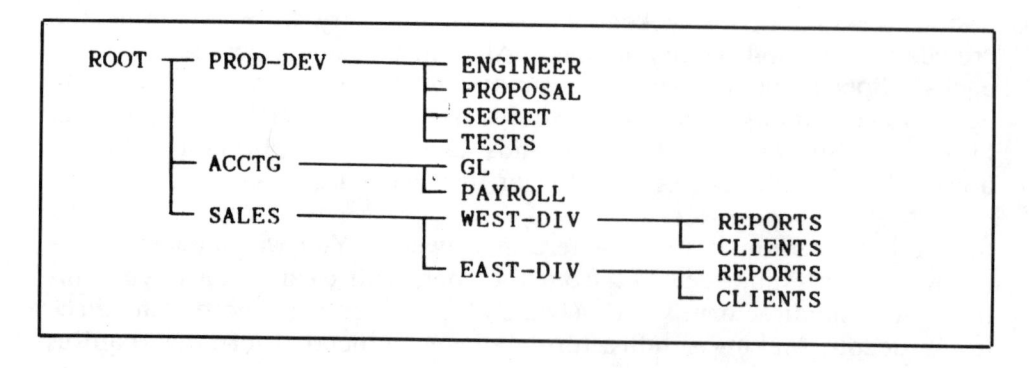

```
ROOT ─┬─ PROD-DEV ─────┬─ ENGINEER
      │                ├─ PROPOSAL
      │                ├─ SECRET
      │                └─ TESTS
      ├─ ACCTG ────────┬─ GL
      │                └─ PAYROLL
      └─ SALES ────────┬─ WEST-DIV ─┬─ REPORTS
                       │            └─ CLIENTS
                       └─ EAST-DIV ─┬─ REPORTS
                                    └─ CLIENTS
```

Figure 3.4 A directory structured along functional lines can be useful in a small company.

A single user may want to divide a disk according to the type of programs used. This structure is shown in Figure 3.5. This directory structure will be used in several examples throughout the Command Reference and Applications sections of this book, so it will be described in greater detail. (If you have a fixed disk system and you have not yet set it up, you may want to follow the instructions in Chapter 11 for setting one up now. This way, you can actually try the examples shown in the rest of this chapter.)

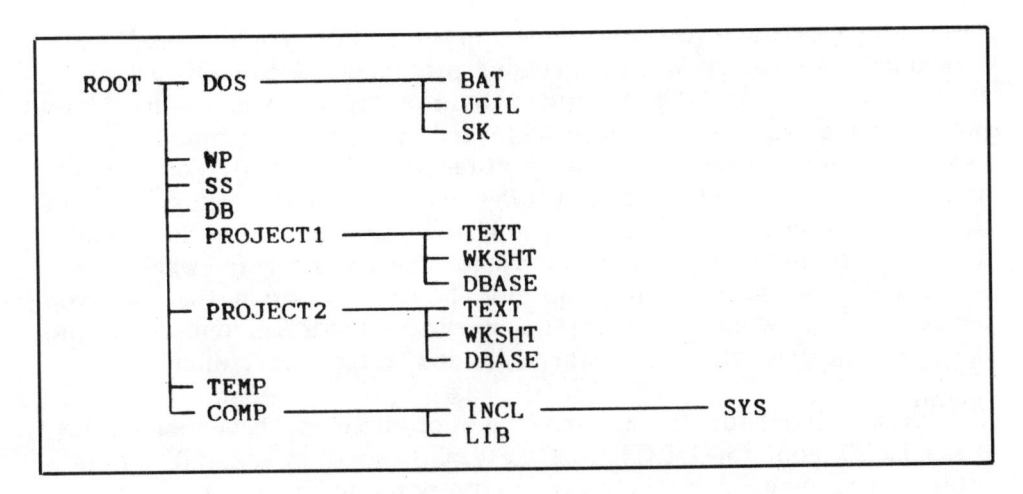

```
ROOT ─┬─ DOS ──────────┬─ BAT
      │                ├─ UTIL
      │                └─ SK
      ├─ WP
      ├─ SS
      ├─ DB
      ├─ PROJECT1 ─────┬─ TEXT
      │                ├─ WKSHT
      │                └─ DBASE
      ├─ PROJECT2 ─────┬─ TEXT
      │                ├─ WKSHT
      │                └─ DBASE
      ├─ TEMP
      └─ COMP ─────────┬─ INCL ───────── SYS
                       └─ LIB
```

Figure 3.5 For the DOS applications presented in this book, a directory structure typical of a single-user system is used.

The root directory contains only the necessary startup files (COMMAND.COM, CONFIG.SYS, and AUTOEXEC.BAT) and several subdirectories. You won't be spending much time in the root directory.

The \DOS subdirectory contains all of the files from your DOS diskette and three subdirectories: \BAT, \UTIL, and \SK. \BAT contains all of the batch files you write (except AUTOEXEC.BAT, which must be in the root directory). \UTIL contains useful utility programs that you acquire to manage your hard disk, change key functions, recover erased files, etc. There are many of these programs available, either commercially (such as Norton Utilities), through electronic bulletin boards, or in magazines. You are bound to pick some up, and this subdirectory is a good place in which to keep them. \SK is used in the example to hold SideKick (a desk utility that pops up with a calculator, appointment calendar, and notepad on your screen) and its related files.

DIRECTORY STRUCTURES

The next three subdirectories shown in Figure 3.5 contain application programs. \WP has a word processing program; \SS contains a spreadsheet program, and \DB holds a data base management program. Many programs require a subdirectory dedicated to their use (some programs even create such a directory during installation; Microsoft Word, for example, creates a directory named \MSTOOLS). Each directory contains the program and its associated files, such as help files and printer drivers—essentially everything that came with the program when it was purchased. These directories do not, however, contain the files you create (such as word processing documents, spreadsheet templates, and data base files), so you will not need to look in them very often.

The next two subdirectories from the root directory have been called \PROJECT1 and \PROJECT2. They can be used to separate different projects you may be working on: a proposal for a major contract, a book, or an experiment to find a cure for the common cold. These subdirectories would not contain any files at all; they would each contain a few subdirectories dividing up the files used in the project. \PROJECT1\TEXT would contain word processing documents associated with project #1; \PROJECT1\WKSHT would contain spreadsheet files, and \PROJECT1\DBASE would contain all the necessary data base files. \PROJECT2 is divided in the same way, and its subdirectories have the same names.

The next directory is named \TEMP, and it is used to hold files temporarily, which can be useful for copying many files from one diskette to another if you have a single-drive system; by copying the files to the \TEMP directory of the fixed disk, and then copying that entire directory to the target diskette, you save a lot of time spent disk swapping. It is also handy if you modify a program or file and want to try the new version before destroying the original; just store the old version in \TEMP until you're sure you won't need it.

The last subdirectory from the root is called \COMP, which could be used by a programmer to contain a program compiler (if you're not a programmer, a compiler converts a program as it's written into a format the computer can understand). The subdirectories shown contain different types of subroutines that can be accessed by the compiler: \COMP\INCL and \COMP\INCL\SYS contain "include" and "system include" files, and \COMP\LIB contains library files.

Of course, you may have different needs or different programs; this example is only a suggestion for a useful structure for a particular situation.

CREATING DIRECTORIES

The first step in using tree-structured directories is creating subdirectories, which is done with the MKDIR (for Make Directory) command. This command can be typed as MKDIR or MD; either format is acceptable. It is more fully explained in Chapter 6, but you can quickly see how it works with this example, which sets up part of the directory structure shown in Figure 3.5. From the C> prompt, type the following commands:

md \project1 ⏎

md \project1\text ⏎

md \project1\wksht ⏎

md \project1\dbase ⏎

ACCESSING SUBDIRECTORIES

Now that you know what a directory structure is, you'll need to know how to maneuver around that structure and access files and programs from the various subdirectories, which can be done by changing the current directory, specifying the path to a file, or using the DOS PATH command.

Changing the Current Directory

An important concept when using tree-structured directories is knowing what the **current directory** is. In Chapter 2, the default drive was discussed; it is the one that shows up at the DOS prompt and the one that DOS always looks at unless you specifically name another. The current directory is similar; it is the directory you are currently working in, and if you type a command, DOS will look only in that directory unless you specify a different directory.

When you start DOS, you are in the root directory of the default drive. To change the current directory to one of the subdirectories, you can use the CD (for Change Directory) command, which is fully described in Chapter 6. Like the MD command, it has a longer version: CHDIR. You can try it now by typing

cd \project1\text ⏎

DOS doesn't tell you that you have changed directories; it merely responds with the usual prompt. If you want to see that you really have changed the current directory, you can use the DIR command to look at the files of the directory you are in. In addition, the DIR command shows the path of the directory at the top of its display. An easier way to see that you changed the current directory is to use the CD command again, this time without any path specification. Type

cd ⏎

The screen will display the following:

    C:\PROJECT1\TEXT

This time, DOS responds with the name of the current directory.

DOS keeps track of a current directory in each drive, not just in the default drive. So if, after the previous example, you change the default drive to A, \PROJECT1\TEXT will still be the current directory on drive C. Any reference you make to drive C will look only at that directory (not the root directory) until you change it or specify another.

Specifying a Path to a File

By specifying the path to a file, most DOS commands and most of the newer application programs allow you to work with files that are not in the current directory. To specify a path, you need to name all of the subdirectories along the branch to a file, followed by the file name, and separate the names with backslashes. For example, you could display a file in \PROJECT1\TEXT by entering

```
type \project1\text\ltr2don.doc
```

There are some special symbols used in path specifications. A backslash at the beginning of the path name tells DOS that the path starts with the root directory. A backslash by itself is a complete path specification; it refers to the root directory.

To be safe, you can always specify a complete path starting at the root directory, as was done in the previous example; this strategy would work no matter what the current directory is. If the root directory is the current directory, you could have entered

```
type project1\text\ltr2don.doc
```

(without the first backslash) and received the same result. If another directory was the current directory, however, DOS would start its search in that directory. It would look for a subdirectory of the current directory named PROJECT1.

Two periods (..) are used as another symbol in path specifications. They indicate the parent directory of the current directory. For example, if the current directory is \PROJECT1\TEXT, then a specification of ..\DBASE is equivalent to \PROJECT1\DBASE. This specification provides a shortcut going back towards the root. Figure 3.6 shows how these symbols can be used to refer to another directory from within any directory.

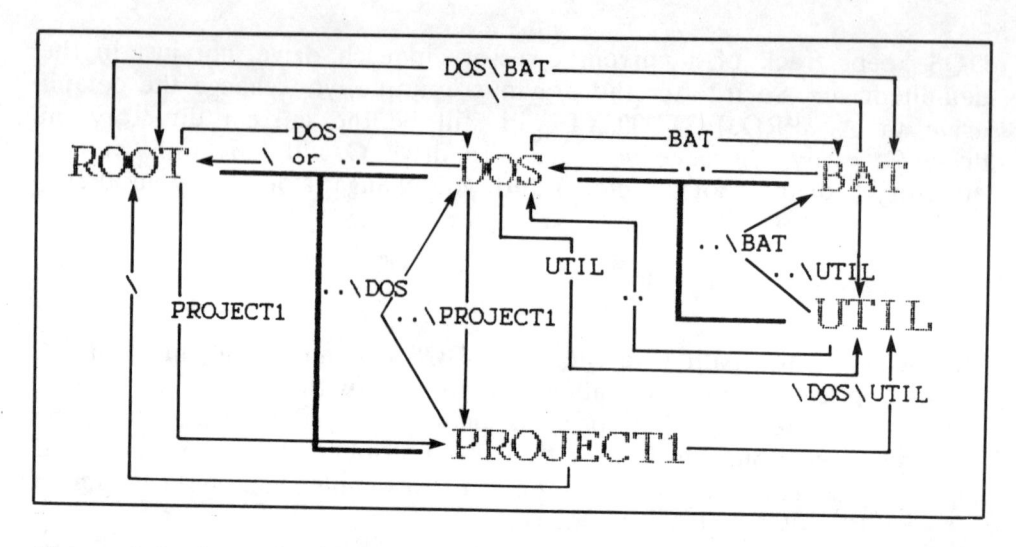

Figure 3.6 Instead of specifying the complete path to a directory, there are shortcuts for referring to other directories from within any directory.

Using the PATH Command

So that you can keep all of your programs together instead of repeating them in each subdirectory where you will be using them, DOS has a method of searching for programs through the use of the PATH command.

This command sets up a search path that DOS will use to find programs that are not in the current directory. It can only be used to search for programs with the extension .COM, .EXE, or .BAT. To see how the PATH command works, enter

chkdsk⏎

The screen will display the following message:

    `Bad command or file name`

Then enter

path c:\dos⏎
chkdsk⏎

The first time you try the command, DOS cannot find the CHKDSK command in the current directory. After using the PATH command, if DOS can't find the program in the current directory, it will look in the path (or paths) specified in the command and then execute the program when it finds it. DOS will keep using this search path until you change it with another PATH command or reboot.

The PATH command can be very powerful and is usually included as part of the AUTOEXEC.BAT program that runs each time you start DOS. You will see how this command works in Chapter 11.

DISPLAYING DIRECTORY STRUCTURES

DOS has a command to help you keep track of tree-structured directories. The TREE command displays a list of the subdirectories (and files if you want to see them) on your disk. It is an external command (a separate program file that DOS must find in order to execute), so make sure that it is in your current directory or on a PATH before you try using it. To display a list of subdirectories and the files they contain, enter

tree /f⏎

If the display scrolls off the screen before you have a chance to read it all, then you'll be interested in the next chapter, for DOS has a solution to this problem.

REMOVING DIRECTORIES

If you later decide that you don't need a directory that you have created, you can remove it with the RMDIR or RD (Remove Directory) command. Before a subdirectory can be removed, it must be empty; it cannot contain any files or subdirectories. For example, if you finish project #1, you can free up some space on your disk by archiving (or copying) those files to diskettes and then removing them from the fixed disk. To do that for the \PROJECT1\TEXT subdirectory, at the C prompt, enter

cd \project1\text ⏎

Then enter

copy *.* a: ⏎

The screen will display the names of the files being saved:

>   OUTLINE.DOC
>   REPORT.DOC
>   2 File(s) copied

Then enter

del *.* ⏎

The screen will respond with the following question:

>   Are you sure (Y/N)?

Type

Y ⏎

and then enter

cd .. ⏎

Finally, enter

rd text ⏎

This series of commands obviously includes a few that haven't been discussed yet, but they are included here to make the example complete. The commands perform the following functions: After changing to the \PROJECT1\TEXT directory, all files in the directory are copied to the diskette in drive A. The next line deletes all files in the directory before changing directories to the parent directory—\PROJECT1 in this example. This command is executed before removing the directory because you cannot remove the current directory; you must change out of it before removing it.

CHAPTER 4

REDIRECTION AND PIPING

By this time, you have used DOS commands enough to know that many commands display information on the screen and ask you to answer some questions by typing at the keyboard. This process involves **standard output** (the display screen) and **standard input** (the keyboard). These are the devices through which DOS normally expects to communicate with you. Beginning with version 2, DOS has a powerful feature called **redirection**.

REDIRECTION

Redirection is the ability to take DOS' standard output or input and redirect it to (or from, in the case of input) a different device or file. This feature has many uses. The DIR (directory) command, for example, can be directed to the printer instead of the screen so that you will have a hard copy to work with. Or it could be directed to a file for future reference or further processing by another program. Anything that a DOS command normally displays on the screen (except standard error output, which is described later in this chapter) can be directed to another device or file; any input normally typed at the keyboard to a DOS command can be directed from another device or file.

Redirection is accomplished with three symbols, which are shown in Table 4.1. The format for using redirection is as follows:

command symbol devicename

or

command symbol filespec

command can be any DOS command that is typed at the DOS prompt. The complete command, including any variables and options, should be typed there. These commands are all described in Chapters 6 and 7. (In addition, a few application programs permit the use of input/output redirection; check the program manual, or try it out yourself.)

symbol is one of the three redirection symbols shown in Table 4.1.

devicename can be any valid DOS device name. Table 2.4 (from Chapter 2) contains a complete list of these names.

filespec is defined as *[d:][path]filename.ext*, which specifies the drive name, directory, file, and extension to which output is sent or from which input is received.

Symbol	Usage
>	Redirects the output of a program
>>	Redirects the output of a program and adds the text to an existing file
<	Redirects the input of a program

**Table 4.1
Symbols used for redirection.**

Redirecting Output

To see how redirecting output works, try the following command, which will print a directory of the root directory of the disk in drive B. Enter

`dir b:\ > prn`⏎

In this example, the output of the DIR command is sent to the PRN device, which is the parallel printer port (refer to Table 2.4 for a list of DOS device names).

Fixed disk users who usually use drive A for diskettes can adjust the command format slightly to print the root directory on drive A. Enter

`dir a:\ > prn`⏎

In fact, you can change any of the examples in this chapter in a similar fashion.

While the printer may be the device to which you most often send data, any output device will work (such as COM1, which could be connected to a modem).

43

Instead of redirecting output to a device (such as the printer), output can be redirected to a file, for example, with this command:

`dir b:\ > dir.txt`⏎

To be sure that this command worked, with the TYPE command, try displaying the file you just created:

`type dir.txt`⏎

A word of caution is in order here. If you direct output to a file, DOS will create a file with the name you specify. If a file already exists with the same name, DOS will *without warning* destroy the old file and create a new one containing the redirected output. *Be sure that the file you name for output does not already exist or does not contain any information you want to save.*

Redirected output can also be **appended** to an existing file. Perhaps you want to create a file containing the names of files in both disk drives. This file could then be sorted or manipulated in some other way to make it easier for you to keep track of your files. The following example will add a directory of the disk in drive A to the file you already created, which contains a directory of drive B. At the prompt, enter

`dir a:\ >> dir.txt`⏎

Now, if you display the DIR.TXT file with the TYPE command, you should see both directories. The original file was not destroyed (as it would if the ">" symbol had been used); instead, the output was added to the end of the existing file.

If the file does not exist on the drive and in the directory named in the command, ">>" will create the file.

Redirecting Input

Some commands and other programs require input from the keyboard, which can be redirected from another device or a file. If the input is to come from a file, the file must contain all the responses in exactly the order the program expects them.

For example, perhaps there are a few important files that you want to check periodically to make sure that nothing (or nobody) has changed them. You can use the COMP (compare) command to verify that the files match your originals. Instead of repeatedly answering COMP's prompts for the names of the files to compare, all the answers could be put in a "script," such as the following (you would press **Return** at the end of each line):

```
copy con comp-in
origfile.001
b:\
Yprogfile.bas
b:\
Ydatafile.dat
b:\
N^Z        (^Z is obtained by pressing the F6 key)
```

The screen would display the following message:

```
    1 File(s) copied
```

Note in the script that the "Y" and "N" responses to COMP's "Y/N" (yes/no) queries are not on lines by themselves because COMP does not expect to find a **Return** keystroke after the answer; it acts immediately after receiving a single letter.

To use the script, all you would need to do is enter the command with redirected input. COMP will look to the file named COMP-IN for answers to its questions. Enter

```
comp <comp-in⏎
```

The screen will display the following:

```
Enter primary file name
origfile.001

Enter 2nd file name or drive id
b:\

A:ORIGFILE.001 and B:\ORIGFILE.001

Files compare ok

Compare more files (Y/N)? Y

Enter primary file name
progfile.bas

Enter 2nd file name or drive id
b:\

A:PROGFILE.BAS and B:\PROGFILE.BAS

Files compare ok

Compare more files (Y/N)? Y

Enter primary file name
datafile.dat

Enter 2nd file name or drive id
b:\

A:DATAFILE.DAT and B:\DATAFILE.DAT

Files compare ok

Compare more files (Y/N)? N

A>
```

Combining Input and Output Redirection

The redirection symbols can be combined in a single command for even more power and flexibility. For example, the DIR.TXT file you created earlier can be used as input to the SORT command, with its output redirected to another file, which creates a file with a list of all the files on both disks, sorted alphabetically. Enter

```
sort < dir.txt > sortdir.txt⏎
```

You can display the contents of the SORTDIR.TXT file with the TYPE command.

There is an easy trick to remembering which redirection symbol to use in each instance: the arrow points the way. For redirected output, the arrow points *to* the file or device where you want output sent. For redirected input, the arrow points *away from* the input file, towards the command where the input goes.

Standard Error

In addition to standard output, DOS sends some messages to **standard error**, which is always the display screen; standard error cannot be redirected. Actually, this result works out for the best, for certain prompts really don't need to be directed to a file or other device; they are intended for the person sitting at the computer. Most of the time, these messages tell the user to insert a new diskette or take similar action.

To see the difference between standard output and standard error, try the DOS BACKUP command. Enter

```
backup a: b: > prn⏎
```

The screen will display the following:

    Insert backup source diskette in drive A:
    Strike any key when ready

    Insert backup diskette 01 in drive B:

    Warning! Files in the target drive
    B:\ root directory will be erased
    Strike any key when ready

Insert a blank, formatted disk in drive B when prompted; all files on drive A will be backed up to that diskette. Note that all the disk change prompts are still displayed on the screen (these are standard error), while a list of the files backed up is redirected to the printer. If you have a fixed disk, the BACKUP command should be used religiously, and this method provides you with a printed directory of your backup diskettes. To see how this command normally works, try entering it without the "> prn" redirection.

PIPING

Piping is similar to redirection. Instead of output being redirected to a file, however, a pipe connects two programs so that the output of one program becomes the input of another program. The symbol used for piping is the vertical bar character (|).

In Chapter 3, you tried the TREE /F command and watched futilely as the list of files scrolled off the screen before you could read them all. You could have used redirection to send the screen output to a file, and then used that file as input to the MORE command, which displays a screenful of text and waits for you to strike a key. That process could be done in two steps by entering

```
tree /f > tree.txt⏎
more < tree.txt⏎
```

An easier way would be to connect the two programs (TREE and MORE) with a pipe, using the output of TREE as the input of MORE. Enter

tree /f ¦ more⏎

MORE is a **filter** program. It takes characters from standard input (redirected from TREE, in this example), processes or filters the characters, and sends them to standard output (the screen). The filtering done by MORE is simple: it merely counts the characters sent to the screen and pauses for you to strike a key when the screen is full. Other filter programs included with DOS are SORT, which rearranges the input information before displaying it, and FIND, which extracts certain information from the input and ignores the rest when sending it to standard output.

When you use piping with DOS, you must have some extra space on the disk for temporary files that DOS will create. In the example above, DOS saves you some keystrokes by combining two commands into one by using piping. Internally, however, it works much like the preceding example; it creates a file that contains output from the first program to be used as input to the second program. DOS will automatically erase the file when it is done, but the space must be available on the disk when you start the command.

COMBINING REDIRECTION AND PIPING

Redirection and piping can be combined for added flexibility. For example, the combined disk directory file (DIR.TXT) can be sorted and displayed one screenful at a time with the following command:

sort < dir.txt ¦ more⏎

As another example, you could take the DIR.TXT file and create a new file that would be an alphabetically sorted directory of all the files created in 1986. At the prompt, enter

find "-86 " dir.txt ¦ sort > 1986dir⏎

Only the lines in DIR.TXT that contain "-86 " (the last part of the date field in the directory) are extracted by the FIND command. These lines become input to the SORT command, which sorts them alphabetically. Finally, the output of the SORT command is redirected to a file named 1986DIR.

Experiment with redirection and piping. They are not the easiest DOS features to understand, but they add tremendous power. You will use them more in the applications section of this book.

SECTION II

HOW TO USE THE DOS COMMANDS

CHAPTER 5

HOW TO USE THE DOS COMMANDS

The first section of this book gave you some basic information about what DOS is and what it does. You even tried using a few DOS commands. Hopefully, it was enough of an introduction so that you have some idea of DOS' capabilities and enough to interest you in learning more about each DOS command. This section discusses each DOS command in detail.

CONVENTIONS USED IN THIS BOOK

Beginning in Chapter 6, each command is described in detail, including all of its options. For easy future reference, each command starts on a new page. The format for all of the command descriptions is the same, and that format will be described here so you'll know the key features to look for.

Command Name and Version Number

At the top of the page, you'll find the name of the command and a brief summary of what it does. Immediately below the summary is a version number. This number indicates the first version of PC-DOS in which the command appeared. None of the early DOS commands have been deleted, so each command is a part of all versions of PC-DOS, starting with the number shown. If you are using a version of DOS earlier than the indicated number, then any reference to that command will not apply to your system.

Some DOS commands have changed slightly over the years. In this book, the latest version (PC-DOS 3.3) is described, but if there are any significant differences in earlier versions, they are mentioned.

Internal and External Commands

Next to the earliest version number is a single word describing the type of command: either **internal** or **external**. Internal commands are actually a part of DOS resident in memory whenever DOS is running. They can be used at the DOS prompt even if a DOS disk is not in the drive.

External commands are separate programs; they are not really part of DOS proper. Like application programs, they are stored on disk until you use them. To see a list of the external command programs, look at a directory of your DOS disk. The command programs do not remain in memory; after a command has been executed, it must be read from a disk if you want to use it again. So whenever you want to use an external command, it must be on a disk currently in a disk drive. With DOS 3, the command program can be in any drive or directory; you can call it by specifying the name of the drive and directory before the command. For example, from the prompt, you would enter

c:\dos\chkdsk⏎

In earlier DOS versions, the command program must be in the current directory of the default drive or in a directory specified with the PATH command; you cannot specify the drive and directory when you invoke the command.

Functions

Beneath the earliest version and internal/external indicators and next to the "Functions" heading is a description of what the command does.

Command Format

The "Format" section shows the syntax of the command. Parts of the command that do not change are shown in uppercase letters, although you do not need to type them that way. You must type the letters or words exactly as shown, except that either upper- or lowercase letters are acceptable (for convenience, lowercase letters are usually used, and all the examples are shown with lowercase letters).

Parts of the command format are shown in *italic* letters. These are called variables and should be replaced with information you provide (usually the name of a file).

Square brackets ([]) are used to enclose parts of the command that are optional. The command will take some action if everything within the brackets is left out, although it may not be what you had in mind. When using the command, do *not* type the brackets; they are included here only to indicate which parts of the command are optional.

A few commands have options that can be one of two possibilities (either ON or OFF, for instance). These two possibilities are shown one above the other, separated by a line. Enter either one (in upper- or lowercase), but not both.

Variables

Most commands require the input of some variable information (the information that will replace the italic terms in the command format section). Each of the variables shown in the command format is described here so that you'll know what to type in place of the variable name.

One variable that shows up in almost all the commands is **filespec** (short for file specification). A complete file specification consists of a drive name (including the colon), the path to a file, the file name, and extension. There should be no spaces within the file specification. Fortunately, you needn't type in the complete file specification every time you want to access a file. If the file is on the default drive, the drive name is not needed. If the file is in the current directory, the path is not needed. Relative path specifications may be used: the path to a file in a subdirectory can start with the current directory instead of the root directory.

Note that in many commands, the file name and extension are shown as optional. In most cases, they are only optional if you specify a drive or path instead of a file name. Then the command will affect all the files in the given directory instead of a single file.

Options

Many DOS commands have optional switches that activate special features. In most cases they consist of a slash (/) followed by a single letter, which may be typed in upper- or lowercase. Each of the options is described in this section.

Some options can be one of two possibilities (either ON or OFF, for instance). These options are also described in this section.

Comments

Following the "Comments" heading is a complete description of how the command works. Use this section to see why the command is used and where it would be most helpful in your situation. In addition, hints and suggestions for the command's practical usage are included here.

Exit Codes

A few DOS commands issue **exit codes** when they finish. These codes are special flags which indicate if everything went normally during command execution, or if there was some type of error condition. The exit code can be tested with the IF ERRORLEVEL batch subcommand, which is explained in Chapter 7.

Messages

Nearly all DOS commands generate some messages that are displayed on the screen. Some are informational; they let you know what the command is doing. Some are warnings; they let you know that the command is about to destroy some information unless you stop it. Many are prompts; they tell you to insert diskettes in the proper drive or ask if you want to proceed. And, of course, some are error messages; they tell you that you did something wrong or that the command can't find the files you specified.

All the messages generated by the command are shown in this section, along with a list of the probable causes and, most importantly, the action you should take if you do encounter one of the messages.

The exact wording of the messages has changed slightly from one version of DOS to another, but you should be able to find any message in this section, no matter which version of DOS you use.

Examples

Perhaps the most important part of each command's description is the examples section. Here, you'll find practical examples (along with explanations) of the command's use.

HOW TO ENTER AND USE THE COMMANDS

All DOS commands should be typed when you see the prompt (which is normally A), or they should be entered through batch files. As previously mentioned, DOS commands can be typed with either lower- or uppercase letters (there are a few exceptions, and they are noted in the command descriptions). DOS doesn't process a command until you enter it by pressing the **Return** key.

DOS Editing Keys

If you are as fumble-fingered as most PC users, you'll sometimes make mistakes when typing DOS commands. If you notice the mistake before you press the **Return** key, there are two ways to correct the error. (Actually, there are three ways if you count using the **F5** key, which will be covered shortly.)

The first is to use the **Backspace** key (above the Return key, it has a left-pointing arrow on it), which will delete the character to the left of the cursor and move the cursor one space to the left. You can use it repeatedly, going back all the way to the left end of the line if necessary. The left arrow key has the same effect as the backspace key in DOS command lines. The second error correction key is the **Escape** key, which cancels everything you have typed on the current line. The line isn't erased from the screen, and the cursor drops to the next line (but not the left end of the line); however, you are starting anew after pressing Escape.

Sometimes, you will see that you made a mistake after you enter a command (which will usually give you an error message). At other times, you will find yourself repeating a command (or a similar command). DOS has some useful features for both of these situations.

DOS stores the most recent command you entered in a buffer and allows you to edit the command and enter it again. You use the function keys F1 through F5 for editing the command line. The key functions are summarized in Table 5.1.

Key	Function
F1	Copies one character from buffer to command line
F2*x*	Copies all characters up to first occurrence of *x*
F3	Copies all characters from cursor to end of line
F4*x*	Skips characters up to first occurrence of *x*
F5	Saves current line in buffer without entering
Ins	Starts insert mode
Del	Deletes one character from the buffer

**Table 5.1
DOS editing keys**

The **F1** key copies characters to the command line from the buffer one at a time. The **F3** key copies all the characters from the current cursor position to the end of the line. If you mistakenly typed "TYEP AUTOEXEC.BAT" (which would generate a **Bad command or file name** message), instead of retyping the whole line, you could edit it. First, press **F1** two times, which will display "T" and "Y" on the command line. Then, type the correct characters ("PE" instead of "EP"). Finally, press **F3** to copy the rest of the buffer to the command line.

The **F2** and **F4** keys can be used for manipulating larger chunks of text from the buffer. Perhaps you'd like to copy a file to two different disk drives. Instead of typing "COPY C:MEXICO.DOC A:" and then typing "COPY C:MEXICO.DOC B:," you could save nearly half the typing with the **F2** key. After entering the first command, press **F2** and **A**, which copies all characters up to (but not including) the first "A" from the buffer to the command line. Then, type "B" (which replaces the "A"), and press **F3** to finish the command. Finally, press **Return** to start the second copy command.

The **F4** key works like the **F2** key, except that it *skips* all characters up to (but not including) the first occurrence of the next character you type. As an example, say you typed the command "DIR M*.DOC /P" because you are looking for a specific file that you think starts with the letter M. If it doesn't show up in that directory search, you could repeat the command without the file specification. First, press **F2** and **M**, which copies "DIR" to the command line. Then, press **F4** /, which skips over "M*.DOC" (nothing is displayed on the screen). Then, finish the command by pressing **F3**, which copies "/P" to the command line, and press **Return**.

Like the Escape key, the **F5** key can be used if you realize that you made a mistake in a line before you press **Return**. Instead of discarding what you have typed, however, **F5** saves it in the buffer so you can edit it with the editing keys. The cursor drops to the next line, but the command is not entered.

Sometimes you will need to add some characters to the previously entered line. The **Insert** key will put you in insert mode until you press another editing key. For example, if you enter the command "TYE MEXICO.DOC," you could correct the error by pressing **F2 E**, pressing **Insert**, typing the missing character ("P"), and then pressing **F3** to complete the line.

The **Delete** key allows you to delete any extra characters you type in a line, one at a time. For example, to correct the line "TYYPE MEXICO.DOC," press **F1**, **Delete**, and **F3**.

WILD CARDS IN FILE SPECIFICATIONS

Many DOS commands require you to enter the name of a file. Often, you will want to process many files, which could be done by repeatedly entering the command, each time with a different file name. Obviously, there must be a better way.

Two special characters can be used by DOS in file specifications: the asterisk (*) and the question mark (?). Often called **wild card characters**, they can be used to represent any character, just like wild cards in poker can be used to represent any card. These characters allow one file specification to represent many files with names that are similar but not the same.

The question mark can be used to represent any single character. Table 5.2 shows some examples of how to use the question mark in file specifications.

File specification	Includes these files
CHAPTER?.DOC	CHAPTER1.DOC, CHAPTER2.DOC, CHAPTER3.DOC
PROG??.BA?	PROG01.BAS, PROG01.BAK, PROG02.BAS, PROGXX.BAT
???SALES.CAL	JANSALES.CAL, FEBSALES.CAL, $$$SALES.CAL
INCOME.?A?	INCOME.BAS, INCOME.CAL, INCOME.BAT, INCOME.DAT

**Table 5.2
Question mark wild card character usage.**

The asterisk wild card character can be used to represent any group of characters. Usually, it is used to find all the files with the same extension or all the files with the same name. Table 5.3 shows how the asterisk can be used.

File specification	Includes these files
INCOME.*	INCOME.JAN, INCOME.FEB, INCOME.86
*.BAT	LOG.BAT, PHONE.BAT, NOTE.BAT, PRINTER.BAT
PET*.DOC	PET.DOC, PET-DOG.DOC, PET-CAT.DOC, PET-BIRD.DOC
.	All files in a directory

**Table 5.3
Asterisk wild card character usage.**

Wild card characters can only be used in file names and extensions; they cannot be used in the drive name or path specifications.

Care should be taken when using wild card characters in DOS commands, especially destructive commands like DEL and ERASE. You should make sure that you know exactly which files will be included in the command. The easiest way is to use the DIR command with the same file specification before you use the file specification in a command that might destroy your important files.

GENERAL DOS MESSAGES

You may encounter a message that applies to DOS in general or to more than one command. These messages are listed here alphabetically along with some timely advice about what each message means and what to do about it. Messages that apply to specific commands are listed under the command name in Chapters 6, 7, and 8.

Access denied. The command you used could not access the file, directory path, or device involved. For example, you may have tried to write to a file that is marked read only.

Bad command or filename. The command you entered could not be executed. There are many possibilities for generating this message. Check the command you are trying to use for its specific requirements. You can also receive this message if the command you entered is not a valid DOS command, if the file was not found, or if the search path named in the PATH command did not include the location of this command.

Bad or missing <filename>. This message appears only at startup and indicates one of the following:

(1) The driver in the DEVICE=<filename> parameter in CONFIG.SYS was not found. Correct the device driver name, or use the diskette that contains the device driver.

(2) A break message was out of bounds for the machine size. Correct the device driver coding.

(3) An error occurred while the driver was being loaded. That driver was not installed by DOS. Correct the device driver coding.

Bad or missing Command Interpreter. COMMAND.COM cannot be found on the disk being booted, or an error occurred while the disk was being loaded. This message can also appear if (1) COMMAND.COM is removed from the directory it was in when DOS was started, or (2) COMSPEC= in the environment points to a directory that doesn't have COMMAND.COM, and DOS is reloading the command processor.

Batch file missing. DOS could not locate the batch file it was processing. The file may not be in the file specification you gave, or the PATH command may not include the drive and directory that contains the batch file. Check the specific requirements for using batch files in Chapter 7.

Cannot load COMMAND, system halted. When DOS attempted to reload the command processor, it was not found in the path specified by COMSPEC, or the area where DOS keeps track of available memory was destroyed. The only solution is to reboot.

Configuration too large. This is a startup error that indicates DOS could not load itself. Use another DOS disk to startup, and change the CONFIG.SYS file on the original boot disk to lower the number of FILES=xx or BUFFERS=xx. Restart DOS with the disk you changed. You may have to install more RAM to solve this problem.

Disk boot failure. DOS could not load IBMBIO.COM or IBMDOS.COM during startup. Try rebooting the disk. If you get the same message, try using another boot disk. If it still fails, the disk drive on which you are trying to boot may be bad.

Divide overflow. This message can occur when you are using a program that has a bug in it or is bad in some way. If you wrote the program, locate and correct the error. If the program is not yours, contact the author. This message may also occur if you try to format a RAM disk. Check to be sure that you are formatting the correct disk, and try again.

Error in EXE file. DOS found an error while trying to load a .EXE program. Try running the program again with a backup copy if you have one. If you still get this message, you can correct the program if you wrote it or contact the author.

Error loading operating system. DOS could not boot on a fixed disk because it found an error. If the error still occurs after several startup attempts, use a DOS diskette to load DOS. Try running DIR or CHKDSK. If you still get an error, you may have a problem with your fixed disk. You can also try copying COMMAND.COM on to the fixed disk and placing a copy of SYS there also. Try rebooting.

Error writing to device. DOS found an I/O error when writing output to a device. Retry the command. If you get the same error, DOS may be having trouble handling the number of bytes requested. Change the amount of data in the file and try again.

EXEC failure. DOS found an error while reading a command or program from the disk, or the FILES command in CONFIG.SYS has too low a value. Increase FILES to 15 or 20 (see Chapter 8) and restart DOS. If this strategy doesn't help, there may be a problem with the disk.

FATAL: Internal Stack Failure, System Halted. The available stack resources were exceeded, which is usually caused by a rapid succession of recursive hardware interrupts. Usually, rebooting will solve the problem. If this problem recurs, you can increase the stack resources in the STACKS command in CONFIG.SYS (see Chapter 8) and restart DOS.

File allocation table bad, drive x
Abort, Retry, Ignore? DOS found a problem in the file allocation table of the disk in drive *x*. Answer **R** for "Retry" (several times if necessary) to see if the problem is solved. If not, answer **A** for "Abort." If you are using a diskette, copy the files to another diskette and reformat the bad one. If you are using a fixed disk, do a complete backup and reformat the disk. Unfortunately, the disk is unusable until it is reformatted.

File creation error. DOS, or another program, tried to add a new file to the directory or replace an existing file, but failed. Run CHKDSK to see if the directory or disk is full or if some other problem exists.

If the file already exists, you can use the ATTRIB command to see if the file is a read-only file. If it is a read-only file, and you want to delete or change it, you can use ATTRIB to remove the read-only marker.

File not found. DOS couldn't find the file you specified. The file may not be on the drive or in the directory you specified. Check the format of the command (see Chapters 6, 7, and 8) to be sure you entered it correctly.

Incorrect DOS version. The command you specified cannot be used with the DOS version you have installed. If you have the correct version of the command on a diskette, copy it over the old version. Try the command again.

Incorrect number of parameters. You used a different number of parameters than the command calls for. Check the format of the command (see Chapters 6, 7, and 8), and try the command again.

**Insert disk with batch file
and strike any key whey ready.** DOS cannot execute the next command in the batch file because the diskette containing the batch file has been removed from the disk drive. You have probably removed it from the drive to perform another task. Insert the diskette with the batch file in the drive and press a key.

**Insert disk with \COMMAND.COM in drive A
and strike any key when ready.** DOS is trying to reload COMMAND.COM but cannot find it on the startup disk. You have probably removed it from drive A to perform another task. Put the diskette with COMMAND.COM in the drive and press a key.

**Insert diskette for drive x and press any key
when ready.** With a one-drive system, this message frequently appears to prompt you to change diskettes so that it can continue processing. The diskette you need will depend on what command you are executing. Insert the correct diskette in the drive and press a key.

Insufficient disk space. The disk does not have enough free space to accommodate the file. Run CHKDSK to determine how much free space is available. There are several ways to solve the problem: use another disk, delete unwanted files to free up space, and so on. Then try the command again.

Insufficient memory. There is not enough free RAM to execute the program or command. You can free up memory by removing memory-resident programs, such as SideKick and VDISK. You can also remove unneeded device drivers and so on that take up RAM. When you have freed up some space, try the command again.

Intermediate file error during pipe. DOS cannot create or write to one of the temporary files used while performing the pipe function. The disk may be full, or it cannot find the temporary files. You can free up disk space by copying files to another disk and then deleting the originals or by deleting unwanted files. You can also copy the files needed to perform the task to a disk that has enough free space.

Sometimes, the program you are running is deleting files on the disk that may include the temporary files used for piping; therefore, DOS cannot find them when they are needed.

Internal stack overflow
System halted. The internal stack was overfilled. Reboot (by simultaneously pressing Ctrl-Alt-Del) your computer. If this error occurs repeatedly, increase the number of stack frames in the STACKS command in your CONFIG.SYS file.

Invalid COMMAND.COM in drive n. The version of COMMAND.COM that DOS tried to load was an incorrect version. This error usually happens with diskettes that haven't been used in a while and contain an older version of COMMAND.COM. You'll also see a message to load the correct version of COMMAND.COM. Insert the disk with the correct version and press a key. You can update your disk with the old copy of COMMAND.COM by copying the correct version to that disk.

Invalid directory. There are several reasons for receiving this message, depending on the command you are trying to execute: (1) the directory doesn't exist or doesn't exist on the drive you specified, (2) you misspelled the directory path, (3) you forgot to use a backslash (\) before the path name or between the directories in the path name. Check the format requirements for the command you want to use and try again.

Invalid environment size specified. The environment size that you gave with the SHELL configuration command is incorrect. Correct the SHELL command in your CONFIG.SYS file and restart DOS.

Invalid disk change. The diskette in the high-capacity disk drive was changed while there were still files open on the diskette. Insert the correct diskette to continue.

Invalid drive in search path. An invalid drive name was found in the PATH command. The drive does not exist on your system. This message appears when a program or batch file tries to access the invalid drive, not when you enter the PATH command. Use the PATH command to correct the drive name (see Chapter 6), and run the program or batch file again.

Invalid drive specification
Specified drive does not exist,
or is non-removable. The command contains an invalid drive name, which could be a drive that does not exist on your system, or you could be using a command for diskettes, but you specified a fixed disk or RAM disk in the command format. Check the requirements of the command (see Chapters 6, 7, and 8) and re-enter a valid drive.

Invalid number of parameters. You gave too few or too many parameters for the command you are using. Check the requirements for the command (see Chapters 6, 7, and 8) and try again.

Invalid parameter. One or more of the parameters you gave in the command is either incorrect or in the wrong order. Check the requirements for the command (see Chapters 6, 7, and 8) and try again.

Invalid partition table. Incorrect disk partition information was detected during startup from the fixed disk. Start DOS from a diskette, and then use FDISK to examine and correct the fixed disk partition information.

Invalid path. The directory path you gave does not exist, the path name contained invalid characters, or it was more than 63 characters. Check the directory path and re-enter.

Invalid STACK parameter. The numbers that you used with the STACKS command in your CONFIG.SYS file are wrong. Correct the STACKS command in your CONFIG.SYS file and restart DOS.

Maximum number of logical DOS drives installed. You have created 24 logical drives. You must delete an existing logical drive before you attempt to define another one.

Memory allocation error
Cannot load COMMAND, system halted. The area in which DOS keeps track of memory has been damaged or destroyed. Restarting DOS should take care of this problem.

Missing operating system. During startup from the fixed disk, the DOS partition was marked bootable, but it did not contain a copy of DOS. Start DOS from a diskette, and try using SYS to place a copy of the operating system on the fixed disk. Restart DOS from the fixed disk. If that doesn't help, restart DOS on the diskette again, use BACKUP to do a complete backup of your fixed disk, and then use FORMAT /S to format and place a copy of the operating system on the fixed disk. Remember to do the backup first because your files will be lost when you format the fixed disk. Finally, use RESTORE to restore your files to the fixed disk.

No free file handles
Cannot start COMMAND, exiting. An attempt to load a second copy of the command processor was unsuccessful because there are too many open files. Increase the number of open files in the FILES command in CONFIG.SYS and restart DOS.

Non-System disk or disk error
Replace and strike any key when ready. You tried to start up DOS on a non-system disk. IBMBIO.COM and IBMDOS.COM must be present on the disk you are starting. This message can also appear when a disk read error occurs. Insert a DOS diskette in drive A, and restart your system. If you are trying to start up a fixed disk, reboot a DOS diskette, and use the SYS command to place a copy of the operating system on the fixed disk.

Out of environment space. DOS could not accept the SET command because it was unable to expand the area where the environment information is kept. This problem usually occurs after a program that makes itself resident is loaded, such as PRINT, MODE, or GRAPHICS. Rebooting DOS will remove these resident programs.

Path not found. The file name or directory path you gave does not exist on the drive specified. Check to be sure you have entered the path correctly and that it exists where you indicate.

Path too long. The directory path and file name you gave are more than 63 characters long. Correct the path if you can. If you can't, you may have to revise your subdirectory structure so that shorter path names can be used. See Chapter 3 for help on directory structures.

Program too big to fit in memory. There is not enough free RAM to load the program you are using. If you have memory-resident programs, such as SideKick and VDISK, you may want to remove them from memory to use the other program. You can also reserve more memory with the BUFFERS command in the CONFIG.SYS file or add additional memory to your system.

Sector size too large in file <filename>. The device driver named in <filename> specifies a device sector size larger than the devices previously defined in DOS. Reduce the sector size to conform with the sector size of DOS. If you purchased this program, contact your dealer.

Syntax error. The format of the command you used is incorrect. Check the requirements of the command (see Chapters 6, 7, and 8) and try again.

Terminate batch job (Y/N)? This message appears when you press **Ctrl-Break** while a batch file is being processed. Answer **Y** for "Yes" and press **Return** if you want to stop the batch file and return to the system prompt. Answer **N** for "No" and press **Return** to continue batch processing with the next command in the batch file (the command being processed when you pressed **Ctrl-Break** is skipped).

xxxx device driver cannot be initialized. The device driver named is bad. Get a new copy of the file named, or take it out of your CONFIG.SYS file.

CHAPTER 6

DOS COMMANDS

APPEND

Define search directories

Version 3.3 External

Functions: Defines the drives and directories that DOS searches for if a file is not found in the current directory.

Formats: APPEND [/X] [/E]

or

APPEND [[*d:*]*path*[;[*d:*]*path*][...]

or

APPEND [;]

Variables: *d:* is a valid drive (one that exists on your system) on which you want DOS to search.

path is a valid directory path in which you want DOS to search.

... indicates the option to add more drives and directory paths to the search.

Typing **APPEND** ; removes the extended search paths (only the current directory is searched).

Using APPEND with no parameters displays the current search paths.

Options: /X tells append to also search for program and batch files (commands).

/E saves the APPEND path in the environment space.

Comments: When DOS (or a program) needs a file that is not in the current directory of the specified (or default) drive, DOS searches the directories you named in the APPEND command.

APPEND will not find program or batch files (files with .COM, .EXE or .BAT extensions) unless you use the /X option.

APPEND lets you access files from any disk drive in any directory without changing the default drive or directory every time.

If you use the /E option, you can view or change the APPEND path with the SET command.

If you use the /X option, APPEND also adds the function of the PATH command: finding programs and batch files.

APPEND's primary use is to find data or overlay files in different directories.

Some software programs use overlay files as part of the program. In some cases (usually with older programs), these overlay files must be in the default directory for the program to find them. APPEND lets you put these files anywhere on your disk. Most programs have been updated so that this problem no longer occurs.

APPEND also lets you put data files anywhere on your disk. In some cases, however, your program won't work exactly as you expect when using data files that are not in the current (or specified) directory. Many programs—especially word processing and spreadsheet programs—actually create a new file every time you save your work. In general, you can recognize programs that work in this way because they leave backup files with the extension .BAK that contain the previous versions of your work. These backup files are actually the previous files that have been renamed. When you use APPEND, these programs will read the file from another subdirectory. But when they save your work, they create a new file in the current directory. You end up with two versions of the same job in two different directories, many times with the same name.

Each path must be a series of valid directories and sub-directories. If you use more than one path, they must be separated by semicolons.

If you do not use a drive name, the default drive is used.

It is recommend that you always specify the drive name and a path name that starts at the root directory, which lets you access a file from any disk drive in any directory.

Errors in the path names are not detected until DOS actually does a directory search. Invalid paths and paths that no longer exist are ignored.

Directories are searched in the order specified in the APPEND command.

Messages: **APPEND / ASSIGN conflict.** You have used the ASSIGN command before using the APPEND command. If you want to use both, you must use APPEND before you use ASSIGN.

APPEND / TopView conflict. You have loaded TopView before using the APPEND command. If you want to use both, you must use APPEND before you start TopView.

Incorrect APPEND version. You are using the wrong version of APPEND. Be sure that you are using the APPEND command that came on your DOS diskette.

Incorrect path or parameter. You specified a path with the /X or /E options. Options can only be used the first time that you use APPEND. If you use an option, you can't specify a path. You must use the APPEND command twice, first with the options, then with a path.

No Append. You entered APPEND, and no APPEND path is set.

Examples: To start APPEND where you want to keep the APPEND path in the environment space, from the C> prompt, enter

append /E ⏎

To define a search path for the directories \DATA and \FILES, enter

append c:\data;c:\files ⏎

To see the current APPEND path, enter

append ⏎

The screen will display the following response:

APPEND=C:\DATA;C:\FILES

To turn off APPEND's search path, enter

append ; ⏎

ASSIGN

Assign disk drive
Version 2.0 External

Functions: Temporarily reassigns disk drive names or restores default drive names.

Format: ASSIGN *d=d*

Variables: *d* is a valid drive name (one that exists on your system). Unlike most other DOS commands, you do not have to enter a colon (:) when naming a disk drive or use spaces between the drive names and the equal sign (=).

You can make more than one assignment at the same time. Use a space between each assignment set (e.g., ASSIGN A=C B=C).

Use ASSIGN with no parameters to return to default drive assignments.

Comments: This command helps you use applications that will not let you change drives in the program itself. For example, you can use ASSIGN to let the program think that a fixed disk (drive C) is really drive A or B. Subsequently, any time you or your program references drive A or B, DOS will substitute drive C. For example, if you type **DIR A:**, DOS will display a directory of drive C.

ASSIGN does not work with all programs; in those programs in which it does not work, the command is simply ignored.

ASSIGN should not be used with the BACKUP, RESTORE, LABEL, JOIN, SUBST, or PRINT commands. It can hide the true device name when the actual drive information is needed.

The FORMAT, DISKCOPY, and DISKCOMP commands ignore any drive reassignments. The command **FORMAT A:**, for example, will format the diskette in drive A, despite any preceding ASSIGN commands.

DOS will accept a drive name that does not exist, without displaying an error message; however, when you try to use that drive, the **Invalid drive specification** message is displayed.

Messages: **Invalid drive specification.** You used an invalid drive as the new drive assignment. (Note: This message appears only when DOS attempts to access the invalid drive, not when you use the ASSIGN command.)

Invalid parameter. You included a colon (:) and/or a space between the drive letter and the equal sign (=).

Examples: To make DOS send all requests for drive A to physical drive C, from the DOS prompt, enter

assign a=c ⏎

To reassign both drives A and B to drive C, enter

assign a=c b=c ⏎

To restore default drive assignments, enter

assign ⏎

ATTRIB

Change file attribute
Version 3.0 External

Functions: Sets or clears the Read-Only and Archive file markers. Can also display the current setting of this marker.

Format: ATTRIB [$\frac{+R}{-R}$][$\frac{+A}{-A}$] /S *filespec*

Variables: *filespec* is defined as [*d:*][*path*]*filename.ext*, which specifies the drive name, directory, file, and extension on which the command is to act.

You can use wild card characters in the file name.

Options:
+R   sets the Read-Only file marker.

-R   clears the Read-Only file marker.

+A   sets the Archive file marker. This option is not valid in versions prior to DOS 3.2.

-A   clears the Archive file marker. This option is not valid in versions prior to DOS 3.2.

To display the current setting of the Read-Only file marker, don't use any of the options (+R, -R, +A, or -A).

/S also processes files in subdirectories of the specified directory.

Comments: The Read-Only file marker is called an **attribute**, which is how this command received its name.

This command allows you to "protect" files from being accidentally deleted or changed. DOS will not allow you to change or delete a file while the Read-Only file marker is set.

If you use the /S command, the files in the specified directory—as well as all its subdirectories—will be processed.

Some programs may not interpret the Read-Only file marker correctly and may give confusing error messages, such as **Disk Full**.

If you attempt to remove (using DEL or ERASE) a file with the Read-Only file marker set, you will receive an **Access denied** message. If you use wild card characters with these commands, you will only receive this message if *all* the files that you specify have the Read-Only file marker set. The files with the Read-Only file markers set will not be removed.

If you try to write over a file that has the Read-Only file marker set, for example, by using COPY or redirecting output to the file, you will receive a **File creation error** message. The file with the Read-Only file marker set will not be changed.

You can change the name of a file with the Read-Only file marker set. The file with the new name will still have the Read-Only file marker set.

You can make a copy (using COPY) of a file with the Read-Only file marker set. The new file will *not* have the Read-Only file marker set.

When a file is created, the archive file marker is set (+A). When the file is backed up with BACKUP or XCOPY /M, DOS automatically resets the archive file marker (-A). If you subsequently modify the file, DOS again sets the archive bit (+A); thus, it is a record of file backup. If the archive bit is off (-A), then the current version of the file has been backed up.

Two DOS commands use the archive bit: BACKUP and XCOPY. If you use the /M option with BACKUP, then only files with the archive bit set (+A) will be backed up. Likewise, the /A and /M options of XCOPY will copy only files with the archive bit set (+A).

Messages: **Invalid number of parameters.** You entered too few or too many parameters. You will receive this message if you enter ATTRIB with no file name following it.

Invalid path or file not found. The file couldn't be found on the path that you specified. The path is the current directory if you don't include a path with the file name. Check the spelling of the file name that you entered. You will receive this error message if you use a directory name instead of a file name. You cannot make a directory read-only.

Syntax Error. You entered the command incorrectly. The +R, R, +A, or -A options must come before the file name.

Examples: To set the file marker of the file named TEXT.DOC to read-only and archive, from the DOS prompt, enter

attrib +r +a text.doc ⏎

To display the setting of the file marker of the file TEXT.DOC, enter

attrib text.doc ⏎

The screen will display the following response:

    R   A A:\TEXT.DOC

The "R" at the left of the line indicates that the Read-Only file marker is set; the "A" indicates that the Archive file marker is set.

To clear the Read-Only file marker from all the files with a file name extension of .DOC in the current directory, enter

attrib -r *.doc ⏎

To display the status of the file markers of all files in the root directory of drive C, enter

attrib c:*.* ⏎

The screen will appear similar to the following:

```
R A  COMMAND.COM
R    AUTOEXEC.BAT
R    CONFIG.SYS
```

Note that directories are not shown in this list.

BACKUP

Back up files
Version 2.0 External

Functions: Backs up one or more files from one disk to another. Commonly used to back up files on a fixed (hard) disk to one or more floppy diskettes.

Format: BACKUP d:[filespec] d: [/S][/M][/A][/D:mm-dd-yy] [T:hh:mm:ss][/F][/L[:logfile]]

Variables: d: is a valid drive name (one that exists on your system). You must use a colon (:). The first drive name is the **source** drive (the drive from which you are backing up). The second drive name is the **target** drive (the drive to which you are backing up).

filespec is defined as [path][filename.ext], which specifies the file that is to be backed up.

You can use wild card characters in the file name.

logfile is defined as [d:][path][filename.ext], which specifies the log file.

You can specify any combination of path, filename, and .ext; if none are specified, all files in the current directory are backed up.

Options: These options can be used separately or combined:

/S   also backs up files in subdirectories of the specified directory. This option will include either the current directory and its subdirectories if path is not used or the directory specified in path and its subdirectories.

/M   backs up only files that have changed since the last backup.

/A   adds files to an existing backup diskette. Without this option, the files already on the diskette are erased.

/**D:***mm-dd-yy*

> includes files created or changed on or after the date *mm-dd-yy*, where
>
> *mm* = month
> *dd* = day
> *yy* = year
>
> You must use a colon (:) after the **/D**. You can use either a minus sign (-) or a slash (/) between the numbers in the date.

/**T:***hh:mm:ss*

> includes files created or changed after the time given on the date specified. The time *hh:mm:ss* is specified as
>
> *hh* = hours (0 through 24)
> *mm* = minutes
> *ss* = seconds
>
> You must use a colon after the **/T** and before the minutes and seconds. The minutes and seconds are optional.
>
> This option was added in DOS version 3.3.

/F formats the target diskettes if they are not already formatted. This option was added in DOS version 3.3.

/**L:***logfile*

> creates a log file of the back up. If a file name is not given, the default is BACKUP.LOG. This option was added in DOS version 3.3.

Comments: The backup diskettes must already be formatted for DOS, unless you use the /F option that was added in version 3.3; otherwise, BACKUP will not work on unformatted diskettes.

If you use the /A option to add files to the diskette you inserted, the correct diskette must already be in the target drive. DOS will not prompt you to insert the diskette after BACKUP is entered.

BACKUP displays the name of each file as it is backed up. Label each backup diskette in numerical order. When the files are restored (with RESTORE), you are prompted to insert the backup diskettes in order.

When the diskette is full, you are prompted to insert the next diskette. Again, be sure you clearly identify your diskettes in numerical order.

Diskettes (both source and target) should not be write-protected because BACKUP needs to mark the files as being backed up (/M).

Do not use BACKUP with a drive name that has been reassigned (with ASSIGN) because BACKUP needs to know the true drive letter that is used.

Do not use BACKUP when JOIN is active because the tree structure may no longer be valid when RESTORE is used.

If the target disk is a fixed disk, backup files are placed in a subdirectory named \BACKUP. If the target disk is a diskette, backup files are placed in the root directory.

The files on the backup diskettes cannot be used for normal processing and should be transferred back to the fixed disk with RESTORE. You cannot restore backup files with COPY (see RESTORE for more details).

If you are sharing files, you cannot backup files that you do not have access to. If you try to back up one of these files, the **Not able to backup at this time** message is displayed.

If you use the /L option, a log file will be created that includes the date and time that you made the backup and a record of each file that was backed up. If the log file already exists, the new information is added to the end of it. You cannot make a log file on the target disk.

Exit Codes:	0	Successful backup completed.
	1	No files were found to be backed up.
	2	Backup was terminated by the user (**Ctrl-Break** or **Ctrl-C**).
	3	Backup was terminated because of an error.

Messages: *** **Backing up files to diskette xx** *** Files are being backed up to the diskette. *xx* is the number of the diskette in the target drive, starting sequentially with diskette #1.

*** **Backing up files to drive x** ***
Number:x. Files are being backed up to target drive *x*. The target number *x* is the number of the diskette that should be inserted in the drive.

Cannot execute FORMAT. BACKUP uses FORMAT to format new diskettes. This message means that either FORMAT is not on the current path or there is not enough memory to run FORMAT. Be sure that FORMAT is on the path, or format your diskettes before running BACKUP.

Cannot FORMAT nonremovable drive X. BACKUP will not format a fixed disk. If you want to back up to a fixed disk, you must prepare it first.

Diskette is not a backup diskette. The diskette you inserted in the disk drive was not created using BACKUP. Check the diskette with DIR; the first file should be BACKUPID.@@@.

Fixed Backup device is full. The fixed disk has no more storage space on it. Possible solutions include (1) freeing up space by deleting unnecessary files from your source so that not as many files will be backed up; (2) copying files off the source and then deleting them; (3) backing up to another target.

Insert backup diskette xx in drive x:
Warning! Diskette files will be erased
Strike any key when ready. When you use BACKUP, this message is displayed each time a new diskette should be inserted. x is the target drive; xx is the number of the diskette to be inserted, starting sequentially with diskette #1. Files already on the diskette will be erased.

Insert backup source diskette in drive x
Strike any key when ready. This message prompts you to insert in drive x the diskette from which you want to back up, and then strike any key.

Insert backup target diskette y in drive x
Strike any key when ready. This message prompts you to insert in drive x the diskette y, to which you want to back up, and then strike any key.

Insert last backup target in drive x. This message prompts you to insert in drive x the last (i.e., highest numbered) diskette you used for the previous backup. This message occurs when you use the /A option.

Invalid drive specification
Source and Target drives are the same. You used the same drive name for both the source and target diskettes. Re-enter with different drive names.

Invalid date. You entered an invalid date with the /D:*mm-dd-yy* option. Also, check to be sure you entered it in the right format.

Invalid path. The file couldn't be found on the path that you specified. Check to be sure the path is an existing one and that you spelled it correctly.

Last backup target not inserted. The /A option was used, but the diskette you inserted was not the highest numbered backup diskette from the latest backup set.

*** Last file not backed up *** The target diskette is full. The partial file that was not completely backed up is deleted. If you want to back up the file, insert a new backup diskette and add this file to it (using the /A option).

*** Not able to back up file *** Files cannot be backed up due to a file sharing conflict. Someone is using the file you want to back up. Try backing up the file later by using the same format specification, but add /M so that the files previously backed up won't be backed up again.

path\filename.ext
Not able to backup at this time. The file is being used by someone else. This problem occurs only when files are shared (DOS 3).

Source and target drives are the same. The two drives cannot be the same for a backup. Re-enter using different drives.

Target cannot be used for backup. You did not use a backup diskette. If you think the diskette is the correct one, try the command again, back up to a different drive, or restart the system and try again.

Target does not contain backup files. The /A option was used, but no previous backup files were found on the diskette. Insert the correct diskette and re-enter the command.

WARNING! No files were found to back up. No files matched your file specification on the source drive. Check your spelling and format. Also, check to see that the files you want to back up are in the directory you named.

WARNING! Target is full. The target diskette has no more storage space on it. Insert a new backup diskette and re-enter.

**Warning! Files in the target drive d:\BACKUP directory will be erased
Strike any key when ready.** BACKUP is going to erase all the backup files on the target diskette. If you want to add files to the target diskette instead of erasing what is there, press **Ctrl-Break** to stop BACKUP and try again using the /A option.

Error opening log file. BACKUP can't open a log file using the name or path you specified. You can't put the log file on the target disk.

Logging to file x. Your backup operation is being logged to the file named.

No source drive specified. You didn't specify a source drive. You must specify both a source and destination for BACKUP.

No target drive specified. You didn't specify a target drive. You must specify both a source and destination for BACKUP.

Examples: To back up all files in the current directory on drive C with the extension .DOC to drive A, at the DOS prompt, enter

backup c:*.doc a:⏎

To back up all the files in all the directories and subdirectories on drive C to drive A, at the DOS prompt, enter

backup c:\ a: /s⏎

To back up all the files on drive C that have changed since the last backup was done to drive A, at the DOS prompt, enter

backup c:\ a: /m/s⏎

To back up all files in the PROGRAMS directory that were created or changed on or after July 15, 1986, enter

backup c:\programs a: /d:7/15/86⏎

This example backs up all files with the extension *.bas* in the PROGRAMS directory and any subdirectories of PROGRAMS that were created or changed March 1, 1986 or later. The files are added to the diskette. At the DOS prompt, enter

backup c:\programs*.bas a: /s/a/d:3-1-86⏎

BREAK

Check for Ctrl-Break
Version 2.0 Internal

Functions: DOS can check for Ctrl-Break whenever it performs a function; this command tells DOS whether or not to check for **Ctrl-Break**.

Format: BREAK [ON / OFF]

Options: **ON** lets you check for Ctrl-Break whenever a program requests any DOS function.

OFF returns checking to normal operation.

Using BREAK alone displays the current state of Ctrl-Break: **Break is on** or **Break is off**.

Comments: Entering Ctrl-Break at the keyboard (by holding down the **Ctrl key** and then pressing the **Scroll Lock/Break** key) is an instruction to end a program. Normally, the only time that DOS checks for Ctrl-Break is during standard input (keyboard), output (display), print, or auxiliary device operations. BREAK can be very useful if you are running an application where it would be better to check for Ctrl-Break at certain points in your program. This feature gives you more control over application processing.

For example, BREAK ON lets you immediately terminate a program such as a compiler (which performs few or no standard device operations) because DOS checks for Ctrl-Break after every operation. Reduced processing speed is negligible.

Messages: **Must specify ON or OFF.** BREAK was entered with something other than **ON** or **OFF**.

Break is on. DOS is checking for Ctrl-Break after every operation. This message is displayed when you use BREAK without an option.

Break is off. DOS is only checking for Ctrl-Break during standard input, output, print, or auxiliary device operations. It is displayed when you use BREAK without an option.

Examples: To instruct DOS to check for Ctrl-Break whenever a program requests any DOS function, enter

break on⏎

To return checking to normal operation, enter

break off⏎

To display the current state of Ctrl-Break (**ON** or **OFF**), enter

break⏎

The screen will display a message such as the following:

    BREAK is on

or

    BREAK is off

CHDIR or CD

Change directory
Version 2.0 Internal

Functions: Changes the current directory of the specified or default drive.

Displays the current directory path of a drive.

Formats: CHDIR [[*d:*]*path*]

or

CD [[*d:*]*path*]

Variables: You can use either CHDIR or CD in the command format.

d: must be a valid drive name; if used without *path*, it shows the current directory path of drive *d:*. The default drive is used if this variable is not included.

path changes the current directory to the directory specified. For example, \DOS\UTILITY\BATCH changes to the BATCH subdirectory.

By using the backslash (\) as the first character in *path*, DOS starts its search in the root directory. If the path name does not start with a backslash, the name indicates a subdirectory of the current directory.

NOTE: Refer to Chapter 3 for a complete explanation of directory structures.

Comments: An invalid directory is a *path* that does not exist, a directory that does not exist, an incorrect format, or a misspelled *path*.

DOS displays the **Invalid directory** message and stays in the current directory.

There are two ways to move through directories: you can start at the root directory and move down, or you can start at the current directory and move up or down.

To move one directory up (called the **parent** directory), you can use two periods (..) rather than typing the directory name. A disk drive name can precede the two periods.

To move more than one directory at a time, separate each directory with a backslash (\). The maximum number of characters in a directory specification is 63.

Messages: **Invalid directory.** You have used a *path* that does not exist, a directory that does not exist, an incorrect format, or a misspelled *path*. If the directory does exist, check that the *path* is correct. Also, check for misspelling and correct use of backslash characters and periods.

Examples: To change the current directory to the PROJECT1 directory on drive C, at the A> prompt, enter

chdir c:\project1 ⏎

or simply

cd c:\project1 ⏎

For the rest of the examples, change the default drive to C by entering at the A> prompt

c: ⏎

From the example above, you can change to a subdirectory of PROJECT1. To change to the TEXT subdirectory on the current drive, at the C> prompt, enter

cd text ⏎

Note that by not starting the path name with the backslash character (\), DOS starts looking in the current directory, which is PROJECT1.

Now, to change to the new subdirectory DBASE (which is also a subdirectory of PROJECT1 from the previous example), at the C prompt, enter

cd ..\dbase ⏎

The new current directory will be \PROJECT1\DBASE. You could have also entered

cd \project1\dbase ⏎

and achieved the same result; however, using two periods (..) saves keystrokes.

To return to the PROJECT1 directory, at the C prompt, enter

cd .. ⏎

or

cd \project1 ⏎

You can also use the Change Directory command to display the current directory path. To show the current directory path on drive C (from the previous examples), enter

cd c: ⏎

or simply

cd ⏎

The screen will display the following response:

    C:\project1

To return to the root directory, enter

cd \ ⏎

CHKDSK

Check disk
Version 1.0 External

Functions: Reports disk and memory status by checking the directory and file allocation table of the designated or current disk.

By using the CHKDSK options, you can also repair errors in the directories or file allocation table.

Format: CHKDSK [*filespec*] [/F][/V]

Variables: *filespec* is defined as [*d:*][*path*]*filename.ext*, which specifies the drive name, directory, file(s), and extension on which CHKDSK is to act. If you use *filespec*, CHKDSK displays the number of contiguous areas occupied by the file(s).

Options:

/F   corrects errors found in the directory or File Allocation Table (FAT). Without this option, CHKDSK continues to act as though it were preparing to correct the disk so that you can analyze possible results of correction; however, it does not actually write the corrections to the disk.

/V   allows CHKDSK to display a series of messages indicating its progress and providing details about each error. It also causes the names of all directories and all files on the disk drive to be displayed.

Comments: CHKDSK begins checking the diskette in the drive you specified as soon as you enter the command.

CHKDSK is helpful in ensuring the integrity of the file structures of a disk. Use it often if the information contained on your disk is critical (along with frequent backups, of course). CHKDSK is also very helpful in monitoring the integrity of your fixed disk files.

If you specify a file name, the number of non-contiguous areas occupied by the file is reported. Badly fragmented files with numerous non-contiguous areas can slow down the performance of the disk when those files are used.

You can tell how badly a disk is fragmented by checking all the files in the specified directory on the disk (*.*). CHKDSK does not check files in the subdirectories of the specified directory.

If lost clusters (allocation units) are found, CHKDSK asks if you want to recover the information into files. If you answer yes, and the /F option is used, each chain of lost clusters is recovered. They are placed in files named FILE*nnnn*.CHK, where *nnnn* is a sequential number starting with 0000. These files are created in the root directory of the specified drive. You can then look at these files to see if they have any useful information. If not, they can be deleted.

You can redirect CHKDSK's output to a file by using a command such as CHKDSK B:>FILENAME. Do not use the /F option in this case.

CHKDSK does not work on network drives or drives where SUBST or JOIN is in effect.

Messages:
All specified file(s) are contiguous. The file or files you named in the command are all written sequentially on the disk, which means you are getting the best performance possible from the file(s).

Allocation error for file, size adjusted. The file just before this message has an invalid cluster number in the file allocation table. Use the /F option to truncate the file at the end of the last valid cluster.

Cannot CHDIR to root. While checking the disk, the command's attempt to change to the root directory failed. This problem is most likely due to a damaged disk.

Cannot CHKDSK a network drive. You cannot run CHKDSK on a network disk or on a disk that is in your computer but is currently being shared on the network. Run CHKDSK on the computer that has the drive, and pause or disconnect the computer from the network.

Cannot CHKDSK a SUBSTed or ASSIGNed drive. The SUBST command changes a subdirectory to a drive name. ASSIGN changes a disk drive to a different drive name. Return all disk drive information to their defaults and run CHKDSK again.

Cannot RECOVER Entry, Processing Continued. The directory *Entry* is damaged and cannot be recovered. Try to copy all the files from this directory to a diskette or to a different directory. Delete the original files and remove the directory. If you find that you have lost some or all of the files in the damaged directory, use your backup files to try to reconstruct the directory.

If the damaged directory is on a diskette, copy all the files possible to another diskette. Reformat the damaged diskette or discard it if necessary.

CHDIR .. Failed Trying Alternate Method. CHKDSK cannot return to a parent directory. Restart DOS and run CHKDSK again. If this step fails, get another copy of CHKDSK from your DOS master diskette, restart DOS, and run CHKDSK again.

Contains xxx non-contiguous blocks. The file just before this message is not sequentially written on the disk. It is written in *xxx* pieces on different areas of the disk.

This message does not mean there is a serious problem; however, because fragmented files take longer to read, you should consider copying badly fragmented files to another disk with the COPY command, which will record the file sequentially, resulting in better performance when the file is read.

If the entire disk is fragmented, you should COPY (not DISKCOPY) the entire disk to a better disk or newly formatted disk. Then, you can reformat the fragmented disk and reuse it.

If you have a fixed disk that is badly fragmented, you should BACKUP your entire hard disk, reFORMAT it, and RESTORE the files to it. Reformatting the hard disk will improve its performance.

Convert directory to file (Y/N)? The directory name just before this message has too much invalid information to be usable. Reply **Y** for "Yes" and press **Return** to convert the directory to a file so that you can examine it and repair the directory if possible. Answer **N** for "No" and press **Return** to continue without converting the directory to a file.

Since there may be several files in the directory that are usable, you may want to answer **N**, and then copy the files to a diskette or to a new directory. Then you can check for files that are usable. Run CHKDSK again, but this time answer **Y** to convert the directory to a file. Check the file to recover as many of the remaining files as you can.

**Directory is joined,
tree past this point not processed.** CHKDSK found a directory that is actually a disk JOINed to the disk you specified in the command format. CHKDSK will skip over this directory and continue.

**Directory totally empty, no . or ..,
tree past this point not processed.** A subdirectory has been found that doesn't have (.) or (..) entries in it. Copy all files in the damaged directory to a diskette or to a new directory, and recover as many files as you can. Some of the files may be lost. Reconstruct the directory with backup files if possible.

Disk error reading FAT X. The File Allocation Table entry indicated by X is invalid. This problem is sometimes caused by a power failure while a file is open. If this message appears twice for FAT 1 and FAT 2, format the disk to make it usable again. If this step fails, discard the disk.

Disk error writing FAT X. A disk error was found while CHKDSK was trying to update the FAT on the specified drive. *X* will be either 1 or 2, depending on which of the two copies of the FAT could not be written. If this message appears twice for FAT 1 and FAT 2, format the disk to make it usable again. If this step fails, discard the disk.

**Entry has a bad attribute
(or size or link)**. This message may begin with either one period (current directory is in error) or two periods (parent directory is in error). Use the /F option to try to correct the error.

**Error found, F parameter not specified
Corrections will not be written to disk.** If you have not used the /F option, CHKDSK still acts as if it is going to fix any errors detected; however, it does not actually write the corrections to the disk.

**File is cross-linked:
on cluster xx.** This message appears twice and displays the two files that are cross-linked. Make copies of both files, delete the originals, and edit the files as is necessary.

**First cluster number is invalid,
entry truncated.** The file, whose name precedes this message, contains an invalid pointer to the data area. If you use the /F option, the file is truncated to a zero-length file.

Has invalid cluster, file truncated. The file just before this message contains an invalid pointer to the data area. To fix this problem, run CHKDSK with the /F option to truncate the file at the last valid data block.

Insufficient room in root directory
Erase files from root and repeat CHKDSK. When you tell CHKDSK to recover lost data into files, these files are created in the root directory. This message indicates that the root directory was full and not all of the lost data could be recovered. Copy the recovered files to another disk or directory, and delete some of the files in the root directory. Then run CHKDSK again to recover the rest of the lost data.

Invalid current directory. An unrecoverable error on the disk was found when CHKDSK tried to read the current directory. No action is required.

Invalid subdirectory. The subdirectory named before this message contains invalid information. If you used the /F option, CHKDSK attempts to correct the error. To find out more about the nature of the error, run CHKDSK again using the /V option.

Non-DOS diskette. The format of the diskette was not compatible with DOS. It was either created by an operating system other than DOS or has been so badly damaged that CHKDSK cannot recognize it. If this diskette is the one you want to check, and the information on it is expendable, format the diskette with the FORMAT command and run CHKDSK again.

Probable non-DOS disk
Continue (Y/N)? Either the diskette is not DOS compatible, or it is damaged. If you did not use the /F option, answer **Y** for "Yes," and CHKDSK will indicate possible corrective actions without actually changing the disk. You should probably take this precaution before using the /F option.

Processing cannot continue. This message is followed by another message explaining why processing cannot continue.

101

Tree past this point not processed. CHKDSK cannot continue past the directory being examined because it has an error. The error will be displayed in the previous message.

Unrecoverable error on directory. CHKDSK found an error while checking the directory. No action required.

xxxx lost clusters found in yyy chains
Convert lost chains to files (Y/N)? Ctrl-Break was entered during a disk Input/Output operation. DOS did not clean up the disk after encountering the Ctrl-Break. If you answer Y for "Yes" and the /F option was used, CHKDSK recovers the chain into a separate file. If /F wasn't used, CHKDSK displays information but takes no corrective action. If you answer N for "No," CHKDSK frees the blocks up so they can be used for new files.

xxxxxx bytes disk space freed. This message is displayed when you free up disk space using the /F option.

Examples: To check the status of the fixed disk (drive C), at the C> prompt, enter

chkdsk ⏎

After the disk is checked, any error messages are displayed, followed by a status report. Following is a sample of what you might see:

```
Volume FDISK created Jul 12, 1986  3:06p

10592256 bytes total disk space
  176128 bytes in 10 hidden files
  163840 bytes in 39 directories
 6971392 bytes in 709 user files
   12288 bytes in bad sectors
 3268608 bytes available on disk

  589824 bytes total memory
  478048 bytes free
```

To check the status of the diskette in drive A, correct any errors, and verify progress, enter

chkdsk a: /f/v ⏎

To see a complete list of the directories and files on a disk and redirect CHKDSK's output to the file DISKDIR.CHK, enter

chkdsk /v >diskdir.chk ⏎

CLS

Clear screen
Version 2.0 Internal

Functions: Clears the display screen.

Format: CLS

Comments: This command clears the display screen and returns the cursor to the home position (the top left corner).

CLS does not affect any current screen characteristics, such as color or column width.

Example: Enter

cls ⏎

COMMAND

Secondary command processor
Version 3.0 External

Functions: Loads a secondary command processor.

Format: COMMAND [*d:*][*path*][/P][/E:*xxxx*][/C *string*]

Variables: [*d:*][*path*] tells DOS in which directory the new command processor is located. Be careful not to start a command processor in one directory and then direct DOS to a different command processor in another directory.

Options:

/P makes the new command processor permanent in memory. If you use /P, the new command processor will remain in memory until you restart DOS.

/C *string*

executes a single command (given by *string*) and then returns to the original command processor.

/E:*xxxx*

sets the size of the environment. The environment is an area in memory where DOS stores information such as the current path and the current prompt. This option allows you to increase the environment space from its normal 127 characters to as much as 32768 characters. The number following the colon is the number of characters that you want to reserve room for in the environment.

To start a semi-permanent secondary command processor, don't use any option. This command processor will function until you issue the EXIT command. The EXIT command will return you to the original command processor.

Comments: Using /P does a partial restart of DOS. It executes the AUTOEXEC.BAT file, but does not clear memory or start device drivers that are in the CONFIG.SYS file. You lose 3280 bytes of memory (with DOS 3.1), which is lost until you re-start DOS.

Using /C provides a one-command secondary command processor. Using no option provides a semi-permanent (until you use the EXIT command) secondary command processor, and /P provides a permanent secondary command processor.

When you start a secondary command processor without any options, it inherits the environment from the previous command processor. You can change the environment of the secondary command processor without affecting the environment of the original command processor. The environment contains the prompt, the path, and the location of the command processor (COMSPEC).

This command is useful for "nesting" batch files. Normally, if you put the name of a batch file as a command in another batch file, the first batch file terminates, and the second takes over unless you use the CALL batch command. Any commands following the "nested" batch file name are ignored. If you put the name of a second batch file in the COMMAND command, the second batch file will execute, and then control will return to the first batch file.

If you use both /C and /P, the /P option is ignored.

Messages: **Specified COMMAND search directory bad.** COMMAND.COM couldn't be found in the directory you specified in the path parameter (or, beyond that, on the path given in your environment); however, the second command processor will still be loaded as if no parameters were given. You must use the EXIT command to return to the first command processor.

Invalid COMMAND.COM
Cannot start COMMAND, exiting. The copy of COMMAND.COM that DOS is trying to load doesn't match what DOS expects. Part of COMMAND.COM is unloaded from memory when programs need more memory. When the program is done, DOS reloads this part of COMMAND.COM.

If the path parameter in your last COMMAND command does not specify the same COMMAND.COM as was specified when you actually started, this error will occur.

This error can also occur if you have changed diskettes while running a program, and the new diskette has the wrong version of COMMAND.COM on it.

DOS exits the highest level command processor and returns you to the next level down.

No free file handles
Cannot start COMMAND, exiting. DOS cannot load a second command processor because there are not enough file handles. Increase the number in the FILES command in your CONFIG.SYS file and restart DOS.

Cannot start COMMAND, exiting. DOS cannot load a second command processor because there is not enough memory. You may have too many memory-resident programs loaded.

Examples: To load a permanent command processor from the \DOS\SYSTEM subdirectory, enter

\dos\system\command /p ⏎

To quickly see how the COMMAND command can be used to chain between batch files, enter the following, pressing **Return** at the end of each line.

```
copy con command1.bat
pause This is the FIRST command processor
command /c command2
pause Now we're back to the FIRST command processor
^Z
```

The screen will display the following response:

    1 File(s) copied

Then enter

```
copy con command2.bat
pause This is the SECOND command processor
^Z
```

Remember to press **Return** at the end of each line. The screen will again display

    `1 File(s) copied`

This process creates two batch files (a batch file consists of a series of DOS commands). The first line "copies" information from the CON (keyboard console) device to a file named COMMAND1.BAT.

To get the ^Z character, press the **F6** key. To try out your demo, enter

command1 ⏎

The screen will display the following information:

```
A>pause This is the FIRST command processor
Strike any key when ready . . .

A>command /c command2

A>pause This is the SECOND command processor
Strike any key when ready . . .

A>

A>pause Now we're back to the FIRST command processor
Strike any key when ready . . .
```

Press a key when prompted. Notice that the program started with the first command processor, switched to the second, and then came back to the first. With complex batch files, this feature can be useful.

To see what would happen without the COMMAND command, re-enter the first batch file with one change (press **Return** at the end of each line):

```
copy con command1.bat
pause This is the FIRST command processor
command2
pause Now we're back to the FIRST command processor
^Z
```

The screen will display the following:

```
    1 File(s) copied
```

Now, try running the demo again. Enter

command1 ⏎

The screen will display the following information:

```
        A>pause This is the FIRST command processor
        Strike any key when ready . . .

        A>command2

        A>pause This is the SECOND command processor
        Strike any key when ready . . .

        A>
```

Notice that the program still chains from the first batch file to the second, but it does not chain back to the first.

COMP

Compare files
Version 1.0 External

Functions: Compares the contents of one file or a set of files (primary files) to the contents of a second file or set of files (secondary files).

Format: COMP [*filespec*] [*filespec*]

Variables: *filespec* is defined as [*d:*][*path*][*filename.ext*].

The first *filespec* specifies the file (or set of files) that you want to compare. It is also referred to as the **primary** file.

The second *filespec* specifies the file (or set of files) that you want to compare with the first file. It is also referred to as the **secondary** file.

You can use wild card characters in *filename.ext*.

Comments: This command is commonly used after a COPY operation to ensure that the two files are identical. To compare two complete diskettes, use the DISKCOMP command.

If COMP is used without parameters, or if the second *filespec* is missing, DOS prompts you for the information. If you do not use a file name, DOS assumes that you want to compare all the files in the specified directory (*.*).

You can also compare all files in one directory with all corresponding files in another directory.

Files are not compared if file sizes are different, if the file matching the secondary *filespec* cannot be found, or if the directory *path* is invalid.

If DOS cannot find the primary *filespec*, it prompts you again for both primary and secondary *filespecs*.

During a comparison, a message appears for any location that has mismatching information in the two files. The message looks like the following:

```
Compare error at offset xxxxxxxx
File 1 = XX
File 2 = XX
```

The message shows the location of the mismatched information (*xxxxxxxx* shown as hexadecimal bytes), the two file names (*File 1* and *File 2*), and the contents of the bytes themselves (*XX*, also in hexadecimal bytes).

After ten mismatches, further comparison is stopped and the **10 mismatches-ending compare** message is displayed. DOS considers further comparison unwarranted.

If no mismatches are found, the **Files compare OK** message is displayed. DOS continues to compare specified files until no more are left. Then, the **Compare more files (Y/N)?** message is displayed. Type **Y** for "Yes" and press **Return** to be prompted for another set of files. Answer **N** for "No" and press **Return** to return to the system prompt.

Messages: **Compare error at offset xxxxxxxx.** There is mismatched information at the offset location (*xxxxxxxx* is in hex bytes). You decide what to do with the information.

Compare more files (Y/N)? Answer **Y** for "Yes" to be prompted for another set of files. Answer **N** for "No" to return to the system prompt.

Enter primary file name. When you enter COMP without any filespecs or if you respond "Yes" to the prompt

Compare more files (Y/N)?, DOS asks you for the first, or primary, filespec. Enter *filespec* as [*d:*][*path*][*filename.ext*]. DOS will then ask you for the second filespec. Use the same format.

Enter 2nd file name or drive id. You haven't entered the second filespec. Enter *filespec* as [*d:*][*path*][*filename.ext*]. If the name of the second file is the same as the first, just enter the second drive name or path name.

EOF mark not found. The files compared OK, but there was no end-of-file marker. This problem usually occurs when comparing non-text files and is not an indication of a problem.

File sharing conflict. One of the two files entered is currently being accessed. Try comparing these files again later. If you are comparing a set of files, DOS will move to the next two files to be compared.

File xxxx AND File yyyy. Displays the two files being compared. *xxxx* is the primary file; *yyyy* is the secondary file. No action is required.

Files are different sizes. If the files are different sizes, then they cannot have the same information. The files are therefore not compared.

Files compare OK. The two files compared have identical information.

10 mismatches-ending compare. Two files are compared, and mismatches are displayed until 10 mismatches occur. At this point, DOS decides that further comparison is unwarranted.

Example: To compare FILE1.DOC to FILE1.BAK on drive A, at the A> prompt, enter

```
comp file1.doc file1.bak ⏎
```

To compare all .ASM files on drive C to .BAK files of the same file name on drive A, at the A> prompt, enter

```
comp c:*.asm *.bak ⏎
```

To compare all .ASM files on drive A to the files with the same names on drive C, at the A> prompt, enter

```
comp *.asm c: ⏎
```

To compare all the files on the drive C in directory UTIL1 to the same files in directory UTIL2, at the C> prompt, enter

comp \util1 \util2 ⏎

COPY

Copy or concatenate files

Version 1.0 Internal

Functions: Copies files or concatenates (combines) files.

Formats: To copy a file:

COPY [*d:*][*path*][*sourcefile.ext*] [*d:*][*path*][*destfile.ext*] [/**V**]

To concatenate (combine) files:

COPY [*d:*][*path*][*sourcefile.ext*]+[*d:*][*path*][*sourcefile.ext*] [*d:*][*path*][*destfile.ext*] [/**V**]

Variables: [*d:*][*path*][*sourcefile.ext*] specifies the file from which you want to copy (the source file).

[*d:*][*path*][*destfile.ext*] specifies the name of the file to which you want to copy (the destination file).

You can use the wild card characters within the file name and extension.

Options:

/**A** Source file: Treated as an ASCII (text) file. The file's data is copied up to, but not including, the first end-of-file marker (Ctrl-Z character) found in the file. The rest of the file is not copied.

Destination file: An end-of-file marker (Ctrl-Z character) is added as the last character of the file.

/**B** Source file: Treated as a binary file. The entire file is copied.

Destination file: No end-of-file marker (Ctrl-Z character) is added.

NOTE: The /**A** and /**B** options can be placed before, between, or after the filespecs. The placement determines to which files the option applies. The option affects the file immediately preceding it and all files after it.

/V   Verifies that information written to the destination file is recorded properly (usually used when critical data is copied). Verification causes slower copying. If VERIFY ON is active, then /V is not needed.

Comments: This command copies one or more files to a different file name on any valid drive or in any valid directory. It also copies or combines one or more files to the same file name on a different drive or directory.

If the destination file is specified as a drive or directory without a file name, files are copied into that directory without changing their names.

When files are copied, the creation date and time recorded for the destination file are the same date and time as those for the source file. They are not the date and time the copy was made.

When the concatenation format is used, COPY combines files into one destination file while copying. The source files are those files from which you want to copy. They are combined by using a plus sign (+) between each file. After the first source file is copied, subsequent source files are added to the end of the previous file.

When files are combined, the date and time recorded for the destination file will be the current date and time. The message indicating the number of files copied is the number of destination files resulting from concatenation.

The COPY command can also be used to transfer data between any of the system devices.

Examples: This example copies all files with the file name FILE plus one character and with the extension BAS from the current directory of drive A to the current directory of drive B. From the DOS prompt, enter

```
copy a:file?.bas b:
```

The screen will display the files that are copied, for example:

```
FILE.BAS
FILE1.BAS
FILE2.BAS
     3 File(s) copied
```

To make a second copy of a file (with a new name) on the same disk and directory, enter

copy sfile.doc dfile.doc ⏎

The screen will display the following:

```
1 File(s) copied
```

This next example copies a file to the same disk and directory and changes the file extension. The file is treated as an ASCII (text) file, and the copy operation is verified. Enter

copy file.bas file.asc /a/v ⏎

The screen will display the following:

```
1 File(s) copied
```

To copy all files from the current drive and directory to the LETTERS directory, from the DOS prompt, enter

copy *.* \letters ⏎

The screen will display the files that are copied:

```
LETTER1.DOC
LETTER2.DOC
LETTER3.DOC
LETTER1.BAK
LETTER2.BAK
LETTER3.BAK
      6 File(s) copied
```

This next example concatenates (combines) the first three files into FILE.TXT in the current directory on the current drive. Enter

```
copy file1.txt+file2.txt+file3.txt file.txt ⏎
```

The screen will display the following:

```
FILE1.TXT
FILE2.TXT
FILE3.TXT
      1 File(s) copied
```

To append the file TWO.ASM to the end of the file ONE.ASM and leave the result in ONE.ASM as an ASCII file, enter

```
copy one.asm+two.asm /a ⏎
```

The screen will display the following:

```
ONE.ASM
TWO.ASM
      1 File(s) copied
```

To combine all files with the extension .TXT and then all files with the extension .REF into one file called ALLFILES.PRN, enter

```
copy *.txt+*.ref allfiles.prn ⏎
```

The screen will display the files that are combined:

```
OUTLINE.TXT
OUTLINE1.TXT
CONTRACT.REF
CONTRACT1.REF
     1 File(s) copied
```

This next example combines all files with the extension .TXT and then all files with the extension .REF; the results are files with the same name but with the extension .PRN. Enter

copy *.txt+*.ref *.prn ⏎

The screen will display the files that are copied:

```
FILE.TXT
FILE.REF
FILE1.TXT
FILE1.REF
FILE2.TXT
FILE2.REF
FILE3.TXT
FILE3.REF
     4 File(s) copied
```

Any valid input device can be used in place of *sourcefile* (for example, CON for keyboard input to create a file). Any valid output device can be used in place of *destfile*. (See Chapter 2 for a list of device names.) To print a file, enter

copy letter.txt prn ⏎

CTTY

Change console
Version 2.0 Internal

Functions: Changes the primary console to a different device name.

Format: CTTY *device-name*

Variables: *device-name* is the new device to be used as the primary console.

Specifying AUX, COM1, or COM2 changes the primary console to one of these device names.

Specifying CON resets the standard console and display screen to the primary console.

Comments: You can use CTTY to install your own character-oriented devices. The device must be capable of both input and output operations. For example, a printer is not a valid device.

Using CTTY lets you control your computer from another terminal—across the room or across town.

CTTY can be used only with programs that use DOS function calls. Other programs that do not use function calls (such as BASIC) cannot use CTTY.

Messages: **Invalid device.** Indicates an invalid device name was used. Check your spelling. DOS may not recognize the device name, or it may not be a character-oriented device.

Example: To use a terminal connected to the asynchronous communications adapter (the serial port) as the primary console, enter

    ctty aux ⏎

119

To change back to the standard console and display screen, at the remote terminal (the one attached to the serial port), enter

ctty con ⏎

DATE

Set system date
Version 1.0 Internal

Functions: Displays and sets the system date.

Format: DATE [*mm-dd-yy*]

Variables: *mm* can range from 1 to 12 (a one- or two-digit number)

dd can range from 1 to 31 (a one- or two-digit number)

yy can be expressed in two ways: it can range from 80-99 when entered as a two-digit number (the leading 19 is assumed), or it can range from 1980-2099 when entered as a four-digit number.

mm, *dd*, and *yy* can be separated by minus signs or slashes.

Enter DATE without variables, and DOS will prompt you for them.

Comments: If you enter DATE with no variables, DOS prompts you with the following message:

    Current date is Day mm-dd-yy
    Enter new date:_

where *Day* is the current day (e.g., Fri.), *mm-dd-yy* is the month, day, and year (e.g., 10-09-86).

You can then enter the new date as *mm-dd-yy* (or *mm/dd/yy*) or press **Return** to keep the date as is.

A valid date within the ranges shown above will be accepted; otherwise, the **Invalid date** message is displayed and the enter date prompt reappears.

DATE will set the date on a built-in permanent clock. Computers such as the AT and the PS/2 have built-in permanent clocks. This feature was added with Version 3.3

Messages: **Invalid date.** You did not enter a valid date, or the format was incorrect. Check the requirements previously listed and re-enter.

Examples: To change the date to September 28, 1986, enter

date 9/28/86 ⏎

To change the date to May 8, 2001, enter

date 5-8-2001 ⏎

DEL

Delete files

Version 1.0 Internal

Functions: Deletes specified files.

Format: DEL *filespec*

Variables: *filespec* is defined as [*d:*][*path*][*filename.ext*], which specifies the drive name, directory path, file name, and extension on which the command is to act.

You can use wild card characters in the *filename* and *ext*ension.

If a path is specified, but *filename* is not given, *.* is assumed.

Comments: The command deletes all the files that match the *filespec*. If no drive or directory is specified, files are deleted from the current directory on the default drive.

WARNING: Wild card characters should be used with extreme caution when deleting files. Many files can be deleted with a single command. If you are unsure about what files will be deleted, first display them using the DIR command with the same file specification. The files listed with DIR will be the files that you will delete with the DEL command (as long as you enter the same filespec).

To ensure that the filespec doesn't change after you see only the directory listing, type DEL and then press the F3 key. DOS will repeat the filespec from the DIR command so you can be sure it isn't mistyped.

When DOS deletes the files you specify in *filespec*, the entry in the disk directory is changed to show "not in use," and the space occupied by the file on the disk is thus freed, which means that until you put information on (write to) that space, you can recover the files you have deleted; however, even with one of the several utility programs available that let you recover lost files (the most well-known of which is *Norton Utilities*), recovery is difficult at best. Once you have written to the space, the files cannot be recovered.

You cannot delete files that are marked as read-only files.

Although you can delete all files in a subdirectory, DEL will not delete a subdirectory itself. Use the RMDIR command to *remove* the subdirectory after all the files have been deleted with the DEL command.

You should return all device names to their true defaults by canceling any changes made with ASSIGN, JOIN, or SUBST before using DEL so that you delete files from the intended drive.

Messages: **Are you sure (Y/N)?** If you use the *filespec* *.* or a path without a file name and extension to delete all the files on a disk or in a directory, this message is displayed to verify that you actually want to delete all files. Type **Y** for "Yes" and press **Return** to delete all files. Type **N** for "No" and press **Return** to return to the system prompt without deleting any files.

File not found. The *filespec* you gave does not exist. Check to be sure you have named the correct drive, directory path, file name, and extension. Also, check your spelling.

Invalid number of parameters. You must use a disk drive, path, or file name with the command.

Example: To delete the file named FILE.DOC from the diskette in drive A, from the DOS prompt, enter

del file.doc ⏎

To delete all the files with the extension .CAL in the SAMPLES directory on drive C, use the DIR command to be sure that you are going to delete only the files you want to delete. Then use DEL to actually delete the files. For example, from the DOS prompt, enter

dir c:\samples*.cal ⏎

The screen will show the files that match the *filespec* you entered:

```
Volume in drive C is VDISK   V3.2
Directory of C:\SAMPLES

Prices    CAL  7936    4-26-86  11:51a
SALES86   CAL  2944    4-26-86  12:22p
     2 File(s)     14464 bytes free
```

Then enter

del ⏎

Press the **F3** key here to have DOS retype the filespec for you. This action ensures that the filespec doesn't change between the DIR and DEL commands. Press **Return** to execute the DEL command.

To delete all the files in the TEMP directory on default drive C, at the C prompt enter

del \temp ⏎

The screen will display the following message:

Are you sure (Y/N)?

125

DOS will prompt you with the **Are you sure (Y/N)?** message before actually deleting any files because you are deleting all the files in the TEMP directory. Type **Y** and press **Return** to delete the files specified. Type **N** and press **Return** to return to the system prompt without deleting any files.

To get the same results, you could have also entered

del \temp*.* ⏎

to which the screen would respond

```
Are you sure (Y/N)?
```

The first format, however, saves keystrokes.

DIR

Directory command
Version 1.0 Internal

Functions: Lists specified files.

Format: DIR *filespec* [/P][/W]

Variables: *filespec* is defined as [*d:*][*path*][*filename* [*.ext*]], which specifies the drive name, directory path, file name, and extension on which the command is to act.

You can use wildcard characters in the *filename* and *ext*.

Options:

/P Pauses when the screen is full. The **Strike any key when ready...** message is displayed. To continue, press any key.

/W Displays the files in a wide (80-column) format. Only the directory names and file names are shown. This option is useful only for 80-column displays.

Comments: The DIR command finds only the files in one directory at a time. Following is a sample directory listing:

```
Volume in drive A is SAMPLE_DIR
Directory of A:\

UTILITY     <DIR>              4-26-86    12:01p
EDITOR      EXE      95104    10-07-84     1:35p
EDITOR      HLP      16200    10-07-84     1:53p
BORDERS     ACS        250     4-01-86    10:46p
FIN-INFO    DOC       2432     4-15-85    10:49p
PHONEDIR    DOC       1408     3-30-86     9:41p
STATETAX    DOC       1024     3-18-86    12:42a
YOSEMITE    DOC       1024     2-24-86    10:54p
      8 Files(s)   241664 bytes free
```

The first two lines include the volume name and the path of the directory being displayed.

Then the file names and extensions that match the *filespec* are listed, along with their size and the date and time the files were created or last modified.

The last line shows total number of files that matched the *filespec* and the amount of free space available on the disk.

Subdirectories are clearly identified with <DIR> in the file size field.

If you do not specify a file name or extension, the *.* filespec is assumed. If you want to list only files that do not have an extension, use the file name followed by a period.

To see a list of all files on a disk, including files in subdirectories, use either the CHKDSK /V or TREE /F command.

If you use the /W option, the file names and directory names are listed five names per line. The file size and date and the <DIR> for subdirectories are not shown.

You can print the directory by using DIR >PRN. You can put the directory into a file by using DIR >*filename*, where *filename* is the name of the file in which you want the directory.

Hidden files (those with the attribute byte set to hidden) are not displayed with DIR.

Messages: **File not found.** The path name or file name does not exist. The path name may not exist, the file name may not exist, or the file may not be in the directory you asked for. Also, check your spelling.

Example: To display files on drive A, at the A> prompt, enter

dir ⏎

To display all files in the DOS directory on drive C, at the C> prompt, enter

dir \dos ⏎

To display all files with the extension .BAS in the PROGRAMS directory on drive C, at the C> prompt, enter

dir \programs*.bas ⏎

To list all files on drive B with the file name FILE, enter

dir b:file ⏎

DOS assumes the extension is .* if none is entered.

DISKCOMP

Compare diskettes
Version 1.0 External

Functions: Compares two entire diskettes.

Format: DISKCOMP [*d:*] [*d:*] [/1][/8]

Variables: *d:* specifies a valid drive name (one that exists on your system). They may be the same drive name or different drives.

If you name only one drive, it will be used for both diskettes. If you don't name any drives, the default drive will be used.

Options:
/1 Compares only the first side of the diskettes, even if the diskettes or the drives are double-sided.

/8 Compares 8 sectors per track, even if the first diskette has 9 or 15 sectors per track.

Comments: You should compare only diskettes that are compatible and formatted with the same number of sides, tracks, and sectors (see Chapter 2).

If you have only one disk drive, you can still compare disks. You will be prompted to insert each disk at the proper time. DISKCOMP waits for you to put the correct disk in and to press a key to continue.

When a disk comparison starts, the number of sides and sectors per track is automatically determined by the characteristics of the first diskette. You can change this number by using the options /1 or /8.

During a disk comparison, DISKCOMP compares all tracks on a track-by-track basis and displays a message if the tracks are not the same. The message shows the track number and the side of the diskette (0 or 1).

If you have made a copy of a diskette with the COPY command, the files produced on the backup copy will be the same but may be placed at different locations on the diskette. In this case, use the COMP command rather than DISKCOMP to compare individual files.

When the comparison is finished, DISKCOMP displays the **Compare more diskettes (Y/N)?** message. Type **Y** for "Yes" and press **Return** to be prompted for another set of diskettes. The same drive names are used. Type **N** for "No" and press **Return** to return to the system prompt.

DISKCOMP does not work when you have changed drive characteristics with SUBST, ASSIGN, or JOIN. DISKCOMP does not work on network drives.

DISKCOMP Demonstration

This demonstration shows the steps for both a successful comparison and a failed comparison. In this demonstration, two copies are made of a diskette. The first copy is made with the COPY command. The second copy is made using the DISKCOPY command.

The original diskette has been in use for some time with several files added, deleted, and modified. It is compared to the two copies.

To begin, enter

```
diskcopy a: b:
```

The screen will display the following:

```
Insert source diskette into drive A
Insert destination diskette into drive B
Strike any key when ready
```

Insert the original disk in drive A, and insert the first blank diskette in drive B. Press any key to start copying, which will erase any information that may have been on this diskette; be sure that the diskette doesn't contain any information you need.

The screen will then display the following:

```
Copying 9 sectors per track, 2 side(s)
Copy complete
Copy another (Y/N)?n
```

Type **N** for "No" and press **Return** to end DISKCOPY and return to the system prompt. Remove the diskette from drive B.

Now you are going to make a copy using the COPY command. If the second blank diskette has already been formatted, you can skip the format command shown next. If the diskette has not been formatted, enter

format b: ⏎

The screen will display the following:

```
Insert new diskette for drive B:
and strike Enter when ready
```

Insert the diskette in drive B and press **Return** to start formatting, which will erase any information that may have been on this diskette; be sure that the diskette doesn't contain any information you need.

When FORMAT is finished, the screen will then display the following:

```
Format another (Y/N)?n
```

Type **N** for "No" and press **Return** to end FORMAT and return to the system prompt.

To copy all files from drive A to drive B, at the
A> prompt, enter

copy a:*.* b: ⏎

The screen will display the following:

>   .....
>   .....
>   (Files being copied are displayed)
>   .....
>   .....
>   x File(s) copied

After all the files have been copied, you will return to the system prompt. Remove the diskette from drive B.

To start comparing diskettes, enter

diskcomp a: b: ⏎

The screen will display the following:

>   Insert first diskette into drive A
>   Insert second diskette into drive B
>   Strike any key when ready

Insert the original diskette into drive A; insert the duplicate diskette made with DISKCOPY into drive B. Press any key to start comparing the diskettes.

The screen will display the following:

>   Comparing 9 sectors per track, 2 side(s)
>
>   Diskettes compare OK
>
>   Compare more diskettes (Y/N)?

The message **Diskettes compare OK** indicates the duplicate diskette made with DISKCOPY is identical to the original. (If they did not compare OK, you should DISKCOPY the diskette again and then repeat DISKCOMP. If they are still not comparing OK, the duplicate diskette is bad and should be discarded.)

Now compare the original diskette to the duplicate made with the COPY command. Type **Y** for "Yes" and press **Return** to request another diskette comparison.

The screen will display the following:

```
Insert first diskette into drive A
Insert second diskette into drive B
Strike any key when ready
```

Insert the second copy in drive B and press any key to start comparing the diskettes.

The screen will then display the following:

```
Comparing 9 sectors per track, 2 side(s)

Compare error on side 0, track 0

Compare error on side 1, track 0
.....
.....
.....
Compare error on side 1, track 39

Compare more diskettes (Y/N)?
```

The diskette comparison failed with this diskette, which is indicated by the **Compare error** messages. When you copy files with the COPY command, they may not be placed in identical locations on the new diskette. There isn't anything wrong with the second diskette; it is just not identical to the original one.

To end DISKCOMP, type **N** and press **Return**.

To verify that the contents of the disk files are actually the same, even though their location on the disk is not, enter

comp a: b: ⏎

This command will compare each file on each of the disks. You should see a **Files compare OK** message after each one.

Messages:

Cannot DISKCOMP to or from a Network drive. You cannot use DISKCOMP to compare files on a network drive or on a resident drive that is being shared. Use COMP *.* instead. If the drive is being shared, you can PAUSE the server, execute DISKCOMP, then CONTINUE the server.

Compare error on side xx, track xx. During DISKCOMP, one or more locations on track *xx*, side *xx* have different information. You may have used COPY to make backups of your files on the source diskette. These files are usually written to the target diskette in different locations, wherever there is space. If you want an exact copy of a diskette, use DISKCOPY instead of COPY.

Compare more diskettes (Y/N)? You may compare more than one pair of diskettes without re-entering the DISKCOMP command. Type **Y** for "Yes" and press **Return** to compare another set of diskettes. You will be prompted to insert the proper one. Type **N** for "No" and press **Return** to end DISKCOMP and return to the system prompt.

Compare process ended. DISKCOMP is finished comparing. No action is required.

Comparing x sectors per track, n side(s). This message tells you how many sectors per track (x = 8, 9, or 15) and how many sides (*n* = 1 or 2) are found on the first diskette. If you use the /8 option, *x* will be 8; if you use the /1 option, *n* will be 1.

Diskette/Drive not compatible. The diskette is not compatible with the drive it is in, which could be caused by an attempt to read a high-capacity diskette in a double-sided drive, for example.

Diskettes compare OK. DISKCOMP was successful. The two diskettes are identical.

Drive or diskette types not compatible. The target diskette or drive is not compatible with the source diskette or drive. For example, you cannot compare a double-sided diskette to a single-sided diskette.

Insert first diskette in drive x
Insert second diskette in drive x. DISKCOMP prompts you to insert the first diskette and the second diskette into the drives you specified in the command format.

Make sure a diskette is inserted into the drive and the door is closed. DISKCOMP is trying to access a drive you named in the command format, and it is either empty or the drive door is open. Make sure you are using the right drives, you have the diskette inserted, and the drive door is closed.

Specified drive does not exist, or is non-removable. One of the drive names you used is either a fixed disk drive (which you can't use to compare), or the drive doesn't exist on your system. Check your command format and re-enter the correct drive name(s). If you have altered true drive information with ASSIGN, JOIN, or SUBST, return all drives to their defaults and retry DISKCOPY.

Unrecoverable read error on drive x
Track xx, side x. If DISKCOMP cannot read any data, it tries a total of four times, and then displays this message if it is unsuccessful. Drive *x*, track *xx*, and side *x* show the drive, the track, and the side of the diskette where it failed.

If the diskette is the second diskette, use DISKCOPY with a new diskette and try DISKCOMP again; otherwise, use COPY *.* to copy all files from the damaged diskette to a new one. Then, reformat the damaged diskette or discard it.

Examples: To compare the diskette in drive A to the diskette in drive B, at the A prompt, enter

diskcomp a: b: ⏎

To perform a single-drive compare on drive A, enter

diskcomp a: a: ⏎

or simply enter

diskcomp ⏎

without any variables. DISKCOMP will ask you to insert the proper diskette at the right time.

To compare only the first side of the diskette in drive A to the first side of the diskette in drive B, enter

diskcomp a: b: /1 ⏎

To compare only 8 sectors per side of the first diskette with 8 sectors of the second diskette, enter

diskcomp a: a: /8 ⏎

or

diskcomp /8 ⏎

This is a single-drive compare.

DISKCOPY

Copy diskettes
Version 1.0 External

Functions: Makes a copy of an entire diskette.

Format: DISKCOPY [*d:*] [*d:*] [/1]

Variables: *d:* specifies a valid drive name (one that exists on your system). They may be the same drive name or different drives.

The first drive name is the **source** drive; the second drive name is the **target** drive.

If the second drive is not given, the default drive is assumed as the target.

If you don't name any drives, the target drive will be used as both source and target.

When only one drive is used, DISKCOPY prompts you when to insert each diskette at the proper time.

Options: /1 Copies only the first side of the diskettes, even if the diskette or the drive is double-sided.

Comments: Using an invalid drive name in the command format will result in an **Invalid drive specification** message.

If you have only one disk drive, you can still perform a disk copy. You will be prompted to insert each disk at the proper time. DISKCOPY waits for you to put the correct disk in and to press a key to continue.

A diskette must be formatted before the disk is actually copied. If the target diskette is unformatted, or if both disks are not formatted the same way, DISKCOPY formats the target diskette the same way the source diskette was formatted. If the /1 option is used, the target diskette is formatted only on one side.

WARNING: *DISKCOPY destroys (overwrites) any information already on the target diskette. Be sure the target diskette is either new, blank, or contains files that you do not want to keep.*

After copying, DISKCOPY prompts you with the **Copy another (Y/N)?** message. Type **Y** for "Yes" and press **Return** to copy another diskette. The same drive names will be used, and DISKCOPY will prompt you to insert the diskettes. Type **N** for "No" and press **Return** to return to the system prompt.

DISKCOPY makes an exact copy of the source diskette. It senses whether the format is one- or two-sided and 8 or 9 sectors per track and formats the target diskette in the same way. The only time this process doesn't happen is when you use the /1 option. Here, the target diskette is formatted as one-sided regardless of the source diskette's format.

It is a good idea to format your target diskettes ahead of time with the FORMAT command. FORMAT will report any bad sectors, and you can either reformat the diskette or use another diskette. DISKCOPY will try to write information to these bad sectors although it will indicate the drive, track, and side where the disk error occurs. The result is that you won't get a clean copy, and performance will be affected. (See FORMAT for details about formatting diskettes.)

WARNING: *Always write-protect your source diskette. If you make a mistake when doing a one-drive DISKCOPY, or you specify the wrong drives, you won't destroy any information on your source diskette.*

A good rule of thumb to observe when doing a DISKCOPY is to watch the drive lights when the operation starts. DISKCOPY will first read information from the source diskette to prepare to copy it to the target diskette. If the wrong drive light comes on first, quickly flip open the drive doors and wait for a read error to occur. If you catch it in time, you won't lose any information. The best precaution, however, is to write-protect your source diskette.

The files on a well-used diskette may be fragmented, resulting in files that are not sequentially stored. Poor disk performance is the result. Using DISKCOPY will result in a second copy with the same fragmentation. In this case, you should use the copy command to copy files to the second diskette (i.e., COPY a:*.* b:). They will be stored sequentially, and disk performance will improve. You can use CHKDSK *.* to check for fragmentation (see CHKDSK for details).

You can run DISKCOMP after DISKCOPY to verify that the diskettes are identical. (See DISKCOMP for details.)

DISKCOPY does not work when you have changed drive characteristics with SUBST, ASSIGN, or JOIN. DISKCOMP does not work on network drives.

DISKCOPY Demonstration

This demonstration shows the steps for making two backup diskettes by using DISKCOPY. The demonstration uses a dual-drive approach. The backup diskettes do not need to be formatted. DISKCOPY will format them.

To begin, enter

diskcopy a: b: ⏎

The screen will display the following:

```
Insert source diskette into drive A
Insert destination diskette into drive B
Strike any key when ready
```

Insert the original diskette in drive A. Insert the first blank diskette in drive B and press any key to start copying, which will erase any information that may have been on the disk in drive B; be sure the diskette doesn't contain any information you need before you start copying.

The screen will then display the following:

```
Copying 9 sectors per track, 2 side(s)
Copy complete
Copy another (Y/N)?
```

Type **Y** for "Yes" and press **Return**.

The screen will then display the following:

```
Insert first diskette into drive A
Insert second diskette into drive B
Strike any key when ready
```

Leave the original diskette in drive A. Remove the first diskette from drive B, and insert the second backup diskette. Press any key to start copying.

The screen will display the following:

```
Copying 9 sectors per track, 2 side(s)
Copy complete
Copy another (Y/N)?
```

Type **N** for "No" and press **Return**. You will return to the system prompt.

DISKCOPY has made two identical copies of the original diskette. You can use DISKCOMP to verify that the copies are identical (see the DISKCOMP command for details).

Messages: **Cannot DISKCOPY to or from a Network drive.** You cannot use DISKCOPY with a network drive or a drive on your system that is being shared. If you are using a network drive, use COPY *.* instead. If your system drive is being shared, wait until it is free and try DISKCOPY again.

Invalid parameter
Do not specify filename(s)
Command format:DISKCOPY d: d: [/1]. The command was entered improperly. Check the format and try again.

Copy another (Y/N)? This message is displayed whenever a copy process has been completed. Type **Y** for "Yes" and press **Return** to copy another diskette. The same drive names will be used, and DISKCOPY will prompt you to insert the diskettes. Type **N** for "No" and press **Return** to return to the system prompt.

Copy complete. All information on the source diskette has been copied to the target diskette. No action is required.

Copying xxx tracks
x Sectors/Track, n side(s). Copying format information is provided in this message. *xxx* will be either 40 or 80 tracks. *x* will be 8 if the diskette was formatted with DOS 1, 9 for DOS 2, and 15 for DOS 3 on a high-capacity drive. *n* will be the number of sides being copied—either 1 or 2.

Diskette/Drive not compatible. The diskette is not compatible with the drive it is in, which could be caused by attempting to read a high-capacity diskette in a double-sided drive, for example.

Drive or diskette types not compatible. The target diskette or drive is not compatible with the source diskette or drive. For example, you cannot copy a double-sided diskette to a single-sided diskette.

Formatting while copying. This message is informational. Either the target diskette is unformatted, or it isn't formatted in the same way as the source diskette. No action is required.

Insert source diskette in drive x
Insert target diskette in drive x. DISKCOPY prompts you to insert the first (source) diskette and the second (target) diskette into the drives that you specified in the command format.

Make sure a diskette is inserted into the drive and the door is closed. DISKCOPY is trying to access a drive you named in the command format, and it is either empty or the drive door is open. Make sure that you are using the right drives, you have the diskette inserted, and the drive door is closed.

Source diskette bad or unusable. DISKCOPY has found errors on the source diskette while trying to read it. The diskette may not be suitable for a DISKCOPY. Try copying all files to the target diskette with COPY *.* instead. If this step doesn't help, your source diskette is probably damaged and unusable.

Source diskette bad or incompatible. DISKCOPY has found errors on the source diskette while trying to read it. The diskette may be bad, or it may be the wrong kind of diskette for the drive you are using. Try copying all the files to the target diskette with COPY *.* instead.

Specified drive does not exist, or is non-removable. One of the drive names you used doesn't exist on your system or is a fixed disk. Check your command format and re-enter the correct drive name(s). If you have altered true drive information with ASSIGN, JOIN, or SUBST, return all drives to their defaults and retry DISKCOPY.

Target diskette bad or unusable. The target diskette is bad, damaged, or poor quality. Try reformatting it with the FORMAT command. If this step doesn't help, use another diskette.

Target diskette may be unusable. This message follows an unrecoverable read, write, or verify error message. The information copied to the target diskette may be incomplete.

If the error is on the target diskette, try reformatting the target diskette with the FORMAT command. If this doesn't help, use another diskette.

If the error is on the source diskette, try copying all the files to a new diskette, reformat the source diskette, and copy the files back. Then try DISKCOPY again.

Target diskette write protected
Correct, then strike any key. You can't copy to a write-protected diskette. You may have reversed the drive names you want to use as source and target drives. Re-enter the command with the correct format.

If the command format is correct, remove the write-protect tab on the target diskette (if that diskette is the one you really want to use as the target diskette). You can also use another diskette that isn't write protected.

Unrecoverable read error on source
Track xx, side x. When a read error occurs, DISKCOPY tries four times to read the information from the source diskette. If it is unsuccessful, DISKCOPY continues, but you may not get an identical copy. Use DISKCOMP to compare the two disks. If they aren't identical, copy the files on the source diskette to another one, reformat the source diskette, copy the files back, and try DISKCOPY again.

Unrecoverable write error on target
Track xx, side x. DISKCOPY tries several times to write information to the target diskette. If it is unsuccessful, DISKCOPY continues, but you may not get an identical copy. Use DISKCOMP to compare the two disks. If they aren't identical, reformat to see if the diskette is usable (no bad sectors). If not, discard it and use a new diskette.

Examples: To copy an entire diskette from drive A to drive B, at the A> prompt, enter

diskcopy a: b: ⏎

To copy an entire diskette with one drive only, enter

diskcopy ⏎

To perform a one-drive COPYDISK on drive A from a fixed disk (drive C), at the C> prompt, enter

diskcopy a: a: ⏎

ERASE

Erase files
Version 1.0 Internal

Functions: Deletes specified files. ERASE is identical to DEL, which is described in detail in this chapter.

FASTOPEN

Reserve memory
Version 3.3 External

Functions: Saves directory information in memory for faster access.

Format: FASTOPEN d:[=nn][d:[=nn]]...

Variables: *d:* is a valid fixed disk drive (one that exists on your system) for which you want to save directory information.

nn is the number of directory entries for which you want to reserve memory. The value of *nn* can range from 10 to 999; the default is 34.

... indicates the option to specify information for as many drives as you have on your system.

Comments: You can only use FASTOPEN once. Include information for all your fixed disks with one command. It is recommended that you include FASTOPEN in your AUTOEXEC.BAT file.

FASTOPEN only works with fixed disks. Since diskettes are removable, it isn't safe for DOS to keep directory information in memory.

The proper value for *nn* varies with the directory structure of your disk and the kind of work that you do. If you select a value that is too small, FASTOPEN won't work to maximum advantage. If you select a value that is too big, it may take more time looking in memory than it does to check the disk.

The value of *nn* should be at least as large as the deepest level of subdirectories that you have, or you will not get any increase in speed.

It is recommended that you start with a value of *nn* = 100.

Each directory entry stored in memory takes 35 bytes.

Messages: **Cannot use FASTOPEN for drive x.** You have attempted to use FASTOPEN on a diskette drive or a drive that has been reassigned with JOIN, SUBST, or ASSIGN. Remove the reassignment and try again. FASTOPEN doesn't work with diskette drives.

FASTOPEN already installed. You tried to use FASTOPEN twice. You must specify all the drives the first time you use FASTOPEN.

FASTOPEN installed. You have successfully started FASTOPEN.

Same drive specified more than once. You specified the same drive letter more than once. Correct your entry and try again.

Too many drive entries. You entered too many drive names. Correct your entry and try again.

Too many name entries. You specified a value of *nn* greater than 999. Correct your entry and try again.

Examples: To set the number to 100 of directory entries to keep in memory for fast reference, enter

fastopen c:=100 ⏎

FIND

Find string filter
Version 2.0 External

Functions: Searches for a text string in a file. This command can find either the lines that match or that do not match. It can optionally report the total number of lines matched and display the line numbers.

Format: FIND [/V][/C][/N] "*string*" [*filespec*] [*filespec*]

Variables: "*string*" is the set of characters for which you want the command to search. The *string* must be enclosed in quotes (").

filespec is defined as [*d:*][*path*][*filename.ext*], which is the drive name, directory path, file name, and extension on which you want the command to act.

You can search in more than one file. A space must be inserted between each *filespec*, and they must all be entered after *string*.

Global characters cannot be used in the file name and extension.

Options: All options, if any are used, must be placed between the command name FIND and the *string* variable. (Most DOS commands use options at the end of the command format.)

/V   searches for lines that do *not* match *string*.

/C   displays a total count of the number of lines that match *string*. If /C is used, /N is ignored.

/N   displays the line number of each match and then displays the actual line.

Comments: If you do not specify a drive name, the default drive is used.

If you do not specify a path name, the current directory is used.

Two quotes within a string are interpreted as a single quote (e.g., *Now is ""the"" time* is interpreted as *Now is "the" time*).

Uppercase characters do not match lowercase characters and vice versa; characters must match *exactly* in order to be found.

You can optionally write the lines found to an output file by adding >*filespec* at the end of the command. The > character redirects the information to another file. *filespec* is defined as [*d:*][*path*][*filename.ext*], which is the drive name, directory path, file name, and extension of the output file.

This command is useful for searching out information in a data base-type fashion and redirecting it to a new output file. For example, an address file for use with a merge letter could be used with FIND to search for addresses with a certain zip code and write them to a new output file; however, because the command searches by lines, your address would have to be contained all in one line in order for the entire address to be redirected.

If the FIND command is used with a pipe (¦), then the output of the preceding command is "filtered" through FIND. In this case, no *filespec* is required since the input to FIND is coming from another command instead of a file. See Chapter 4 for a complete explanation.

Messages:

FIND: File not found filename. The file *filename* could not be found. Make sure you have given the correct drive, directory path, file name, and extension. Also, check your spelling.

Most DOS commands use options at the end of the command. FIND uses them before *string*. If you put them at the end of the command, FIND will think that the option (/C, /N, or /V) is the file name and will give you the **File not Found** message.

FIND: Invalid number of parameters. You didn't give FIND enough information to act on the command. You need to specify at least FIND *string filespec*. Re-enter the command with the required parameters.

FIND: Invalid parameter x. You used an invalid option. /V, /C, and /N are the only options you can use. Re-enter the command.

FIND: Syntax error. You didn't use the correct format. Check the format, especially *string*. Remember, *string* must be enclosed in quotation marks ("). Also, a single quote within a string must be entered with two quotes (e.g., *Now is "the" time* must be entered as *Now is ""the"" time*).

Examples: To display all lines that contain the string "DOS Reference Manual" in CHAPTER1.DOC, enter

```
find "DOS Reference Manual" chapter1.doc
```

The screen might display the following:

```
---------- chapter1.doc
the DOS Reference Manual further describes
refer to the DOS Reference Manual for more
in the DOS Reference Manual, you'll find
is described in the DOS Reference Manual
```

To display all lines that contain the string "refer to Appendix A" in CHAPTER1.DOC, CHAPTER2.DOC, and CHAPTER3.DOC, enter

```
find "refer to Appendix A" chapter1.doc chapter2.doc chapter3.doc
```

The screen might display the following:

```
---------- chapter1.doc
for more details, refer to Appendix A
refer to Appendix A for the code conversions
---------- chapter2.doc
you can refer to Appendix A to convert
about code conversions, refer to Appendix A
---------- chapter3.doc
to convert the ASCII codes, refer to Appendix A
```

In the rest of the examples, MESSAGES.TXT contains a list of all the DOS messages. Each line is "tagged" according to the DOS command it applies to.

To display the lines that have the string "BREAK" in MESSAGES.TXT, enter

find "BREAK" messages.txt ⏎

The screen will display the following:

```
---------- messages.txt
BREAK - Must specify ON or OFF
BREAK - BREAK is On
BREAK - BREAK is Off
```

The result is that all BREAK command messages are displayed.

To count the lines that have the "BREAK" string, enter

find /c "BREAK" messages.txt ⏎

The screen will display the following:

```
---------- messages.txt: 3
```

To count the lines that have do *not* have the "BREAK" string, enter

`find /c/v "BREAK" messages.txt` ⏎

The screen will display the following:

```
---------- messages.txt: 523
```

To display and number the lines that contain the "BREAK" string, enter

`find /n "BREAK" messages.txt` ⏎

The screen will display the following:

```
---------- messages.txt
[24]BREAK - Must specify ON or OFF
[25]BREAK - BREAK is On
[26]BREAK - BREAK is Off
```

To find the lines that contain the "BREAK" string and output them to the file BREAKMSG.SRT, enter

`find "BREAK" messages.txt breakmsg.srt` ⏎

The four lines that were displayed on the screen in the first example are written to BREAKMSG.SRT. To display them, enter

`type breakmsg.srt` ⏎

The screen will display the following:

```
---------- messages.txt:
BREAK - Must specify ON or OFF
BREAK - BREAK is On
BREAK - BREAK is Off
```

FORMAT

Format a disk
Version 1.0 External

Functions: Initializes a diskette or fixed disk and checks for defective tracks. Optionally places the operating system on the disk.

Format: FORMAT *d:* [/S] [/1] [/8] [/V] [/B] [/4][N:*xx* T:*yy*]

Variables: *d:* is a valid drive name (one that exists on your system) that contains the disk you want to initialize. Starting with version 3.2, this variable is a required entry. With earlier versions, if you do not specify a drive name, the default drive is used.

Options:

/S   places a copy of the operating system on the initialized disk, which makes the disk "bootable."

/1   formats only the first side of the diskette.

/8   formats an eight-sector diskette (for use with DOS version 1).

/V   writes a volume label on the disk.

/B   formats an eight-sector diskette and leaves space in the directory for a copy of the operating system (which can be placed there later with the SYS command).

/4   formats a diskette in a high-capacity disk drive for double-sided (320K/360K) use. This option was added in DOS version 3.

/N   sets the number of sectors to format.

/T   sets the number of tracks to format.

Some options cannot be combined, for example,

/V with /8

> The /8 option creates diskettes that are usable with DOS 1, which does not recognize labels.

/V or **/S** with **/B**

> The **/B** option creates diskettes that have space reserved for any version of DOS. Since DOS 1 doesn't recognize labels, you can't use the **/V** option. The **/S** option actually transfers DOS to the diskette, so it defeats the purpose of **/B**.

/1, /4, /8, or **/B** with a high-capacity diskette or a fixed disk

> These options all affect the configuration of a standard diskette and have no meaning when applied to other drives.

Comments: Both diskettes and fixed disks must be formatted or **initialized** before they can be used. See Chapter 11 for the procedure for formatting a fixed disk.

If the diskette has been used, FORMAT will destroy any information already on the diskette. A good rule of thumb is to list the files with the DIR command before you format a used diskette. If you don't want to destroy all of the files, you can either copy them to another disk or format a different disk.

Unless you tell it differently, DOS formats the diskette to the maximum capacity of the drive (single- or double-sided, and 8, 9, or 15 sectors per track).

The **/N** and **/T** options must be used together. If you use only one, you will receive the **Invalid parameter** message. The **/N** and **/T** options don't work with 5-1/4" single- or double-sided drives.

DISKCOPY automatically formats diskettes as it copies, so you do not need to use FORMAT before you use DISKCOPY.

When you first enter the command to format a diskette, the message

```
Insert new diskette for drive d:
and strike ENTER when ready
```

is displayed. *d* is the drive containing the disk you want to format. When you have inserted the new diskette, press **Return** to start formatting. (On versions of DOS before 3, pressing any key will start formatting.) If you decide you do not want to format a disk at this point, press **Ctrl-Break** to return to the DOS prompt.

During the format process, the following message is displayed:

```
Head: 0 Cylinder: 0
```

Versions of DOS before 3.2 display this message instead:

```
Formatting . . .
```

When the disk is formatted, DOS displays the message

```
Format complete
```

Information about the diskette, such as the following, is displayed:

```
362496 bytes total disk space
362496 bytes available on disk
```

If the disk contains any bad sectors, the number of bytes are displayed as **xxxx bytes in bad sectors**. If you transfer the operating system with the **/S** option, the number of bytes it uses is displayed as **xxxxx bytes used by system**, which will lessen the total number of bytes available on the disk by *xxxxx* bytes.

After displaying this information, the message

    `Format another (Y/N)?`

gives you the option of formatting more than one diskette without retyping the FORMAT command. Type **Y** for "Yes" and press **Return** to format another diskette. DOS will prompt you to insert the next diskette. Type **N** for "No" and press **Return** to terminate FORMAT and return to the system prompt.

You can use the options to format your diskette differently than it normally would be formatted.

Use the **/S** option to place a copy of the operating system (DOS) on the diskette. The files IBMBIO.COM and IBMDOS.COM are hidden files that make the diskette "bootable." The COMMAND.COM file is also placed on the diskette.

If these files are not on the default disk, DOS displays the following prompt:

    `Insert DOS disk in drive d:`
    `and strike Enter when ready`

Insert your DOS diskette (which contains the operating system files) and press **Return** to continue.

Use the **/1** option to format only one side of the diskette (even if it is a double-sided diskette). If used with **/B**, your diskette will be compatible with all versions of DOS and IBM computers using 5-1/4" diskettes.

Use the **/8** option to format your diskette with 8 sectors per track. Your diskette will be compatible with DOS version 1.

Use the **/V** option to write a volume label on the diskette. When formatting is complete, the following prompt will appear:

    `Volume label (11 characters, ENTER for none)?`

The volume label can be up to eleven characters long. You can use the same characters that are allowed for naming files, plus the space (see Chapter 2 for details). Key in the name you want and press **Return**. If you do not want to add a volume label, just press **Return.**

Use the **/B** option to format an 8-sector diskette and reserve space in the correct place on the diskette for the operating system (DOS). This option does not, however, actually place a copy of DOS on the diskette.

The **/B** option is used to create diskettes that can have DOS added later. This is the type of diskette that many programs are on when you buy them. If you give or sell programs to someone else, you should use this type of diskette. The DOS licensing agreement does not allow you to give away or sell copies of DOS.

If you are using a computer with a fixed disk, always specify the drive name in the FORMAT command. If you don't specify a drive name, you may accidentally reformat the fixed disk and lose all your information. In newer versions, DOS has added more warnings to prevent accidental formatting of a fixed disk.

NOTE: Earlier versions of DOS, including DOS 2, give little or no warning when they are about to format the fixed disk. If you are using DOS 2, it is recommended that you follow the procedure given in Chapter 14 for preventing accidental formatting.

Version 3.2 of DOS added one more level of protection when you try to format a fixed disk; the following prompt appears:

```
Enter current Volume Label for Drive C
(Press Enter for none):
```

If you enter an incorrect label, FORMAT will respond with the message **Invalid Volume ID**, and FORMAT will quit.

All versions of DOS after version 3 display the following message:

```
Warning! All data on non-removable disk drive x
will be lost
Proceed with Format (Y/N)?
```

If you specifically want to format the fixed disk, answer **Y** and press **Return**. If you don't want to format the fixed disk, answer **N** and press **Return**.

Once formatting begins, it's too late to stop it; you will lose all the information on the fixed disk. Hopefully, you'll have backup diskettes to minimize the loss.

Table 6.1 shows which types of media can be formatted in the different types of diskette drives available.

Drive type	Diskette types	Options
5-1/4" Single-sided (160/180KB)	180KB Single-sided 160KB Single-sided	None /8
5-1/4" Double-sided (320/360KB)	360KB Double-sided 320KB Double-sided 180KB Single-sided 160KB Single-sided	None /8 /1 /1 /8
5-1/4" High-Capacity (1.2MB)	1.2MB Double-sided 360KB Double-sided 320KB Double-sided 180KB Single-sided 160KB Single-sided	None /4 /4 /8 /4 /1 /4 /1 /8
3-1/2" (720KB)	720KB Double-sided	None
3-1/2" (1.44MB)	1.44MB Double-sided 720KB Double-sided	None /N:9 /T:80

Table 6.1
FORMAT compatibility

NOTE: Diskettes formatted with the /4 option in a high-capacity drive may not be read from or written to reliably in a single- or double-sided drive.

You cannot format a RAM disk (VDISK), a network disk, or a disk made active with ASSIGN, SUBST, or JOIN.

Exit Codes: Beginning with version 3.2, the FORMAT command sets exit codes that indicate errors. These codes can be used with IF ERRORLEVEL in batch files to take different actions, depending on the success or failure of the FORMAT command. The exit codes produced by FORMAT are as follows:

0   Successful completion of the FORMAT command.

3   FORMAT was terminated by the user (Ctrl-Break).

4   FORMAT was terminated due to an error.

5   FORMAT was terminated due to a "N" response before formatting a fixed disk.

FORMAT Demonstration

This demonstration shows you how to format new diskettes using two disk drives (A and B). The DOS diskette is placed in drive A and the unformatted diskette in drive B.

If you have a one-drive system (with no fixed disk), you can still format diskettes. Type **FORMAT B:** and press **Return** with the DOS diskette inserted in the A drive. DOS will tell you when to switch between the DOS diskette and the new, unformatted diskette. You may have to switch the diskettes several times to complete the format procedure.

If you are using a fixed disk, you can format new diskettes in the A drive. Type **FORMAT A:**, press **Return**, and insert the blank diskette in the A drive.

This hypothetical demonstration formats three new diskettes. The first diskette will show a successful format with no bad sectors; the second diskette will contain several bad sectors. The third diskette will use the /S and /V options to transfer a copy of the operating system and write a volume label.

If you typed

format b: ⏎

The screen would display the following

```
Insert new diskette for drive B:
and strike ENTER when ready
```

Press **Return**. The screen would display the following:

```
Format complete

    362496 bytes total disk space
    362496 bytes available on disk

Format another (Y/N)?
```

Type

y ⏎

The screen would then display the following:

```
Insert new diskette for drive B:
and strike ENTER when ready
```

Press **Return** or any other key. The screen would display the following:

```
Format complete

    362496 bytes total disk space
      7680 bytes in bad sectors
    354816 bytes available on disk

Format another (Y/N)?
```

Type

n ⏎

Then, from the A prompt, enter

format b: /s /v ⏎

The screen would display the following:

>   Insert new diskette for drive B:
>   and strike ENTER when ready

Press **Return**. The screen would display the following:

>   Format complete
>   System transferred
>
>   Volume label (11 characters, Enter for none)

Enter

accts rec ⏎

The screen would display the following:

>   362496 bytes total disk space
>   62464 bytes used by system
>   300032 bytes available on disk
>
>   Format another (Y/N)?

Type

n ⏎

Messages: **Attempted write protect violation.** The diskette you are trying to format is write-protected. Check the diskette; if it has a tab covering the write-protect notch, you must remove the tab to format the diskette. Be sure that this diskette is the one you want to format. It may be write-protected for a reason. If the diskette doesn't have a tab on it, check to be sure you specified the correct drive in the FORMAT command.

Bad Partition Table. There is no DOS partition on the fixed disk, or the partition table is bad. Use FDISK to create a DOS partition.

Cannot find system files. The hidden files IBMBIO.COM and IBMDOS.COM cannot be found on the current drive, and the drive is not removable. Change to the drive that has the system files in the root directory and try again.

Cannot FORMAT a Network drive. You cannot format a drive that is a network drive or a drive that is currently being shared on the network. If the drive is being shared, you can either try again later or PAUSE the server, complete the FORMAT, then CONTINUE the server.

Cannot FORMAT a SUBSTed or ASSIGNed drive. Return all drive assignments to their defaults and try again.

Disk not compatible. The disk you are trying to format is not a compatible disk as described in this command reference. Insert a compatible diskette and try again.

Disk unsuitable for system disk. A defective track was found where the system files were to be placed. FORMAT a different diskette. The unsuitable diskette can still be used for storing information.

Drive letter must be specified. You must enter a drive letter when starting FORMAT.

Error reading partition table. An error occurred while FORMAT was reading the partition table. Use FDISK to create a DOS partition and try again.

Error writing partition table. An error occurred while FORMAT was writing the partition table. Use FDISK to create a DOS partition and try again.

Format failure. A disk error was encountered. Try the command again. If you get the same message, for some reason, the diskette is damaged and unusable. Discard the damaged diskette and FORMAT another.

FORMAT not supported on drive d. You have attempted to format a drive that can't be formatted, such as a VDISK. If this error occurs when using a fixed disk or diskette, load a new copy of DOS and try again.

Insert DOS disk in x:
and ENTER when ready. FORMAT is trying to load the DOS files, but the drive *x* does not contain the DOS diskette. Insert the DOS disk in drive *x* and press **Return** to continue. (With earlier DOS versions, the message reads **strike any key when ready**. You can strike any key, not just the **Return** key, to start formatting.)

Insert new diskette for drive x:
and strike ENTER when ready. This message instructs you to insert the new diskette you want to format in drive *x*. Press **Return** to start formatting. (With DOS versions before 3, you can press any key to continue.)

Insufficient memory for system transfer. There is not enough memory available to accommodate the operating system. Try removing some memory-resident programs, such as SideKick or VDISK.

Invalid characters in volume label. Volume labels contain one to eleven characters. Valid characters are the same as those used for file names and spaces. Most punctuation marks can't be used. Re-enter a valid volume label.

Invalid device parameters from device driver. The DOS partition is invalid. Use FDISK to create a DOS partition and try again.

Invalid media or track 0 bad - disk unusable. The diskette type and drive type may be incompatible. You may have tried to format a double-sided 320/360K diskette in a high-capacity 1.2MB drive or a high-capacity 1.2MB diskette in a double-sided 320/360K drive. If you are using DOS version 3.2, retry FORMAT with the /4 option.

Track 0 is where the boot record, file allocation table, and directory must reside. If track 0 is bad, the disk is unusable. Try FORMAT again. If you get the same message, use another diskette.

Invalid Volume Label. The volume label that you entered doesn't match the volume label of the disk you are trying to format. Use the VOL command to check the volume label and try FORMAT again.

Parameters not compatible. You tried to use two options that cannot be combined. Refer to the previous "Options" section for compatibility, and re-enter the command.

Parameter not compatible with fixed disk. You tried to use an option that cannot be used with a fixed disk. They include the /1, /4, and /8 options. Re-enter the command.

Press any key to begin formatting x: In DOS version 2, this message will be displayed if you try to format a fixed disk. Use **Ctrl-Break** to terminate if you do not want to format the fixed disk. Press any key if you do want to format the fixed disk.

Reinsert diskette for drive x and strike Enter when ready. This message prompts you to re-insert the new diskette you are formatting. This message will appear when you are using a single-drive FORMAT or when you reinsert the DOS diskette to transfer the system files.

System transferred. This message is informational, verifying that the operating system files IBMBIO.COM, IBMDOS.COM, and COMMAND.COM were placed on the newly formatted disk.

Unable to write BOOT. The boot record cannot be placed on track 0. The disk is therefore unusable. Try the command again. If it still doesn't work, use another diskette.

Volume label (11 characters, ENTER for none)? This message prompts you to enter the disk's volume label. The volume label can be eleven characters long. The rules that apply for naming files also apply to volume labels (see Chapter 2 for details). Key in the name you want and press **Return**. If you do not want to name a volume label, just press **Return**.

Warning! All data on non-removable disk drive x will be lost
Proceed with Format (Y/N)? You are about to format the fixed disk. If you really want to format the fixed disk, answer **Y** and press **Return**. If you don't want to format the fixed disk, answer **N** and press **Return**.

Examples: To format a diskette in drive B, at the DOS prompt, enter

format b: ⏎

To format a diskette in drive B and write a volume label, at the DOS prompt, enter

format b: /v ⏎

To format a diskette in drive A from the fixed disk, transfer the system files, and write a volume label, at the C> prompt, enter

format a: /s /v ⏎

GRAFTABL

Load graphics table
Version 3.0 External

Functions: Loads a table of graphics characters into memory.

Format: GRAFTABL

Comments: This command lets you use the extended character set with a color/graphics adapter in graphics mode.

The characters in the extended character set have ASCII codes from 128 through 255.

This command increases the size of DOS in memory by 1328 bytes (with DOS 3.1).

This command description covers the default operation of GRAFTABL. GRAFTABL can also load foreign language code pages, as described in the IBM DOS reference manual.

Messages: **Graphic characters loaded.** The GRAFTABLE command sucessfully loaded the character table.

Graphic characters already loaded. The GRAFTABL command has been previously executed.

Example: The following example loads the table of graphics characters. From the active drive prompt, enter

```
graftabl ⏎
```

Table 6.1 shows the characters that can be used and their corresponding ASCII codes. To display one of these characters on the screen, hold down the **Alt** key, type the ASCII code on the 10-key numeric pad (don't use the numbers at the top of the keyboard), and then release the **Alt** key.

128	Ç	129	ü	130	é	131	â
132	ä	133	à	134	å	135	ç
136	ê	137	ë	138	è	139	ï
140	î	141	ì	142	Ä	143	Å
144	É	145	æ	146	Æ	147	ô
148	ö	149	ò	150	û	151	ù
152	ÿ	153	Ö	154	Ü	155	¢
156	£	157	¥	158	₧	159	ƒ
160	á	161	í	162	ó	163	ú
164	ñ	165	Ñ	166	ª	167	º
168	¿	169	⌐	170	¬	171	½
172	¼	173	¡	174	«	175	»
176	░	177	▒	178	▓	179	│
180	┤	181	╡	182	╢	183	╖
184	╕	185	╣	186	║	187	╗
188	╝	189	╜	190	╛	191	┐
192	└	193	┴	194	┬	195	├
196	─	197	┼	198	╞	199	╟
200	╚	201	╔	202	╩	203	╦
204	╠	205	═	206	╬	207	╧
208	╨	209	╤	210	╥	211	╙
212	╘	213	╒	214	╓	215	╫
216	╪	217	┘	218	┌	219	█
220	▄	221	▌	222	▐	223	▀
224	α	225	β	226	Γ	227	π
228	Σ	229	σ	230	μ	231	τ
232	Φ	233	θ	234	Ω	235	δ
236	∞	237	ø	238	∈	239	∩
240	≡	241	±	242	≥	243	≤
244	⌠	245	⌡	246	÷	247	≈
248	°	249	·	250	-	251	√
252	ⁿ	253	²	254	■	255	

**Table 6.1
Graphics characters
available with GRAFTABL**

GRAPHICS

Screen print
Version 2.0 External

Functions: Lets you print the contents of the graphics display screen on a printer capable of printing bit-image graphics.

Format: GRAPHICS [*printer*] [/R][/B]

Variables: *printer* selects the type of IBM PC printer, or compatible printer, that you are using as follows:

- **COLOR1** selects the IBM PC Color Printer with a black ribbon.

- **COLOR4** selects the IBM PC Color Printer with an RGB (red, green, blue, and black) ribbon.

- **COLOR8** selects the IBM PC Color Printer with a CMY (cyan, magenta, yellow, and black) ribbon.

- **COMPACT** selects the IBM PC Compact Printer.

- **GRAPHICS** selects the IBM PC Graphics Printer.

- **THERMAL** selects the IBM PC Convertible Printer.

If you do not specify a printer type, the IBM PC Graphics Printer is assumed.

Options:
- /R reverses print colors so that the image on the paper matches the screen image (white characters on a black background).

- /B prints the background color of the display screen, which works only for the **COLOR4** and **COLOR8** parameters.

Comments: Printers that are not IBM PC Printers must be compatible with the type of IBM PC printer selected.

You must have a Color/Graphics Adapter to display graphics and activate the GRAPHICS command. Without one, the command has no effect.

After you use the GRAPHICS command, you can print the graphics screen contents by using the **Shift-PrtSc** keys.

The GRAPHICS command stays in effect until you restart, or reboot, your computer. It affects only the graphics mode and has no effect on the text mode.

If you are in the graphics mode, the screen print will take several minutes (the text mode only takes a few seconds).

In the 320×200 color graphics mode, non-color printers will print in four shades of gray (instead of four colors).

In the 640×200 color graphics mode, the screen is rotated 90 degrees to the left (the upper right corner of the screen is printed on the upper left corner of the paper). The screen is printed in black and white.

Examples: To select the IBM PC Color Printer with an RGB (red, green, blue, and black) ribbon, enter

graphics color4 ⏎

To select the same printer as in the previous example but have the screen's background color also printed, enter

graphics color4 /b ⏎

After using the command, to print a graphics screen, hold down one of the **Shift** keys and press the **PrtSc** key.

JOIN

Join directory to a drive
Version 3.1 External

Functions: Connects one drive to a directory on another drive, producing a single directory.

Format: JOIN *d: d:\directory*

or

JOIN *d:* /D

Variables: *d:* specifies the drive to which you want to connect a directory on another drive.

d:\directory specifies the drive and directory to which you want to connect. The directory must be empty, start at the root, and be only one level deep. If the directory doesn't exist, DOS will create it. You must include the backslash (\).

Options: /D removes a connection. With this option you give the drive name that you no longer want connected.

JOIN entered alone will display the current connections.

Comments: The directory path that you use can't be the root (\) directory.

The entire tree of the disk that you connect is joined, starting at the root.

Don't use the following commands while you are using connections: ASSIGN, SUBST, BACKUP, DISKCOMP, DISKCOPY, FORMAT, and RESTORE.

Messages: **Invalid Parameter**. Indicates one of three problems: (1) you typed an incorrect drive name, (2) you tried to connect to the current directory, or (3) you specified /D without specifying which drive connection to remove.

Cannot JOIN a network drive. Indicates that you entered the name of a network drive. Try again with a different name. Remember, neither name can be that of a network drive.

Invalid drive specification. Indicates that you have referred to a drive that has been connected by JOIN. You must remove the connection (use the /D option) or refer to the directory to which you have connected the drive.

Example: To connect drive B to the directory C:\LETTERS, at the DOS prompt, enter

join b: c:\letters ⏎

Then, if you want to access any of the information on drive B, you would find it in the \LETTERS subdirectory of drive C.

To display the current connections, enter

join ⏎

The screen will display the following response:

    B: => C:\LETTERS

To remove the connection of drive A, enter

join a: /d ⏎

LABEL

Volume label
Version 3.0 External

Functions: Puts a label on a disk. Can also change or remove a label.

Format: LABEL [*d:*][*volume-label*]

Variables: *d:* defines the drive that you want to label. If you don't enter a drive, you will use the default drive.

volume-label is the label that you want to add to the disk. If you don't enter a volume label you will be prompted for one.

Comments: A volume label may contain spaces, but only if you enter the label in response to the prompt. You cannot have spaces within a volume label entered on the command line.

A volumn label may contain spaces, but only if you enter the label in response to the prompt. You cannot have spaces within a volumn label entered on the command line.

A label can be one to eleven characters long. The same characters are allowed in a volume label as are allowed in a file name, plus the space character. All letters are automatically capitalized by the LABEL command.

You should not try to change the volume label on a SUBSTituted drive because the label of the actual drive will be changed.

Don't use LABEL on ASSIGNed or network drives.

Messages: **Cannot LABEL a Network drive.** You tried to label a drive that is part of a network. DOS doesn't allow you to do this.

Delete current volume label (Y/N)? Appears only if the disk already has a volume label, and you don't enter a new volume label. Press **Y** and then **Return** to remove the old volume label, or press **N** and then **Return** to keep the old volume label.

Invalid characters in volume label. You used an improper character in the volume label that you have specified. You will be asked to enter a new volume label.

No room in root directory. There isn't an empty directory entry in the root directory to hold the volume label. The volume label is actually a hidden directory entry, so if the root directory is full, DOS can't add the volume label.

Volume in drive X has no label. The disk that you specified doesn't have a label. This message is displayed if you don't give a volume label on the command line.

Volume in drive x is xxxxxxxxxx. Shows the existing label of the disk in the drive you specified. This message is displayed if you don't give a volume label on the command line.

Volume label (11 characters, Enter for none)? This message asks you to enter a new volume label. If you don't want to add a new volume label, just press **Return**.

Example: To add a new label to the default drive, enter

```
label ⏎
```

The screen will display the following information:

```
    Volume in drive A has no label
    Volume label (11 characters, ENTER for none)?
```

Enter

```
my label ⏎
```

To put a new label on drive A without verifying any existing label, from the DOS prompt, enter

label a:data base ⏎

MKDIR or MD

Make a directory

Version 2.0 Internal

Functions: Creates a new subdirectory on the specified disk.

Format: MKDIR [*d:*]*path*

or

MD [*d:*]*path*

Variables: *d:* is a valid drive name (one that exists on your system) where you want to create the new subdirectory. If you do not specify a drive name, the default drive is used.

path is the directory path for the new subdirectory you want to create.

Comments: MD is the abbreviated form of MKDIR. The commands work identically.

By specifying a complete directory path, a new subdirectory will be created anywhere you want it to be; otherwise, a subdirectory is created in the current directory.

You can create as many subdirectories as you want. You are limited only by disk space; however, the maximum length of a directory path specification is 63 characters, including the backslashes.

The subdirectory name can be from one to eight characters with an optional extension. The name must conform to the rules for file names (see Chapter 2 for details).

You cannot name a subdirectory with the same name as a file in the parent directory. For example, if a file named UTILITY resides in the DOS parent directory, you cannot create a subdirectory named UTILITY; however, if the file has an extension such as UTILITY.ASM, then you could create a UTILITY subdirectory.

Messages:	**Unable to create directory.** This message can occur for several reasons: (1) the directory already exists, (2) one of the path names you specified is incorrect, (3) a file already exists with the same name, or (4) either the root directory or the disk itself is full.
	Check these problems for the directory you want to create and try again.
Examples:	The following examples use drive C as the default drive.

CAUTION: If an ASSIGN, JOIN, or SUBST command is in effect, and you create a directory with MKDIR, it will be created as a subdirectory on the actual disk.

To create the subdirectory called ACCOUNTS in the root directory, enter

```
mkdir \accounts
```

Instead, you could enter

```
md \accounts
```

If you were in the root directory, you could enter

```
md accounts
```

without the backslash (the backslash tells DOS to start in the root directory, which is the current directory in this case).

To create subdirectories of ACCOUNTS called RECV and PAY, enter

```
md \accounts\recv
md \accounts\pay
```

If ACCOUNTS is the current directory, you could simply enter

md recv ⏎

md pay ⏎

MODE

Redirect printer output
Version 1.1 External

Functions: Redirects printer output to the asynchronous communications adapter for use with a serial interface printer.

Format: MODE LPT#[:]=COM#[:]

Variables: # is the printer number: for LPT (the parallel printer), the value of # is 1, 2, or 3; for COM (the serial device), the value of # is 1, 2, 3, or 4. The colon (:) is optional.

Comments: For many programs, this command is required when using the asynchronous adapter for a serial printer. All output that is normally sent to LPT1 or PRN (including **Shift-PrtSc**) is sent to the serial printer instead of the parallel printer port. The MODE COM#: command is used to set the protocol characteristics of the serial printer.

You must use a valid number for both the parallel printer and the serial device.

This command can be canceled with the MODE LPT#: command, where # is 1, 2, or 3.

Messages: **LPT#: rerouted to COMn:** This message indicates that subsequent output will be sent to the serial device instead of the parallel printer. *n* is the number of the serial device (COM1, COM2, COM3, or COM4).

Must specify COM1, COM2, COM3, or COM4. COM1, COM2, COM3, and COM4 are the only valid serial devices. Re-enter the command using either COM1, COM2, COM3, or COM4.

Resident part of MODE loaded. When you use the MODE command to redirect printer output, part of it remains in memory until DOS is restarted.

Examples: To redirect printer output from LPT1 to COM1, enter

mode lpt1:=com1: ⏎

You could also enter

mode lpt1=com1 ⏎

without the colons.

MODE

Set asynchronous communications options

Version 1.1 External

Functions: Sets the protocol characteristics of the asynchronous communications adapter.

Format: MODE COM # [:]*baud*[,*parity*[,*databits*[,*stopbits* [,**P**]]]]

Variables: # is the adapter number: 1, 2, 3, or 4. The colon (:) is optional.

baud sets the baud rate. The value of baud can be 110, 150, 300, 600, 1200, 2400, 4800, or 9600. You can enter just the first two characters; the rest are ignored. For example, to set the baud rate to 4800, enter **baud = 48**.

parity selects the parity checking: N = no parity check, O = odd parity, E = even parity. The default value is E.

databits sets the number of data bits. The value of *databits* can be either 7 or 8. The default value is 7.

stopbits sets the number of stop bits. The value of *stopbits* can be either 1 or 2. The default value is 1.

Options: P selects continuous retries on time-out errors when the asynchronous adapter is being used for a serial interface printer. Press **Ctrl-Break** to stop the retry loop. To cancel this option, you must re-enter this MODE command without the **P**.

Comments: You must specify an adapter number (1, 2, 3, or 4), but the colon is optional.

You must specify a baud rate. Parameters other than the baud rate are optional. If you use more than one parameter, they must be separated by commas. You can select the default value for a parameter by entering the comma without the parameter.

If you enter an invalid parameter, the **Invalid parameter** message appears, and the protocol characteristic remains unchanged.

Using the **P** option causes a portion of MODE to remain resident in memory.

Messages: **COMn: bbbb,p,d,s,t initialized.** This message displays the protocol characteristics as follows:

n	adapter number (COM1, COM2, COM3, or COM4)
bbbb	baud rate (110, 150, 300, 600, 1200, 2400, 4800, or 9600)
p	parity check (e = even, o = odd, and n = none)
d	data bits (7 or 8)
s	stop bits (1 or 2)
t	type of serial device (p = serial printer, timeouts retried; or - = other serial device, timeouts not retried)

Illegal Device Name. You used a device name other than COM1, COM2, COM3, or COM4. Re-enter the command.

Invalid baud rate specified. You must enter one of the baud rates previously shown. Remember that only the first two characters are needed (although entering more than two will not cause this error message; they are simply ignored).

Invalid parameters. This message indicates the following: (1) you gave an incorrect parameter, (2) you skipped a required parameter, or (3) you used the wrong format for a parameter. Check the command and the requirements described in this section and try the command again.

Resident part of MODE loaded. When you use the **P** option, part of the MODE command remains in memory until DOS is restarted.

Must specify COM1, COM2, COM3, or COM4. You entered the command incorrectly. Retype the command using the correct syntax.

Examples: To set the serial communications protocol on COM1 to 1200 baud, no parity, 8 data bits, and 1 stop bit, enter

mode com1:12,n,8,1 ⏎

To set COM2 to 4800 baud and select the default values for all other parameters, enter

mode com2:48,,,,p ⏎

Note that this command also selects continuous retries for timeout errors. Using the **P** option indicates that the asynchronous adapter is being used for a serial interface printer.

MODE

Set color/graphics options

Version 1.1 External

Functions: Switches the display between monochrome and color/graphics adapter (or enhanced graphics adapter), and sets the graphics adapter characteristics.

Format: MODE [*char/line*][,*shift*][,T]

Variables: *char/line* selects the characters per line to one of the following:

- **40** selects a 40-column display with the color/graphics adapter.

- **80** selects an 80-column display with the color/graphics adapter.

- **BW40** switches the active display to the color/graphics adapter, and selects a black and white (cancels color), 40-column display.

- **BW80** switches the active display to the color/graphics adapter, and selects a black and white (cancels color), 80-column display.

- **CO40** switches the active display to the color/graphics adapter, and selects a color, 40-column display.

- **CO80** switches the active display to the color/graphics adapter, and selects a color, 80-column display.

- **MONO** switches the active display to the monochrome display adapter (cancels the color/graphics adapter).

shift shifts the display right (shift = **R**) or left (shift = **L**) one character in the 40-column mode and two characters in the 80-column mode. This parameter works only with the color/graphics adapter and not with enhanced graphics or monochrome adapters (an error message is displayed).

Options: T   requests a one-line test pattern for aligning the display screen. This parameter works only with the color/graphics adapter and not with enhanced graphics or monochrome adapters.

Comments: The MODE command switches the active display if you have more than one type of display adapter installed in your computer. You can include the command in your AUTOEXEC.BAT file to set the display when you turn on, or restart, your computer.

The *shift* and **T** parameters are usually used together to align the screen and test the alignment. A prompt is displayed to determine if the screen is properly aligned. If *shift* = **R**, DOS displays the **Do you see the rightmost 9? (Y/N)** prompt; if *shift* = **L**, the prompt **Do you see the leftmost 9? (Y/N)** is displayed. Answer **Y** for "Yes" to return to the system prompt. Answer **N** for "no" to repeat the process and shift the screen again, either one character (40-column display) or two characters (80-column display). This method lets you shift the display screen repeatedly until it is properly aligned, without having to re-enter the MODE command each time.

When you use this command, the display screen is cleared (and the cursor moves to the top left position).

If you do not have the correct display on your system, the **Invalid parameter** message is displayed.

When *char/line* is **CO40** or **CO80**, color is not automatically shown but will be activated by programs that use color.

Messages: **Do you see the leftmost 9? (Y/N)**

or

Do you see the rightmost 9? (Y/N). These messages prompt you to verify that the screen is properly aligned when you use the *shift* and **T** parameters. If you shift left, the first message is displayed; shifting right displays the second message.

Answer **Y** for "Yes" to return to the system prompt.

Answer **N** for "no" to repeat the process and shift the screen again, either one character (40-column display) or two characters (80-column display). This method lets you shift the display screen repeatedly until it is properly aligned, without having to re-enter the MODE command each time.

Invalid parameters. This message indicates the following: (1) you gave an incorrect parameter, (2) you skipped a required parameter, or (3) you used the wrong format for a parameter. Check the command and the requirements described in this section and try the command again.

Resident part of MODE loaded. When you use the *shift* variables, part of the MODE command remains in memory until DOS is restarted.

Unable to shift screen right
or
Unable to shift screen left. You cannot use the MODE command to shift the display when using enhanced graphics or monochrome adapters.

Examples: To change the display screen to 40 columns and activate color for a color/graphics adapter, enter

mode C040 ⏎

To change the display screen to 80 columns, shift right one character, and display the one-line test pattern, enter

mode 80,r,t ⏎

To change the active display to a monochrome display attached to a monochrome display adapter, enter

mode mono ⏎

MODE

Set printer options
Version 1.1 External

Functions: Sets the parallel printer characteristics.

Format: MODE LPT # [:][*char/line*][,[*lines/in*][,**P**]]

Variables: # is the printer number: 1, 2, or 3. The colon (:) is optional.

char/line sets the number of characters per line. The value of *char/line* can be either 80 or 132. The default is 80.

lines/in sets the number of lines per inch. The value of *lines/in* can be either 6 or 8. The default is 6.

Options: **P** selects continuous retries on time-out errors. Press **Ctrl-Break** to stop the retry loop. To cancel this option, you must re-enter this MODE command without the **P**.

Comments: This command controls the printing characteristics of IBM and Epson printers, as well as printers with compatible control codes.

You must give a printer number (1, 2, or 3), but the colon is optional.

All other parameters are optional. If you use more than one parameter, they must be separated by commas. You can leave a parameter unchanged by entering just the comma.

If you enter an invalid parameter, the **Invalid parameter** message appears, and the printer characteristic remains unchanged.

char/line sets the print pitch to either pica (*char/line* = 80) or condensed (*char/line* = 132).

lines/in sets the line spacing to either 1/6" (*lines/in* = 6) or 1/8" (*lines/in* = 8).

When you use the **P** option for continuous retries on timeout errors, the computer internally loops to wait for the printer to be "ready." The printer is ready when it is connected, turned on, and on line. Until then, the computer appears to be "locked up." You can stop the retry loop one time by pressing **Ctrl-Break**. To cancel this option, you must re-enter the MODE command without the **P**.

Using the **P** option causes a portion of MODE to remain resident in memory.

Messages: **Illegal Device Name.** You used a device name other than LPT1, LPT2, or LPT3. Re-enter the command.

Infinite retry on parallel printer time-out. This message is informational, confirming that you used the **P** option.

Infinite retry not supported on network printer. The **P** option cannot be used with a printer attached to a network. Use the command without **P**, or use a non-network printer.

Invalid parameters. This message indicates the following: (1) you gave an incorrect parameter, (2) you skipped a required parameter, or (3) you used the wrong format for a parameter. Check the command and the requirements described in this section, and try the command again.

LPT #: not rerouted. Any previous reassignment for the printer has been canceled by using the MODE command. # is either 1, 2, or 3.

LPT #: set for 132. The printer is set for 132 characters per line (condensed). # is either 1, 2, or 3.

LPT #: set for 80. The printer is set for 80 characters per line (pica). # is either 1, 2, or 3.

No retry on parallel printer time-out. This message is informational, confirming that the **P** option is not in effect.

Printer error. The MODE command would not set the printer characteristics. The printer may be off, not connected, or off line. It may not be compatible with the IBM or Epson printer control codes.

Printer lines per inch set. The line spacing has been set to either 6 or 8 lines per inch. If the attempt to set the line spacing fails, the **Printer error** message also appears.

Resident part of MODE loaded. When you use the **P** option, part of the MODE command remains in memory until DOS is restarted.

Examples: To specify LPT3 and set the printer characteristics to condensed pitch at 1/8-inch line spacing, enter

mode lpt3:132,8 ⏎

To specify LPT1, set the printer characteristics to pica pitch at 1/6-inch line spacing, and select the continuous retry on timeout errors, enter

mode lpt1:80,6,P ⏎

MORE

More output filter
Version 2.0 External

Functions: Displays a screenful of information from the standard input device, and waits for a keystroke to display another screenful.

The message **--More--** is displayed on the last line of the screen while MORE pauses for a keystroke.

Format: MORE

Comments: The MORE command is useful for displaying a screenful of information without the user having to manually pause the screen (with **Ctrl-NumLock**).

A screenful of information is 23 lines of either 40 or 80 characters per line; however, one line in a file can take more than one line on the screen, so the display may not be a full 23 lines from the file.

After displaying a screenful of information, MORE waits for a keystroke while it displays the **--More--** message on the last line. Pressing any character key causes another screenful of information to be displayed. This process continues until there is no more information to display.

The standard input to MORE, as with most DOS commands, is from the keyboard. So if you type MORE, the display will stop when you have keyed in a screenful of information, which obviously has no practical use; however, by redirecting the input to MORE from a file, the file is displayed one screenful at a time. The format for this procedure is: MORE <*filespec*, where *filespec* is *[d:][path]filename.ext*.

You can use the MORE command to filter the output of other DOS commands, such as the TREE command. The output of the command is then displayed one screenful at a time. The format for this procedure is *command* ¦ MORE, where *command* is the DOS command.

Messages: --**More**-- After displaying a screenful of information, MORE pauses and displays this message on the last line. To display more information, press any character key.

Examples: To display the contents of LIST.TXT, enter

more <list.txt ⏎

If LIST.TXT was in the CORRES directory of drive C, you would enter

more <c:\corres\list.txt ⏎

To pipe the output of the TREE command to the MORE filter, enter

tree /f ¦ more ⏎

PATH

Define search directory
Version 2.0 Internal

Functions: Defines the drives and directories that DOS searches for if a program or batch file is not found in the current directory.

Format: PATH [[*d:*]*path*][;[*d:*]*path*][;...]

Variables: *d:* is a valid drive (one that exists on your system) that indicates the drive on which you want DOS to search.

path is a valid directory path in which you want DOS to search.

... indicates the option to add more drives and directory paths to the search.

Entering **PATH** ; returns the search path to no extended search (only the current directory is searched).

Using PATH with no parameters displays the current path.

Comments: When you enter a command that is not found in the current directory of the specified (or default) drive, DOS searches the directories you named in the PATH command. This method applies only to program files (those with .COM and .EXE extensions) and batch files (.BAT).

PATH lets you access these programs from any disk drive in any directory without changing disk drives or directories every time. You can include PATH in your AUTOEXEC.BAT file so that the command is always active, which is especially helpful for fixed disk users (see Chapter 10 for details).

If you do not use a drive name, the default drive is used.

Each path must be a series of valid directories and subdirectories. If you use more than one path, they must be separated by semicolons.

It is recommended that you always specify the drive name and a path name that starts in the root directory, which will allow you to access a file from any disk drive in any directory.

Syntax errors in the command format are not detected until DOS actually performs a directory search. Invalid paths and paths that no longer exist are ignored. Invalid drive names produce the **Invalid drive in search path** message.

Directories are searched in the order specified in the PATH command.

If the file cannot be found in the current directory or the search paths in PATH, the **Bad command or filename** message is displayed.

Messages: **Invalid drive in search path.** You specified a disk drive that does not exist. This message is displayed when DOS searches for a program or batch file, not when you enter the PATH command. Enter PATH to see what the current search path is, find the error, and retype the command with the correct format.

Bad command or filename. DOS cannot find the file in the current directory or in the search path. Check to see if (1) you typed the correct file name, (2) the command is a program or batch file, or (3) your search path includes the drive and directory where the file is located.

Examples: To define the search path for the fixed disk (drive C) and its directories (DOS and its subdirectories UTIL and BATCH, MSTOOLS, and CALC), at the C prompt, enter

```
path c:\dos;c:\dos\util;c:\dos\batch;c:\mstools;c:\calc ⏎
```

To see the current path settings, enter

path ⏎

The screen will display the following response:

    PATH=C:\DOS;C:\DOS\UTIL;C:\DOS\BATCH;C:\MSTOOLS;C:\CALC

To turn off the path search, enter

path ; ⏎

PRINT

Print files
Version 2.0 External

Functions: Sends a file (or files) to the printer, allowing you do other tasks on the computer at the same time.

Format: PRINT [/D:*device*][/B:*buffsize*][/U:*busytick*]
[/M:*maxtick*][/S:*timeslice*][/Q:*quesize*]
[*filespec1*][/P][/T][/C] [*filespec2*] [/P][/T][/C] ...

Variables: *filespec1*, *filespec2*, and so on are defined as *[d:][path]filename.ext*, which is the disk drive, directory path, file name, and extension that you want to print. You can print more than one file at a time.

You can use wild card characters (? and *) in *filename.ext*.

Options: The first three options can be used with DOS versions 2 and higher. The command has been improved in DOS 3 to include all of the following options.

If you use the /P, /T, or /C options, they will act on the preceding file and all files thereafter.

- /P adds specified files to the print queue for printing. The file preceding the /P option and all subsequent files are added to the queue until a /C option is encountered or until you press **Return**.

    The /P option is the default if none of the /P, /T, or /C options are specified.

- /T terminates printing and displays the **All files canceled by operator** message. All files in the print queue that have not been printed are canceled.

- /C cancels printing and displays the **File canceled by operator** message. The file preceding the /C option and any subsequent files entered are canceled. Printing resumes with the first file remaining in the print queue.

DOS 3 Only

The remainder of the options must be specified at the beginning of the command format, before *filespec* is given.

/D:*device*

> specifies which device to use for printing. *device* is any valid DOS device name.

/B:*buffsize*

> sets the size of the memory buffer to use while printing. *buffsize* can range from 1 to 32767. The default value is 512 bytes. (More about calculating buffer size later.)

/Q:*quesize*

> sets the maximum number of files that can be in the print queue at one time. *quesize* can range from 1 to 32. The default value is 10. If you queue more than ten files, the **Print queue is full** message is displayed, and the command is ignored.

/U:*busytick*

> sets the amount of time (number of clock ticks) that PRINT waits whenever the printer is busy or unavailable. *busytick* can range from 1 to 255. The default value is 1.

If you have a slow printer (less than 4800 baud for a serial printer; less than 100 characters per second for a parallel printer), you should increase this value.

/M:*maxtick*

> sets the amount of time (number of clock ticks) PRINT has to send characters to the printer whenever it gets a turn. *maxtick* can range from 1 to 255. The default value is 2.

NOTE: A **tick** is the smallest measure of time used on personal computers with PC-DOS (or MS-DOS). A tick occurs every 1/18.2 (0.0549) seconds.

/S:_timeslice_

sets the number of slices in each second. _timeslice_ can range from 1 to 255. The default value is 8.

Comments: The PRINT command is used to print files while you use the computer to complete other tasks. The files are "queued up" and are printed as free time becomes available.

When you are at the system prompt, PRINT is allotted almost all of the free time to print files that are placed in the queue. While you are using other programs, the options you use (other than /D) control how much of the free time PRINT is allotted.

PRINT works best on files stored in ASCII format. If you try to print program files (files that end in .COM or .EXE), the results will be unpredictable.

Queued files are printed in the order entered. If you use wild card characters, files are printed in the order that they are listed in the directory.

When each file is finished printing, the paper is advanced to the top of the next page.

Tab characters are replaced with spaces to advance the printhead to the next eight-character boundary. If you do not name a disk drive, the default drive is used.

If you do not name a directory path, the current directory is used.

If you do not specify a file name, the printing queue status is displayed.

The resident size of DOS in memory is increased by about 5K (depending on which options are used) the first time you use PRINT. It stays that way until you reboot the computer.

The /D, /B, /U, /M, /S, and /Q options are used only when the PRINT command is first given. The /D option, if given, must be the first option in the command format.

If you try to use these options without /D, the **Name of list device [PRN]:** prompt is displayed. You have two options:

(1)   Press **Return** to send the files to PRN, which is the same as LPT1.

(2)   Enter a valid DOS device name other than PRN, such as LPT2, LPT3, COM1, COM2, or AUX. Printing is directed to the device you name. If the device is not valid (if it doesn't exist on your system), results are unpredictable.

You cannot change the device assignment until you reboot the computer.

If you try to enter any options again, the **Invalid parameters** message is displayed. These options can be used again once your system is rebooted.

When you use the /C or /T option to cancel printing, the printer stops (even if a file is currently being printed), the paper is advanced to the top of the next page, and the printer's alarm sounds. If /C has been used, printing resumes with the first file remaining in the print queue.

If PRINT cannot read a file due to a disk error, it cancels the file. The disk error message is printed, the paper is advanced to the top of the next page, and the printer's alarm is sounded. PRINT then moves on to the next file.

As long as PRINT has control of the printer, you cannot print anything else with another program (such as DOS, BASIC, or a word processor). You will receive a **Device not ready** message, and the attempt to print will be ignored.

Do not delete or change a file that is being printed or files that are still in the print queue. They will be treated as either a disk error, or the correct copy of the file might not be printed.

You must enter the command as NET PRINT to print on a printer that is part of a network.

You can use the /**B**:*buffsize* option to change the size of the print buffer, which affects the number of times PRINT must read from the disk. Increasing this number increases throughput to the printer, and results in faster printing speed.

The value of *buffsize* is always a multiple of 512 (1024, 2048, and so on). The default value is 512, which is fine for most cases; however, using a value of 4096 (expressed as /B:4096) can significantly improve printing speed.

Calculating Percentage of Free Time

Increasing the amount of the computer's free time taken up by PRINT can increase the speed at which the files in the print queue are printed but decrease the processing speed of other programs. Increasing *maxtick* gives PRINT more time; increasing *timeslice* gives PRINT less time.

Messages: **All files canceled by operator**. You used the /T option to cancel all files in the print queue.

Cannot use PRINT - use NET PRINT. You cannot use PRINT to print a file on a network printer. Re-enter the command using NET PRINT instead.

Errors on list device indicate that it may be off-line. Please check. The device you named in the command is not connected, turned on, or on line. Check your printer and cables to correct the problem.

filename File not in print queue. You tried to cancel a file, but it was not found in the print queue. If this is really the file you want to cancel, it may have already been printed, or you misspelled the file name.

File filename canceled by operator. This message is printed out when you cancel printing of a file. *filename* is the name of the file you canceled.

filename is currently being printed filename is in queue. This message shows you what file is being printed and a list of the files that are on line to be printed. It is displayed whenever you add new files to the print queue or when you use PRINT without any parameters.

List output is not assigned to a device. You gave a device name that is not recognized by DOS. Re-enter the command with a valid device name (one that exists on your system).

Name of list device [PRN]: This prompt appears when you do not name a device in the command format. You can press **Return** to name PRN as the default device, or you can enter an alternate device, such as LPT1, LPT2, LPT3, COM1, COM2, or AUX.

Pathname too long. The length of the file specification was more than the 63-character limit. PRINT skips this file and moves on to the next file in line.

Print queue is full. You cannot add more than the maximum number of files the print queue will accept. Files are added until the maximum is reached. Once a file has been printed, another can be added to the queue. The default maximum is ten files. It can also be changed with the /Q:*quesize* option (*quesize* can range from 1 to 10).

Print queue is empty. This message tells you that there are no files waiting to be printed. It is displayed when you request the queue status by using PRINT without any parameters.

Resident part of PRINT installed. When you use the PRINT command for the first time, this message verifies that PRINT has been installed and will remain resident in memory.

xxxx error on file yyyy. When a disk error occurs, the file cannot be printed (or finish being printed). This message is printed, showing the type of error and the file specification. The paper is then advanced to the top of the next page, the printer's alarm is sounded, and PRINT continues to the next file.

Examples: To send FILE.TXT on drive B to the printer, at the DOS prompt, enter

```
print b:file.txt ⏎
```

The screen will display the following response:

```
Name of list device [PRN]:
```

DOS prompts you for the device name. Press **Return** to send the output of FILE.TXT to the printer.

To cancel printing of FILE.TXT and add the files FILE1.TXT, FILE2.TXT, and FILE3.TXT to the print queue, enter

```
print b:file.txt /c b:file?.txt /p ⏎
```

To terminate printing, enter

```
print b:file2.txt /t ⏎
```

PROMPT

Set the system prompt
Version 2.0 Internal

Functions: Customizes the DOS system prompt, commonly referred to as the A prompt (A>).

Format: PROMPT *prompt*

Variables: *prompt* is the string of text to be used for the new system prompt. You may enter standard characters or special characters defined by a **meta-string**.

A meta-string is a group of characters representing a special character or characters. A meta-string begins with a dollar sign, followed by a character or group of characters. Rules for using meta-strings are explained later.

Comments: Using the command without *prompt* returns the system prompt to the default: A> (where "A" indicates the name of the default drive).

Any string of characters (as well as the specified meta-strings) can be used in a DOS prompt.

The new system prompt remains until you restart DOS or use the PROMPT command again.

Using the SET command displays the current PROMPT format.

Using Meta-Strings:

A meta-string is a group of characters defined in the PROMPT command that lets you display characters and symbols in your prompt that would normally be interpreted by DOS. Piping and I/O redirection symbols, such as ¦, <, and > are good examples. DOS would normally try to interpret these symbols; when used in meta-strings, however, they can be displayed simply as characters without being interpreted.

You can start the prompt with a character that is normally a DOS delimiter (such as a blank space, semicolon, or comma) by preceding the character with a null meta-string, that is, a character that has no meaning to PROMPT, such as $A.

All meta-strings begin with a dollar sign, followed by a character. Unlike most DOS commands, upper- and lower-case letters are not interchangeable. The meta-string characters must be entered exactly as shown. Following are the meta-string characters you can use:

Character	Produces a character
$	$
b	|
g	>
l	<
q	=
e	Escape (ASCII 27)

Character	Performs a function
_ (underline)	newline (1st column of next line)
d	displays the date
h	backspace (ASCII 8), erases the previous character
n	displays the default disk drive
p	displays the default disk drive and current directory path
t	displays the time
v	displays the DOS version

Any other character will be ignored (called **null** meta-strings).

Since the PROMPT command is so versatile, prompt strings can become very long and involved. Once you've established the prompt you like, you can include it in your AUTOEXEC.BAT file or in a separate batch file that can be run whenever you want to use that PROMPT format.

If you include a meta-string that displays the current directory ($p), DOS reads the disk drive before displaying your customized prompt. In this case, there must be a diskette in the drive, or the message

```
Not ready error reading drive d:
Abort, Retry, Ignore?
```

is displayed when DOS reaches this meta-string and tries to read the drive.

Examples: These examples are progressive in nature. Each time the PROMPT is changed, the subsequent example shows the new system prompt rather than the standard A prompt, A>.

To make the standard system prompt a bit more understandable, at the A prompt, enter

```
prompt The default drive is $n:
```

The screen will display the following response:

```
The default drive is A:
```

DOS first displays the phrase **The default drive is**, followed by the meta-string $n, which is actually the default drive. To see how the new prompt changes as you change the default drive, enter

```
b:
```

The screen will display the following response:

```
The default drive is B:
```

If you don't have a drive B, you can change it to drive C by typing **c:** instead. Notice that DOS now displays the meta-string $n as B (or C) instead of A.

To return to drive A and add a second line to the previous example, enter

a: ⏎

The screen will display the following response:

`    The default drive is A:`

Enter

`prompt The default drive is $n$_Please enter a command:` ⏎

The screen will display the following response:

`    The default drive is A`
`    Please enter a command:`

In the previous example, $n displays the default drive and $_ starts a new line. By now, you should be starting to see the possibilities. This one simple command can provide you with some very useful information (instead of a cryptic system prompt) and make life with DOS much easier.

Try a few more examples. To show what drive you are on and what directory you are in, enter

`prompt $p$_$n$g` ⏎

The screen will display the following response:

`    A:\DOS\UTIL`
`    A>`

The meta-string $p displays both the drive and directory path information; $_ starts a new line, and ng displays the standard system prompt ($n is the default drive and $g is >).

To add the date and time to the first line, enter

prompt $d; thhhhh$h p_ng ⏎

The screen will display the following response:

    Thu   7-03-1986;   9:51   A:\DOS\UTIL
    A>

The time is displayed only in hours and minutes by using hhhhhh, which backspaces six times to erase the seconds and hundredths. Seconds and hundredths are not necessary in most cases and merely clutter up the display.

For the adventurous, the ultimate system prompt is defined in Figure 11.2 (see Chapter 11). Try it out.

Now, to return to the standard prompt, enter

prompt ⏎

The screen will display the following response:

    A>

RECOVER

Recover a file or disk directory
Version 2.0 External

Functions: Recovers a file with bad sectors or recovers a file from a disk with a damaged directory.

Format: RECOVER *filespec*

or

RECOVER *d:*

Variables: *filespec* is the name of the file with the bad sectors that you want to recover. *filespec* is defined as *[d:][path]filename.ext*, which specifies the drive name, directory path, file name, and extension of the file.

Wild card characters should not be used in *filename.ext*. If a wild card character is used, RECOVER uses only the first file that matches.

d: is the name of the drive that contains the disk with the damaged directory you want to repair.

Comments: RECOVER does not restore erased files.

If you specify only the drive name, RECOVER attempts to recover the damaged directory on the disk drive you named.

If you do not specify a drive name, the default drive is used.

If you do not specify a path name, the current directory is used.

RECOVER attempts to recover the file by skipping the bad sectors and recovering as much of the information in the file as possible.

RECOVER should not be used when the ASSIGN, SUBST, and JOIN commands are active. Return them to their default values before using the RECOVER command.

RECOVER cannot be used with network drives or with files that are currently being shared.

Messages: **Cannot RECOVER to a network drive.** You cannot recover files that are on a network drive or that are on a drive on your system but are currently being shared. If the file is being shared, you can PAUSE the server, RECOVER the file, then CONTINUE the server.

Invalid drive or filename. This message indicates that (1) you specified a drive that doesn't exist on your system, (2) you didn't give a file name, or (3) the syntax of the command was incorrect. Recheck the command and try again.

Press any key to begin recovery of the file(s) on drive d: This message prompts you to insert the diskette to be recovered in drive *d:*; then press a key to start the recovery.

Warning-directory full xxx files recovered. There is insufficient directory space to recover more files. Copy some of the files to another disk and run RECOVER again.

xxxxxx of xxxxxx bytes recovered. Tells you the number of bytes that were recovered from the damaged file.

Examples: To recover information from the file ACCOUNTS.CAL on drive A, at the A prompt, enter

recover accounts.cal ⏎

To repair the directory of the contents of a disk in drive B, enter

recover b: ⏎

RENAME

Rename a file
Version 1.0 External

Functions: Changes the name of a file.

Format: REN[AME] *oldname newname*

Variables: *oldname* is the file you want to rename. It is specified as *[d:][path]filename.ext*, which is the drive name, directory path, file name, and extension.

newname is the new name you want for the file. It is specified as *filename.ext*, which is the file name and extension. The drive name and file name are not used in *newname* because the file remains in the same directory on the same drive after its name has been changed.

You can use either RENAME or REN in the command format.

Comments: If you do not use a drive name, the default drive is used.

If you do not specify a path name, the current directory is used.

You must specify both *oldname* and *newname* in the command format. If you don't, the **Missing file name** message is displayed.

If *newname* already exists on the disk drive and/or directory you specified, the **Duplicate filename or File not found** message is displayed. The name is not changed.

You can use wild card characters (? and *) in *filename.ext*. As with many other DOS commands, caution should be used when renaming multiple files. Be sure you want to rename all the files that meet the file specification containing the wild card characters.

Messages: **Duplicate filename or File not found.** This message indicates that (1) the file you tried to change does not exist on the drive or directory you specified, or (2) the new file name you gave already exists. Re-enter with the correct format.

Invalid number of parameters. You specified the file names incorrectly. Check the command format above and try again.

Missing file name. You left out the *newname* parameter. Re-enter the command.

Examples: To rename CHAPTER6.TXT to CHAPTER7.TXT, enter

rename chapter6.txt chapter7.txt ⏎

To change the extensions of CHAPTER1.TXT, CHAPTER2.TXT, AND CHAPTER3.TXT on drive B in the \ROMANCE directory to .ASC, enter

ren b:\romance\chapter?.txt chapter?.asc ⏎

If these files were the only files in the \ROMANCE directory on drive B, you could also enter

ren b:\romance*.txt *.asc ⏎

The results would be the same; however, if there were other files with the .TXT extension, they would also be renamed.

REPLACE

Replace or add files
Version 3.2 External

Functions: Replaces or adds files of the same name from one disk to another.

Format: REPLACE *filespec* [*d:*][*path*] [/A][/P][/R][/S][/W]

Variables: *filespec* is defined as *[d:][path]filename.ext*, which is the source drive name, directory path, file name, and extension. The files that match this specification are replaced on or added to the target disk. *filespec* cannot be more than 63 characters long.

You can use wild card characters in *filename.ext*.

[d:][path] is the target drive name and directory path that contain the files that are to be replaced. If /A is used, files that do not exist in the target are added.

Options:

/A adds only those files that do not exist on the target. You cannot use /A with /S.

/P prompts you for each file that matches *filespec*, which lets you select the files you want to replace or add.

/R replaces files that are read-only on the target.

/S searches all directories on the target for files that match *filespec*. You cannot use /S with /A.

/W prompts you to insert a diskette before searching for files that match *filespec*. Without this option, REPLACE starts immediately.

Comments: REPLACE is a useful command for upgrading to a new version of DOS or an application program. Without the /A option, it replaces any existing files with new files of the same name. With the /A option, it adds any new files included on the new program disk.

211

If you do not name a disk drive, the default drive is used.

If you do not name a directory path, the current directory is used.

If you use /W without /A, the **Press any key to begin replacing file(s)** message is displayed. Insert the source diskette and press a key.

If you combine /W and /A, the **Press any key to begin adding file(s)** message is displayed. Insert a source diskette and press a key.

Without the /W option, REPLACE begins as soon as you enter the command.

REPLACE ignores hidden and system files.

Exit Codes:
- **0** Successful completion.
- **2** No source file(s) were found.
- **3** The source or target directory path was invalid or not found.
- **5** The access code for reading or writing a file is not correct. Try again using /R.
- **8** Not enough memory to load REPLACE.
- **11** Invalid format: incorrect parameter or combination of parameters.
- **15** The disk drive doesn't exist on your system.
- **22** REPLACE does not exist for the version of DOS you are using.

Messages:

Add d:\path\filename? You used both the /P and /A options, which let you decide if each file that matches *filespec* should be added to the target. Answer **Y** for "Yes" to add the file; answer **N** for "No" to skip the file without adding it.

Adding d:\path\filename. The /A option to add files was used; *d:\path\filename* indicates the file that is currently being added to the target.

No files added. The /A option to add files was used, but no files were found on the source that matched *filespec*.

No files found. Files were found on the source that matched *filespec*, but files with the same file name and extension were not found on the target. The /A option to add files was not used.

No files replaced. No files could be found on the source that matched *filespec*. The /A option to add files was not used.

Press any key to begin adding files. Both the /W and /A options were used, which prompt you to insert the source diskette that contains files that match *filespec* and are to be added to the target.

Press any key to begin replacing files. The /W option was used, which prompts you to insert the source diskette that contains files that match *filespec* and are to be replaced on the target. The /A option to add files was not used.

REPLACE d:path\filename (Y/N)? You used the /P option which lets you decide if each file that matches *filespec* should be replaced on the target. Answer **Y** for "Yes" to replace or add the file; answer **N** for "No" to skip the file without replacing or adding it. The /A option to add files was not used.

Replacing d:path\filename. Indicates the file that is currently being replaced on the target. The /A option to add files was not used.

Source path required. You must give REPLACE a source path. Try using REPLACE again, and include a source path.

xxx files added. The /A option to add files was used; *xxx* indicates the number of files that were added to the target.

Examples: These examples use the fixed disk (drive C) as the default drive.

To copy the new version of your word processing program from the diskette in drive A to the \WP directory on drive C, at the C> prompt, enter

replace a:*.* \wp ⏎

Then to add any new files included with the program, enter

replace a:*.* \wp /a ⏎

The example above copies all files from drive A that do not already exist in the \WP directory.

To replace CASHRCPT.CAL on drive A with the file of the same name in the \ACCOUNTS directory on drive C, enter

replace \accounts\cashrcpt.cal a: ⏎

To replace all .CAL files on drive A with the files of the same name in the \ACCOUNTS directory on drive C, enter

replace \accounts*.cal a: ⏎

To replace all other copies of CHAP1.TXT on your fixed disk with CHAP1.TXT in the PROJ1 directory on drive A, enter

replace a:\proj1\chap1.txt c:\ /s/p ⏎

In the previous example, REPLACE searches all directories and subdirectories of the root directory to find CHAP1.TXT files. REPLACE prompts you for each match to confirm that you want to replace the CHAP1.TXT file in that directory.

RESTORE

Restore backup files
Version 2.0 External

Functions: Restores one or more backup files from a diskette or a fixed disk to another diskette or fixed disk. The backup files are created with the BACKUP command.

Format: RESTORE d: [filespec] [/S][/P][/B:mm-dd-yy] [/A:mm-yy-dd][/M][/N][/L:hh:mm:ss][/E:hh:mm:ss]

Variables: *d:* is a valid drive (one that exists on your system) that contains the backup files.

filespec is defined as *[d:][path][filename.ext]*. *filespec* specifies the drive name, directory path, file name, and extension of the files you want to restore and where you want to restore them.

Options:

/S   restores all files in the directory specified and in all its subdirectories.

/P   lets you confirm whether or not you want to restore a file that (1) has changed since it was last backed up, or (2) is marked as a read-only file.

/B:*mm-dd-yy*

      restores all files modified on or before the date given.

/A:*mm-dd-yy*

      restores all files modified on or after the date given.

/M   restores all files modified or deleted since they were backed up.

/N   restores files that don't exist on the target.

/L:*hh:mm:ss*

      restores only files modified at or after the time given.

/**E:**hh:mm:ss

> restores only files modified at or before the time given.

Comments: Only files that were saved with the BACKUP command can be restored with RESTORE.

RESTORE version 3.3 will restore backup files saved with earlier versions of BACKUP.

The /B, /A, and /N options should not be used together.

If you do not specify a directory path, the current directory of the disk receiving files is used.

If you specify a directory path, you must also specify a file name and extension, unless you want to restore all the files in the directory (the same as using *.*).

Wildcard characters can be used in the file name and extension. They cause all files matching the file name to be restored.

RESTORE prompts you to insert the next diskette after restoring files on each backup diskette.

RESTORE prompts you to insert the diskettes containing the backup files in order (diskette #1, #2, #3, and so on). If you insert a diskette out of order, RESTORE displays the **WARNING! Diskette is out of sequence** message. You can insert the correct diskette or leave the current diskette in if you know there are no files that match the file specification on the diskettes you skipped.

If you use the /S option, RESTORE re-creates any subdirectories removed since the files were backed up that are necessary to restore files to the disk. The files are then restored in these subdirectories.

RESTORE version 3.3 will not restore the system files (IBMBIO.COM, IBMDOS.COM, and COMMAND.COM). This feature prevents you from overwriting DOS with an earlier version.

If you are restoring files that were backed up using a previous version of DOS, you should use the /P option, which will prompt you to verify restoring files. Answer N for "No" to avoid replacing the DOS files with older versions. (This step is especially necessary for the DOS system files, IBMBIO.COM and IBMDOS.COM; replacing them would make the disk unbootable. You also want to avoid replacing DOS files that have new and enhanced features and may be incompatible with other DOS versions.)

The ASSIGN, SUBST, and JOIN commands should be returned to their defaults before using RESTORE.

If you are sharing files on a network, you can only restore files that you have access to at the time you use the command. If you attempt to restore a file that is being shared, the **Not able to restore at this time** message is displayed along with the path name and file name you are trying to restore.

Exit Codes: 0   Successful restore completed.
                   1   No files were found to restore.
                   2   Restore was terminated by the user (Ctrl-Break or Ctrl-C).
                   3   Restore was terminated because of an error.

Messages:

Backup file sequence error. A file to be restored was backed up on more than one diskette. The diskette you inserted does not contain the first part of the file. Find the correct diskette and insert it in the disk drive.

Files were backed up mm/dd/yy. This message is informational, telling you the date the files were backed up.

Insert backup diskette xx in drive d:
Strike any key when ready. RESTORE prompts you to insert backup diskettes in sequence (#1, #2, #3, and so on). *xx* is the number of the diskette; *d:* is the name of the drive in which to insert the diskette. When you've inserted the correct diskette (don't worry, RESTORE will tell you if you've got the diskette out of sequence), press any key to continue.

Insert restore source diskette in drive d:
Strike any key when ready. RESTORE prompts you to insert the diskette that contains the backup files (the source). *d:* is the name the drive in which to insert the source diskette.

Insert restore target diskette in drive d:
Strike any key when ready. RESTORE prompts you to insert the diskette that is to receive the restored files (the target). *d:* is the name of the drive in which to insert the target diskette. This message appears only when you are restoring files onto removable diskettes.

Invalid drive specification. This message indicates you gave a drive name that (1) does not contain the backup files, (2) does not exist on your system, or (3) has been altered with the ASSIGN, SUBST, or JOIN commands. Check each of these causes and try RESTORE again.

Restore file sequence error. The file was not restored because the diskettes were not inserted in sequential order (#1, #2, #3, and so on). Try again, inserting the diskettes in the proper order.

Source and target drives are the same. The disk drive holding the backup files is the same as the drive that will receive the restored files. Check the rules for entering drive names and re-enter the command. If you are using a system with only one diskette drive, enter the command using drives A and B instead of A and A.

Source does not contain backup files. This message indicates one of several possibilities:

(1) RESTORE couldn't find any files created with the BACKUP command. Try DIR on the diskette and look for the BACKUPID.@@@ file. If the file is missing, this diskette is not a backup diskette.

(2) The backup files may be damaged and unreadable. In this case, the backup files would be unusable.

(3) The \BACKUP subdirectory couldn't be found while files were being restored from a fixed disk. Look for the \BACKUP subdirectory on the fixed disk. If you can't find the subdirectory, the disk doesn't have any backup files on it.

System files restored
The target disk may not be bootable. You have restored the DOS system files, IBMBIO.COM, IBMDOS.COM, and COMMAND.COM from the backup disk. These files may have been from a previous DOS version, which will make your disk unbootable. If this occurs, run SYS to place the current version of the three files onto the disk.

Target is full
The last file was not restored. The disk receiving the restored files is full and cannot hold the complete file listed in the message. The partially restored file is deleted. The file (and any subsequent files) must be restored to a different disk.

Warning! Diskette is out of sequence
Replace the diskette or continue
Strike any key when ready. Files are restored using the same sequence of diskettes as when they were backed up. If you insert a diskette that is out of sequence, such as #1, #3, #2 instead of #1, #2, #3, this message prompts you to put in the right diskette. You have two options:

(1) You can continue with the out-of-sequence diskettes if you are sure that the skipped diskette(s) does not contain any files that match the file specification used in the command. In this case, simply strike any key to continue.

(2) You can insert the next diskette in the sequence and press any key to continue.

This message will continue to be displayed if you are in the middle of restoring a file. RESTORE needs the rest of the file from the next diskette to completely restore the file.

Depending on the DOS version you are using, this message may appear as

```
Warning! Source is out of sequence
Replace source or continue if okay
Strike any key when ready
```

**Warning! File filename
is a read only file
Replace the file (Y/N)?** The file, indicated as *filename*, is a read-only file. If you want to replace it, answer **Y** for "Yes" and press **Return**; otherwise, answer **N** for "no" and press **Return**. This message is only displayed if you use the **/P** option.

**Warning! File filename
was changed after it was backed up
Replace the file (Y/N)?** The file being replaced, indicated as *filename*, was changed since the file was last backed up. Answer **Y** for "Yes" and press **Return** if you want the backed up version to replace the newer version; otherwise, answer **N** for "No" and press **Return**. This message is only displayed if you use the **/P** option.

**Warning! Files in the target root directory will be erased
Strike any key when ready.** This is a warning message that tells you the files in the root directory will be erased. If you do not want to erase these files, press **Ctrl-Break**; otherwise, strike any key to continue.

Warning! No files were found to restore. There weren't any files found on the backup diskettes that matched the file specification you gave in the command.

Warning! Target is full. The disk receiving the restored files is full and cannot hold any more files.

*** Not able to restore file *** The file could not be completely restored because (1) the file is being shared, or (2) you sent a **Ctrl-Break** to stop RESTORE.

*** Restoring files from diskette d: *** This message is informational and is displayed while the files are being restored to the target disk. *d:* is the drive name from which the files are being restored.

*** Restoring files from drive d: ***
Source: d: This message is informational and is displayed while the files are being restored to the target disk. *d:* is the drive name of either the target or source diskette.

Examples: To restore the files with the extension .BAS from the backup diskette in drive A, at the DOS prompt, enter

restore a: c:*.bas ⏎

To restore all files, including subdirectories, from the backup diskette in drive A to drive C, enter

restore a: c:*.* /s/p ⏎

The /P option lets you decide whether or not to restore read-only files or files that have changed since the backup was performed. RESTORE prompts you when one of these files is encountered.

This example uses the fixed disk (drive C) as the default drive. To restore the ACCTREC.DAT file from the backup diskette in drive A to the \GL\AR directory, at the C> prompt, enter

restore a: \gl\ar\acctrec.dat ⏎

RMDIR or RD

Remove a directory
Version 2.0 Internal

Functions: Removes an empty directory.

Format: RMDIR [d:]path

or

RD [d:]path

Variables: *d:* specifies a valid drive name (one that exists on your system).

path is the name of the directory you want to remove. The last directory named in path is the one that is removed (e.g., RMDIR \REPORTS\PROJ1 removes the PROJ1 subdirectory but not the REPORTS directory).

Comments: RD is the abbreviated form of RMDIR. The commands work identically.

The directory must be empty before it can be removed. You can delete all the files in the directory with DEL *.* while the directory you want to remove is the current directory (the "." and ".." entries will remain). Be sure that you do not want any of these files before you delete them.

You cannot remove directories that contain hidden files. Hidden files are not displayed in directories; they are sometimes created as part of a copy-protection scheme.

The root directory cannot be removed.

You cannot remove a directory that you are currently in.

You cannot remove a directory if it has been substituted with the SUBST command.

The RMDIR command should be used with caution while ASSIGN or JOIN are active; make sure you know which actual drive you are referring to in the command.

Messages: **Invalid path, not directory or directory not empty.** This message indicates that (1) you entered a directory path that doesn't exist or is not on the drive you specified; (2) you entered a directory that doesn't exist or is not on the drive you specified, or (3) the directory you want to remove still has files in it. Re-enter the correct drive and path name. Make sure you are removing the correct directory. If it still has files, delete them, and re-enter the command.

Examples: These examples use drive C as the default drive.

To remove the TEMP directory on the default drive, at the C> prompt, enter

rmdir \temp ⏎

Using the format

rd \temp ⏎

will achieve the same results.

To remove the TEXT subdirectory of PROJECT1 on drive A, enter

rd a:\project1\text ⏎

SET

Set system environment
Version 2.0 Internal

Functions: Changes the command processor's environment or displays the current environment.

Format: SET [*name*=[*parameter*]]

Variables: *name*= is the name of the parameter you want to change or add to the system environment. If you specify *name*= without a parameter, DOS deletes the name from the environment.

parameter is the string of information you want to place in the system environment.

If you use SET without any variables, the current system environment is displayed.

Comments: The SET command is a versatile feature that puts information into the command processor's environment for later use with invoked programs. A good example is the use of SET to provide directory path information for requested files. When the application program is loaded, it searches the environment for the information that tells it the directory path to use to find the requested files.

The proper name to use is determined by the application program.

Any lowercase characters in *name* are changed to uppercase when placed in the system environment.

The characters in *parameter* remain unchanged.

SET can be used as an alternative to (1) setting the system prompt with PROMPT, (2) defining the directory path search with PATH, or (3) changing the location of COMMAND.COM with COMSPEC.

When a resident program such as PRINT, MODE, or GRAPHICS is loaded, DOS cannot expand the system environment beyond 127 bytes (characters). You can still use SET to add up to 127 characters; however, if the command would expand the environment area beyond 127 characters, the **Out of environment space** message is displayed, and the environment remains unchanged.

Messages: **Out of environment space.** DOS cannot expand the system environment enough to process the SET command. The maximum that DOS can expand is 127 bytes (characters) when resident programs such as PRINT, MODE, and GRAPHICS are active. If feasible, remove any resident programs and retry the SET command.

Examples: To add the string LIB=\COMP\LIB to the system environment, enter

```
set lib=\comp\lib
```

When the application program is loaded, it can search the system environment for the name LIB and use the \COMP\LIB directory to find the necessary files.

To display the system environment, enter

```
set
```

The screen will display the following information:

```
PATH=
COMSPEC=A:\COMMAND.COM
LIB=\comp\lib
```

Notice that the lowercase letters "lib" in name were converted to uppercase, but the parameter for the directory "\comp\lib" remains in lowercase letters.

To remove lib=\comp\lib from the environment, enter

```
set lib=
```

SHARE

File sharing
Version 3.0 External

Functions: Loads support for file sharing.

Format: SHARE [/F:*space*][/L:*locks*]

Options: /F:*space*

>sets the amount of memory reserved for recording file sharing information. The default value is 2048. Each open file requires the length of the full file name plus 11 bytes.

/L:*locks*

>sets the number of locks you want. The default is 20.

Comments: The SHARE command loads the routines that DOS needs to handle file sharing. If two or more programs use the same file at the same time, there is a possibility that the file could become corrupted if the use of the file is not coordinated.

Messages: **SHARE already installed.** The SHARE command has already been used.

Not enough memory. There is not enough free memory to use the SHARE command. The SHARE command needs a certain amount of memory (5776 bytes with the default settings) to keep track of file sharing. You currently don't have enough free memory. Possibly, you have too many memory-resident programs or too large a VDISK loaded.

Incorrect parameter. You used an incorrect option with the SHARE command, or the values that you specified are too large. Try entering the command again. The maximum value for both options is 65535.

Sharing buffer exceeded. The buffers that SHARE creates to keep track of file sharing are full. Choose **Retry**. If the error repeats, increase the values for the /F: and /L: options.

Unrecoverable file sharing error. The file sharing routines have become hopelessly confused.

Examples: To load the file sharing function using the default values, at the C> prompt, enter

share ⏎

SORT

Sort string filter
Version 2.0 External

Functions: Reads information from the standard input device, sorts the information, then writes it to the standard output device.

Format: SORT [/R][/+n]

Options: /R   reverses the order of sort (e.g., Z comes before A).

/+n   starts the sort at column n.

Comments: This DOS command is a general-purpose sorting program that is fairly flexible but does have its limitations.

SORT works best when sorting files containing straight ASCII text. Files created with special formats (those created with word processing formats, compressed codes, etc.) only hamper the pure sorting capabilities of this command. If you need to do more complicated sorting, there are several commercial data base programs available that perform more sophisticated sorting routines.

Unless you redirect the input from a file, SORT reads information from the keyboard (standard input device).

The SORT result is written to the display screen (standard output device) unless it is redirected to the printer or to another file.

Use the /R option to sort in reverse order; otherwise, the file is sorted in ascending order.

Use the /+n option to start sorting at column n. The plus sign (+) must be included or the **Invalid parameter** message is displayed. n must be a positive integer. The default value of n is 1 (the first character on a line). If you do not use this option at all, SORT starts at column 1.

If you use the input and output files, their names must be different.

SORT sorts the entire physical file, discarding the end-of-file marker and all information beyond.

The maximum file size is 63K (64,512 characters).

The information is sorted in ASCII order (A comes before Z) or in reverse order (Z comes before A).

In DOS version 3, lowercase letters (a-z) are considered the same as uppercase letters (A-Z). In version 2, all uppercase letters are placed before any lowercase letters; therefore, in version 2, uppercase A comes before uppercase Z as expected, but uppercase Z comes before lowercase a-z. For example, "WORDS" comes before "words, " "Words," "WoRdS," "WORDs," etc.

SORT looks at numbers as characters; thus, 1 always comes before 2, 3, 4, or 9. The number 0 comes before 1. Unfortunately, because numbers are usually read from right to left rather than left to right, numbers can only be sorted logically if they are right-justified. Consider the differences in the numbers sorted below:

Left-justified	Right-justified
0942482318	9
12345	38
38	846
8378934	12345
846	96239
9	8378934
96239	0942462318

In DOS version 3, some characters with ASCII values from 128 to 255 are collated differently. The SORT sequence is shown in Table 6.3.

ASCII value		Sort value	
Decimal	Character	Decimal	Character
128	Ç	67	C
129	ü	85	U
130	é	69	E
131	â	65	A
132	ä	65	A
133	à	65	A
134	å	65	A
135	ç	67	C
136	ê	69	E
137	ë	69	E
138	è	69	E
139	ï	73	I
140	î	73	I
141	ì	73	I
142	Ä	65	A
143	Å	65	A
144	É	69	E
145	æ	65	A
146	Æ	65	A
147	ô	79	O
148	ö	79	O
149	ò	79	O
150	û	85	U
151	ù	85	U
152	ÿ	89	Y
153	Ö	79	O
154	Ü	85	U
155	¢	36	$
156	£	36	$
157	¥	36	$
158	₧	36	$
159	ƒ	36	$
160	á	65	A
161	í	73	I
162	ó	79	O
163	ú	85	U
164	ñ	78	N
165	Ñ	78	N
168	¿	63	?
173	¡	33	!
174	«	34	"
175	»	35	#
225	β	83	S

Table 6.3
SORT values for ASCII codes 128 to 255.
ASCII values not shown in this table will sort in normal sequence.

DOS version 3 handles the sorting of ASCII codes 128 to 255 somewhat more intelligently, including foreign characters and symbols. Version 3 can accomodate most files with foreign language text.

Messages: **Invalid parameter.** You entered a parameter that SORT couldn't recognize. Check the format for variables and options and try again.

SORT: Insufficient disk space. There was not enough disk space to complete the SORT, which creates some temporary workfiles on the default drive. Either transfer or delete some files to free up disk space or use another disk and try the command again.

SORT: Insufficient memory. You do not have enough unused memory to run the SORT. If you have memory that can be freed up by deleting memory-resident programs, do so and try the command again. (**Note:** You may need to delete the commands from your AUTOEXEC.BAT file that load the programs into memory, and then reboot your computer.)

Examples: To sort the lines in NAMES.TXT and output them to the display screen, enter

```
sort <names.txt ⏎
```

To sort the lines in NAMES.TXT in reverse order and output them to a file named REVNAMES.TXT, enter

```
sort <names.txt >revnames.txt /r ⏎
```

To display a directory sorted by file size, enter

```
dir ¦ sort /+14 ⏎
```

The pipe symbol (¦) causes the output of the DIR command to be used as input to the SORT command. In the directory listing, column 14 starts the file size. Because the file sizes are right-justified, the numbers are sorted in the proper order (see Chapter 4 for further details on piping).

SUBST

Substitute drive for path
Version 3.0 External

Functions: Substitutes a different drive name for another drive or for a path.

Format: SUBST *d: d:path* [**/D**]

Variables: *d:* is a valid drive name that you want to use as the substitute.

d:path is a valid drive name and directory path that you want to change. The path you specify should start at the root directory.

Using SUBST without any parameters displays all the current substitutions.

Options: **/D** deletes a substitution. You must specify the drive name you used as the substitute (e.g., if you substituted drive G for the path C:\GAMES1, to delete the substitution, enter **SUBST g: /d**).

Comments: The SUBST command is helpful when you use applications that do not recognize path names. Whenever you want to access that directory path, just enter the name of the substituted drive.

The drive letter (*d:*) you specify depends on the value of the LASTDRIVE configuration command used in CONFIG.SYS (see Chapter 8). The default value of LASTDRIVE is E, which means *d:* can be any letter from A through E. Values greater than the default value must be specified in LASTDRIVE. For example, to use drive G, the value of LASTDRIVE must be greater than or equal to G.

You cannot use the same drive names in the format SUBST *d: d:path*. The first drive cannot be the same as the default drive. If you specify a path, it starts from the root directory.

If you use this command with a network drive, the **Cannot SUBST a network drive** message is displayed.

The ASSIGN, BACKUP, DISKCOMP, DISKCOPY, FDISK, FORMAT, JOIN, LABEL, and RESTORE commands should not be used when a substitution exists.

Use SUBST without parameters to display all current substitutions. They are displayed as follows:

G: => D:\PATH

Messages: **Cannot SUBST to a network drive.** You tried to use the SUBST command to substitute a drive for a network path or substitute a network drive for a local path. Re-enter the command only using local drives and paths.

Invalid parameter. This message indicates that you (1) typed an incorrect drive, (2) used the default drive, or (3) used the /D option to delete a substitution, but you didn't specify the drive letter to delete. Re-enter the correct information.

Invalid path. You specified a path name that does not exist. Re-enter the correct path name.

Examples: For the following examples, assume the default drive is A and LASTDRIVE=H.

To substitute drive F for C:\PROJECT1\TEXT, at the DOS prompt, enter

subst f: c:\project1\text ⏎

To list the directory of C:\PROJECT1\TEXT, enter

dir f: ⏎

To display the current substitutions, enter

subst F: = C:\PROJECT1\TEXT ⏎

The screen will display the following information:

    F: => C:\PROJECT1\TEXT

If you were using a word processing program that did not recognize directory paths, you could now load a file from C:PROJECT1\TEXT. For example, to load the document PROPOSAL.TXT from the subdirectory C:PROJECT1\TEXT, enter

`f:proposal.txt` ⏎

when the program prompts you to enter the document name.

To delete the substitution, enter

`subst f: /d` ⏎

SYS

Transfer operating system
Version 1.0 External

Functions: Transfers the operating system to a disk.

Format: SYS *d:*

Variables: *d:* is a valid drive name (one that exists on your system). DOS transfers the operating system to the disk in the specified drive.

Comments: The SYS command lets you transfer a copy of the operating system files to an application program diskette that already has the required space reserved but does not actually contain the files.

The operating system consists of three files. Two of them are hidden—IBMBIO.COM and IBMDOS.COM (or IO.SYS and MSDOS.SYS if you are using MS-DOS). The third file is COMMAND.COM. A disk must have all three files on it to be bootable.

SYS places a copy of IBMBIO.COM and IBMDOS.COM in the reserved space on the disk you name in the command format. SYS does not place a copy of COMMAND.COM on the disk. You must copy this file into the root directory of this diskette, using the COPY command.

The disk directory must be either (1) completely empty, (2) formatted with the command FORMAT *d:*/S, or (3) formatted with FORMAT *d:*/B. DOS startup requires IBMBIO.COM and IBMDOS.COM to be the first two directory entries in the root directory. They are called hidden files because they are not displayed with the DIR command. Also, IBMBIO.COM must reside on consecutive sectors on the disk.

If these criteria are not met, DOS will not load properly when you boot the disk.

You cannot use the SYS command on a network drive.

If a shared drive on your computer is currently being used, the system transfer will not take place.

Messages: **Cannot find system files.** The hidden files IBMBIO.COM and IBMDOS.COM were not found on the default drive. Change the default drive to the one with these files and try again.

Cannot SYS to a network drive. You cannot transfer the operating system to a network drive or to a drive on your computer that is currently being shared.

Incompatible system size. The target diskette contains a copy of DOS that is smaller than the one being copied. No files are transferred. Format a blank diskette with **FORMAT /S** and copy any files to the new diskette.

Insert System disk in x and strike any key when ready. This messages prompts you to insert the DOS diskette with the hidden files IBMBIO.COM and IBMDOS.COM. Insert the proper diskette and strike any key to continue.

Insufficient memory for system transfer. There is not enough memory to place the operating system on the diskette. Reboot your computer without loading any memory-resident programs, such as VDISK, RAM drives, print spoolers, Sidekick, or Superkey.

No room for system on destination disk. The target diskette does not have the proper space reserved for DOS. No files are transferred. Format a blank diskette with **FORMAT /S** and copy any files to the new diskette.

System transferred. DOS has successfully transferred a copy of the operating system.

No system on default drive. You must have the system files on the default drive for SYS to work.

Examples: To transfer the operating system from the diskette in drive A to the diskette in drive B, at the A> prompt, enter

sys b: ⏎

TIME

Set or display the time
Version 1.0 Internal

Functions: Sets the internal clock's time. Alternately displays the time.

Format: TIME [*hh:mm*[:*ss*[.*xx*]]]

Variables: *hh* sets the hours based on a 24-hour clock. *hh* can range from 0 to 23 (a one- or two-digit number).

mm sets the minutes. *mm* can range from 0 to 60 (a one- or two-digit number).

ss sets the seconds. *ss* can range from 0 to 60 (a one- or two-digit number).

xx sets the hundredths of seconds. *xx* can range from 0 to 99 (a one- or two-digit number).

Enter TIME without any variables, and DOS will display the current time and prompt you to either enter a new time or leave it unchanged.

Comments: TIME is used to set the internal clock of your computer. Both the time and the date are important in recording when files are created or changed.

If you do not enter the time with the TIME command, the following message is displayed:

```
Current time is hh:mm:ss:xx
Enter new time _
```

If you just press **Return**, the time will not be changed. If you enter a valid time, such as 11:45:30.15, it will be changed when you press **Return**.

You must enter a valid time within the ranges previously described. You must use colons (:) between the hours, minutes, and seconds. You must use a period (.) between seconds and hundredths of a second.

241

To change the time, you must at least enter *hh* and *mm*. *ss* and *xx* are both optional; and if you enter *ss*, *xx* is still optional. If you do not change *ss* or *xx*, they default to 0.

If you don't enter a valid time or use the wrong format, the **Invalid time** message is displayed, and you are prompted to re-enter the time.

If you don't set the time when you start up, or reboot, your computer, the time defaults to 00:00:00.00.

If you have a battery-powered clock/calendar board in your computer, you won't need this command except to reset the clock for daylight-saving time. Most such boards require the use of a short program that can be included in AUTOEXEC.BAT or a device driver included in CONFIG.SYS to let DOS know about the board's existence.

TIME will set the time on a built-in permanent clock. Computers like the AT and the PS/2 have built-in permanent clocks.

Messages: **Invalid time**
Enter new time. You entered a time that does not exist, or you used the wrong format. Re-enter a valid time.

Examples: To change the time to 8:30 A.M., enter

time 8:30 ⏎

To change the time to 10:23 and 30 seconds P.M., enter

time 22:23:30 ⏎

Remember that the clock is a 24-hour clock, so 10 P.M. is expressed as hour 22. To add 30 hundredths of a second to the previous time, enter

time 22:23:30.30 ⏎

TREE

Display directory path
Version 2.0 External

Functions: Displays all the directories on a disk; optionally displays all the files in each directory.

Format: TREE [*d:*] [/F]

Variables: *d:* is a valid drive name (one that exists on your system). If *d:* is not given, the default drive is used.

Options: /F   displays all the files in the root directory and in all subdirectories.

Comments: The TREE command provides you with the convenience of displaying all the directories on a disk without having to use the DIR command to display each directory and its subdirectories.

Using the /F option displays all the files with their full path names. (The file's date, time, and size, however, are not displayed. Use the DIR command in each directory to find this information.)

The TREE command can be useful for making a printed copy of a fixed disk backup. After completing the backup, use **TREE c: /F>PRN**, and all the file names will be printed. >PRN redirects the screen output to the printer.

Messages: **Dir path listing for volume xxxxxx.** This message is informational, telling you the volume label of the disk.

Invalid path. TREE couldn't access a subdirectory, indicating something is wrong with the directory file. Use CHKDSK to try to determine the problem, and take corrective action (see CHKDSK for details).

No subdirectories exist. The directory you specified doesn't have any subdirectories. If you think some have been previously created, use the DIR command in the directory to look for them.

Examples: These examples use the fixed disk (drive C) as the default drive.

To display all the directories on drive C, at the C> prompt, enter

tree ⏎

To display all the directories and all the files on drive C, enter

tree /f ⏎

To display all the directories and all the files on drive C and output the results to the printer, enter

tree /f>prn ⏎

TYPE

Display file contents
Version 1.0 Internal

Functions: Displays the contents of the file on the screen.

Format: TYPE *filespec*

Variables: *filespec* is defined as *[d:][path]filename.ext,* which specifies the drive name, directory path, file name, and extension on which the command is to act.

You cannot use wild cards in the file name or extension.

Comments: This command is used to quickly display the contents of a file.

If you do not specify a drive name, the default drive is used.

If you do not specify a directory path, the current directory is used.

You must specify a file name that can be found on the drive and in the directory specified.

>PRN redirects the output of TYPE to the printer. (You can also print what is displayed with TYPE by pressing **Ctrl-PrtSc** before using the TYPE command. Press **Ctrl-PrtSc** again to turn off the printing.)

When you TYPE a file, all characters including control characters are displayed. Tab characters (Ctrl-I or ASCII 9) are expanded to the next eight-character boundary, that is, columns 8, 16, 24, and so on.

If you try to TYPE program files, most of the time, strange characters will appear on the screen, and your computer will probably beep a lot. DOS is trying to display the machine-language instructions of the program as ASCII characters.

If you try to print the output of a program file that has these strange characters (with **>PRN** or **Ctrl-PrtSc**), the result is unpredictable. Many control codes that TYPE is sending to the printer actually control printer functions such as form feeds, underlining, and so on.

Messages: **Invalid filename or file not found.** You used a file name that does not exist, is not on the specified drive, or is not in the specified directory. This message also appears if you try to use wild card characters (? and *).

Examples: To display the contents of CONFIG.SYS found on the default drive, enter

```
type config.sys
```

The screen will display the following:

```
device=\dos\system\mouse.sys
device=\dos\system\ansi.sys
device=\dos\system\astclk.sys
buffers=20
files=12
```

To print the contents of ENDSPELL.BAT found on drive C in the BATCH subdirectory, enter

```
type c:\util\batch\endspell.bat >prn
```

VER

Display DOS version
Version 2.0 Internal

Functions: Displays the version of DOS with which you are working.

Format: VER

Comments: Sometimes, it is important to know which version of DOS you are using. Most external DOS commands, for example, operate properly only when used with the same version of DOS they were distributed with. Some application programs require a certain version of DOS (or higher). This command provides a quick way to find out if you have the right version.

If you try to use a DOS external command from a different version of DOS, you will receive the **Incorrect DOS version** message.

Example: To display the version of DOS you are using, enter

ver ⏎

The screen will display a message similar to the following:

IBM Personal Computer DOS Version   3.20

VERIFY

Verify disk output
Version 2.0 Internal

Functions: Verifies that information written to the disk has been correctly recorded.

Format: VERIFY [$\frac{ON}{OFF}$]

Options:
- **ON** lets you confirm that information has correctly been written to the disk.

- **OFF** lets you increase the speed of writing information to a disk because that information is not being verified.

Using VERIFY alone displays the current state of VERIFY: **VERIFY is on** or **VERIFY is off**.

Comments: Normally, when the system is turned on or when DOS is rebooted, VERIFY is off. If VERIFY is off, DOS will not check the information it writes to the disk.

When VERIFY is on, information is checked to be sure that it has been correctly recorded. This checking is done as the command writes the information to the disk, then reads the information back from the disk to make sure it is the same. Data integrity is assured with VERIFY on, but that information is written to the disk much more slowly.

VERIFY only affects disk output; it does not affect any other DOS operation.

VERIFY does not work with information written to a network disk.

If you are not working on critical information, it is usually safe to turn VERIFY off. It is a good idea, however, to turn VERIFY on when performing critical operations such as backing up a fixed disk or making important copies on diskettes.

The degree of performance between VERIFY on and off is less apparent when verifying information written to a fixed disk as compared to a floppy diskette.

Messages: **Must specify ON or OFF.** VERIFY was entered with something other than **ON** or **OFF**.

Verify is on. DOS is verifying the information that it writes to the disk. The message is displayed when you use VERIFY without an option.

Verify is off. DOS is not verifying information that it writes to the disk. The message is displayed when you use VERIFY without an option.

Examples: To have DOS verify information written to a disk, enter

verify on ⏎

To turn VERIFY off so that it doesn't verify information written to a disk, enter

verify off ⏎

To display the current state of VERIFY, enter

verify ⏎

The screen will display a message such as the following:

```
VERIFY is off
```

VOL

Display volume label
Version 2.0 Internal

Functions: Displays the volume label of the disk, if there is a label.

Format: VOL [*d:*]

Variables: *d:* is any valid drive (one that exists on your system).

Comments: Adding volume labels to your disks and diskettes is an important part of effective file management. Volume labels are given to a disk or diskette by using FORMAT or the LABEL command.

VOL lets you quickly determine the label on any disk or diskette, if it has a label.

If you do not specify a drive, the default drive is used.

Messages: **Volume in drive d has no label.** The disk or diskette doesn't have a label. No action is required.

Examples: To display the volume label of the diskette in the default drive, enter

vol ⏎

The screen will display a message such as the following:

    Volume in drive A is BUDGET86

To display the volume label of the fixed disk (drive C), enter

vol c: ⏎

The screen will display a message such as the following:

    Volume in drive C is SALES_DEPT1

XCOPY

Copy files and directories

Version 3.2 External

Functions: Copies files and directories.

Formats: XCOPY[*d:*][*path*][*sourcefile.ext*][*d:*][*path*][*destfile.ext*]
[/A] [/D:*mm-dd-yy*] [/E] [/M] [/P] [/S] [/V] [/W]

Variables: *[d:][path][sourcefile.ext]* specifies the drive, directory, or file(s) from which you want to copy (the source). You can specify a file, a group of files using wild card symbols, a directory, a drive, or any combination of the three.

[d:][path][destfile.ext] specifies the drive, directory, or file(s) to which you want to copy (the destination). This specification also indicates the directory (and file name) where XCOPY starts copying files.

You can use the wild card characters within the file name and extension.

Options:

/A copies only those files that have changed since the last backup (those with the archive attribute set). The archive attribute of the source files is not changed.

/D:*mm-dd-yy*

copies only those files that have changed since the date given.

/E creates subdirectories on the destination even if they end up being empty.

/M copies only those files that have changed since the last backup (those with the archive attribute set). Marks the source files that it copies as "backed up" by clearing the archive attribute, which allows XCOPY to be used in a backup procedure.

/P stops before copying each file and asks you to confirm that you want to copy it.

/S   copies all subdirectories below the source directory. The XCOPY command will create directories on the destination disk if it needs to, but it will not create directories that will end up empty unless you use the /E option also.

/V   verifies that information written to the destination is recorded properly (usually used when critical data is copied). Verification causes slower copying. If VERIFY ON is active, then /V is not needed.

/W   waits for you to insert diskettes before searching for the source files. The **Press any key to begin copying file(s)** message is displayed.

Comments: This command copies one or more files and/or directories to a different file name on any valid drive or in any valid directory. It also copies one or more files and/or directories to the same file name on a different drive or directory.

If the destination is specified as a drive or directory without a file name, files are copied into that directory without changing their names.

If you include a file name (with or without wild card characters) in the source, only files matching that file name will be copied, even if you use the /S option.

If you do not specify a source path, XCOPY will start in the current directory.

If you do not specify a source file name, all the files in the specified directory will be copied. In other words, the default file name is *.*.

If the specified destination path does not exist, XCOPY will create it before copying files to it.

When files are copied, the creation date and time recorded for the destination file is the same date and time as that for the source file. It is not the date and time the copy was made.

The XCOPY command can only be be used to transfer data between disk devices, not to or from the reserved device names, CON or LPT.

The XCOPY command cannot copy hidden files and cannot copy to read-only or write-protected files on the destination.

To make a backup copy of a directory that will not fit on one diskette, use the /M option. As each diskette fills up, you will receive the **Disk full** message, and XCOPY will stop. Insert another diskette and repeat the command. Since the /M option marks the copied files as backed up, the same files will not be copied. Repeat the command with additional diskettes until all the files are copied.

The XCOPY command cannot make a backup copy of a single file that is bigger than the capacity of a diskette. Use the BACKUP command.

Messages: **Cannot perform a cyclic copy**. You have specified a destination that is part of the source. When you use the /S option, the destination cannot be a subdirectory of the source.

Cannot XCOPY from a reserved device. XCOPY can only copy from a file. You cannot use the reserved device names with XCOPY.

Cannot XCOPY to a reserved device. XCOPY can only copy to a file. You cannot use the reserved device names with XCOPY.

Does pathname specify a file name or directory name on the target (F=file, D=directory)? XCOPY did not find a directory named *pathname* on the destination. You must tell XCOPY whether to create a file (enter **F**) or a directory (enter **D**) by this name. If you are copying more than one file, you probably want to create a directory.

File cannot be copied onto itself. You have specified the same source and destination.

Lock violation. A source file is locked against reading. Network files can be locked by another user to prevent you from receiving incorrect data. Wait a short time and try again.

Press any key to begin copying files. You specified the /W option, and XCOPY is waiting for you to change diskettes. When you have inserted the proper diskette, press a key to proceed.

Sharing violation. Either a source or destination file has been opened on the network in a sharing mode that prevents reading from or writing to it. Wait until the file is closed and try again.

Too many open files. There are not two file handles available for XCOPY. Put a FILES=20 command in your CONFIG.SYS file and restart DOS.

Examples: To copy all the files in all the directories from a diskette in drive A to a diskette in drive B, use the following command:

xcopy a:\ b:\ /s ⏎

To copy from drive C to drive A all the files with a WKS extension that have changed since the last backup and mark them as backed up, enter

xcopy c:*.wks a:\ /s/m ⏎

If DOS gives the **Disk full** message, insert another formatted, empty diskette and repeat the command (use the **F3** editing key to repeat the command exactly). The **/M** option will prevent the same files from being copied again.

This example shows how to move a directory and its subdirectories into a different position on the tree of the destination than they were on the tree of the source. On the source disk, the PROJECT1 directory is in the root. On the destination, it is in the CLIENT1 directory (see Figure 6.1). Enter

```
xcopy c:\project1 a:\client1\project1 /s ⏎
```

```
destination disk: before XCOPY

ROOT ─┬─ CLIENT1 ────────── PROJECT1
      └─ CLIENT2


destination disk: after

ROOT ─┬─ CLIENT1 ────────── PROJECT1 ─┬─ TEXT
      │                               ├─ WKSHT
      │                               └─ DBASE
      └─ CLIENT2
```

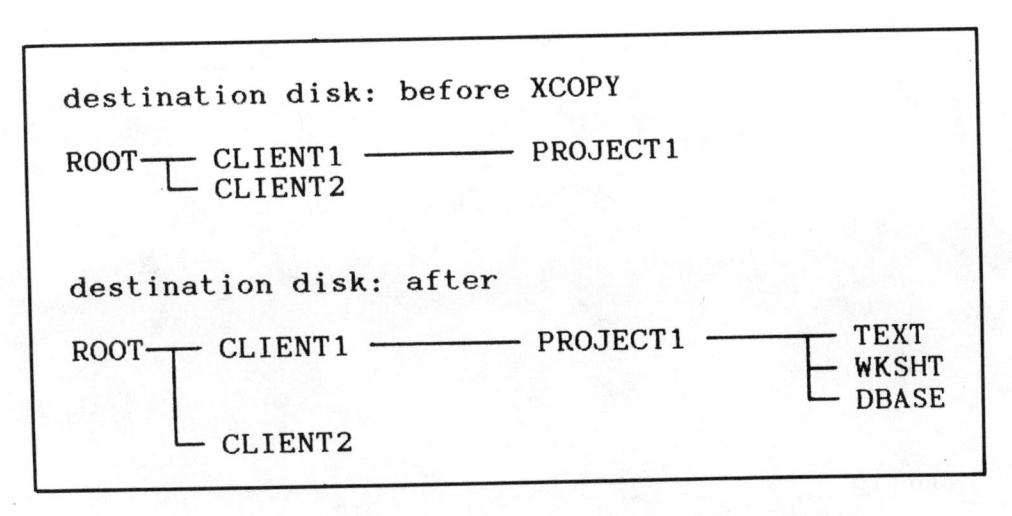

Figure 6.1 Moving Directory Positions with XCOPY

CHAPTER 7

BATCH FILE COMMANDS

BATCH COMMAND

Execute batch file
Version 1.0 Internal

Functions: Executes one or more commands contained in a batch file.

Format: *filespec [parameters]*

Variables: *filespec* is defined as *[d:][path]filename*[.BAT], which specifies the batch file you want to use and its location.

All batch file names must end with the extension .BAT; however, using the extension is optional when you execute the batch command.

You can pass *parameters* to the batch file when it is executed. In this way, the file can process different data during each execution.

Executing Batch Files:

A batch file contains one or more commands that DOS executes one at a time. Any command that can be entered at the DOS prompt can be used in a batch file, including any DOS command, the name of an application program, or another batch file name.

Batch files always use a file name extension of .BAT. To execute a batch file, simply type its name. For example, to execute COMPUTE.BAT, type

COMPUTE ⏎

If you do not specify a drive name, the default disk drive is used.

If the batch file is not in the current directory, the directories specified by the PATH command are searched. If the batch file is not found, the **Bad command or file name** message is displayed.

The commands in a batch file are executed one line at a time. The specified parameters in the batch command format are included as the lines containing the parameter markers are executed.

Up to 10 replaceable parameters can be used in one batch file, and they are numbered %0 to %9. You can add more than 10 parameters by using the SHIFT subcommand. Replaceable parameters are demonstrated in the batch file examples.

While all DOS commands can be used in a batch file, there are also batch subcommands that are usually used only in batch files (see "Batch File Subcommands" later in this chapter).

If DOS finds an incorrect subcommand when running a batch file, the **Syntax error** message is displayed, and the batch file is terminated (the system prompt appears).

You can manually stop executing a batch file with **Ctrl-Break**. When you press **Ctrl-Break**, the **Terminate batch job (Y/N)?** message appears. Answer **Y** for "Yes" and press **Return** to terminate the batch file (the system prompt appears). Answer **N** for "No" and press **Return** to continue batch processing (the current command being executed is skipped).

DOS remembers which diskette holds your batch file so that if you have to replace it with another diskette, DOS will ask you to return the original diskette to continue batch file processing.

You can execute a second batch file immediately after the first by using the second batch file name as the last command in the first file.

Creating Batch Files:

Batch files can be created using the COPY command, EDLIN (the DOS line editor), or any other text editor or word processor that can save a file as ASCII text.

Rules for naming batch files are the same as for any other file name; however, a batch file name should not be the same name as a program file (a file ending with .COM or .EXE) or a DOS command. DOS will not know which file to execute because you do not type the extension when executing the batch file.

All batch files must have the extension .BAT.

The percent sign has special meaning within a batch file (which is explained below). If one of the commands or files used in the batch file contains a percent sign in its name, you must enter the percent sign twice (e.g., CALC%.EXE = CALC%%.EXE).

Replaceable Parameters:

When you use a batch file, anything that you type after the file name is a **parameter**. Parameters are separated by spaces, and the first one is inserted anywhere that "%1" appears in the batch file; the second is inserted anywhere that "%2" appears. You can use replaceable parameters %1 thrugh %9.

The replaceable parameter %0 is special; it is set to the name of the batch file that you are using.

Using Environment Variables:

The command processor's environment space stores some information needed by several functions of DOS. For example, the path is stored there. You can store your own information in the environment space with the SET command.

You can use environment variables in batch files by surrounding the variable name with percent signs.

For example, to use the current path name in a batch file, enter it as "%PATH%". The current path (not the word PATH) will be substituted in the batch file when it is used.

Rules for the AUTOEXEC.BAT File:

When DOS is booted, it automatically executes the AUTOEXEC.BAT file. This file must always be called AUTOEXEC.BAT and must reside in the root directory of the boot disk.

Rules for creating batch files also apply to creating AUTOEXEC.BAT.

The date and time are not automatically requested when AUTOEXEC.BAT is executed unless they are included as DATE and TIME commands in the AUTOEXEC.BAT file.

When you make changes to AUTOEXEC.BAT, you must reboot the system for them to take effect. It is a good idea to keep the most recent version in a backup file named AUTOEXEC.BAK until you are certain that the changes work properly.

Batch File Subcommands:

Batch file subcommands are mostly used only within batch files. They are summarized next and are described in more detail in the rest of this chapter (under the name of each command).

CALL *filename*

  executes the batch file called *filename* and then returns.

ECHO [**ON** / **OFF**]

  turns the screen display on or off.

ECHO *message*

  displays *message* whether ECHO is **ON** or **OFF**.

FOR *%%variable* IN (*set*) DO *command*

    executes *command* for each member of *set*.

GOTO *label*

    transfers processing to *label*.

IF **[NOT]** *condition command*

    provides conditional execution of *command*.

PAUSE *[remark]*

    displays *remark* and suspends processing until a key is pressed.

REM *[remark]*

    displays *remark*.

SHIFT

    shifts parameters one position to the left.

:*label*

    defines a *label*.

Messages: **Bad command or file name.** The batch file name cannot be found. Check to be sure you have entered the name correctly and that the batch file is in the correct directory. The current directory is searched first; then the directories specified by the PATH command or the APPEND /**X** command are searched.

For cannot be nested. More than one FOR subcommand was found on a command line. Delete one of the subcommands and run the batch file again.

Label not found. A GOTO subcommand named a label that did not exist, and the batch file was terminated. Correct the label and run the batch file again.

Syntax error. A subcommand has been used incorrectly. Correct the file and re-execute.

Terminate batch job (Y/N)?. This message occurs when you manually stop a batch file with **Ctrl-Break**. Answer **Y** for "Yes" and press **Return** to terminate the batch file (the system prompt appears). Answer **N** for "No" and press **Return** to continue batch processing (the current command being executed is skipped).

Examples: Batch files can be quite lengthy, as you will see in Section IV, but they can be well worth the effort. You will start with an easy one consisting of just one line; its purpose is to show you a directory of drive A just by typing "A" and pressing the **Return** key. Enter

```
copy con a.bat ⏎
dir a: /p ⏎
^Z ⏎
```

The screen will display the following:

    1 File(s) copied

Be sure to press **Return** at the end each line.

NOTE: The ^Z character is a single character that is a signal to DOS that you are at the end of the file being created. You get this character by pressing **F6** and then pressing **Return**.

Now, try running the batch file. Enter

a ⏎

DOS should display a directory of drive A and pause after each screen of information.

263

Too easy, you say? Try another batch file before continuing. Press **Return** after each line:

```
copy con d.bat
@echo off
cls
dir %1 /p
^Z
```

Note: If you are using Version 3.2 or earlier, omit the @ sign before the ECHO command.

This batch file can be used to display a directory (or subdirectory) of any disk. To see the current directory, enter

d ⏎

To see the current directory of drive B, enter

d b: ⏎

You can display any directory, for example,

d c:\dos ⏎

Or, any subdirectory, such as the following:

d c:\dos\util ⏎

While still very simple, this batch file introduces some common techniques for batch files. The first is the use of ECHO OFF and CLS at the beginning, which provide for a cleaner display (try it without them to see the difference).

More important then the first two lines, however, is the use of the replaceable parameter (%1) in the third line. When you use a batch file, anything you type after the batch file name is a parameter. Parameters are separated by spaces; the first one is inserted anywhere "%1" appears in the batch file. In this case, when you enter the command "d b:" to run the batch file, the third line "dir %1 /p" becomes "dir b: /p" when it is executed.

Try this last example to see how to use environment variables:

```
copy con showcom.bat
@echo The command processor is: %comspec%
^Z
```

The environment variable COMSPEC tells DOS where to look for COMMAND.COM. This batch file shows you what DOS knows. The environment variable %COMSPEC% is replaced by the location of COMMAND.COM when the batch file is run.

CALL

Execute batch file
Version 3.3 Internal

Functions: Executes a batch file from within another batch file and then returns.

Format: CALL *filename*

Variable: *filename* is the name of a batch file.

Comments: CALL allows you to call one batch file from within another batch file and return to the first batch file. If you don't use CALL, processing will stop when the second batch file is finished.

CALL is easier to use and requires less memory than the COMMAND command.

A batch file can call itself, but be sure that it eventually ends.

Examples: In this example, the CALL command in FILE1.BAT calls FILE2.BAT. When FILE2 is done, processing returns to FILE1. Press **Return** after each of the following lines:

```
copy con file1.bat
@echo off
echo This is File 1
call file2
echo Back to File 1
^Z
```

Then, enter

```
copy con file2.bat
echo Now in File 2
^Z
```

Press **Return** after each line.

266

The results should resemble the following. First, enter

file1 ⏎

The screen will display

    This is File 1
    Now in File 2
    Back to File 1

ECHO

Display message

Version 2.0 Internal

Functions: Turns the screen display on or off when DOS commands are executed in a batch file, or displays a message.

Formats: [@]ECHO [$\frac{\text{ON}}{\text{OFF}}$]

turns the screen display on or off.

ECHO *message*

displays *message* whether ECHO is on or off.

Variables: *message* is displayed on the screen whether ECHO is on or off.

Using ECHO without any options causes the current state of echo (on or off) to be displayed.

Putting @ in front of the ECHO command keeps it from displaying on the screen. This feature was added in DOS 3.3.

Options: **ON** (default) displays all commands and the messages they produce as they are executed.

OFF displays only messages produced while commands are executed.

Comments: Commands in batch files are normally displayed as they are executed. A batch file starts with ECHO on. When you use the **OFF** option, batch commands (including REM) are no longer displayed on the screen. Put @ in front of the ECHO OFF command to keep it from displaying on the screen.

ECHO off is only active while the batch file is being executed. If one batch file starts another batch file, the subsequent batch file starts with ECHO on.

ECHO *message* can be used to display messages in a batch file whether ECHO is on or off. By using ECHO *message*, you can display specific messages on the screen, regardless of the current state of ECHO.

Messages that are produced when DOS commands are executed or when other programs are run are displayed whether ECHO is on or off.

ECHO can also be used to display a blank line, which often helps the readability of screen displays. To display a blank line, follow the ECHO command with a space and a null character. The null character (which displays as "^@") can be accessed in EDLIN with the **F7** function key.

Examples: In this batch file, ECHO is first turned off so that the REM command and the first COPY command are not displayed; however, the DOS message produced by the command is still displayed. When ECHO is turned on again, DOS displays the REM command, the COPY command, and the message COPY produces.

Enter the batch file, pressing **Return** following each line:

```
copy con echotest.bat
@echo off
rem *** echo is now off
copy a:chapter1.doc b:
echo on
rem *** echo is now on
copy a:chapter1.doc b:
^Z
```

Test it by entering

echotest ⏎

The screen should display the following:

```
        1 File(s) copied
   A>rem *** echo is now on
   A>copy a:chapter1.doc b:
        1 File(s) copied
   A>
```

FOR..IN..DO

Repeat command
Version 2.0 Internal

Functions: Allows you to repeat processing of a DOS command by executing *command* for each member of (*set*).

Format: FOR %%*variable* IN (*set*) DO *command*

Variables: *variable* can be any single letter, and it is sequentially set to each member of *set*.

set is one or more file specifications expressed as [*d:*]*filename.ext* on which that command is to act. Each file name must be separated by a space. Wild card characters are allowed.

command is the DOS command to be performed in each file named in *set*.

Comments: If a member of *set* is an expression involving the wild card characters (* and/or ?), then %%*variable* is set to each matching file name.

Beginning with DOS 3.2, directory paths can be used with file names shown in *set*; earlier DOS versions will work in the current directory only. Each file must be in the current directory of either the default drive or the specified drive.

When using the FOR command in a batch file, you must put two percent signs before each occurrence of the variable letter. If you are using the FOR command from the DOS prompt (occasionally, this is useful for repeating a command), only use one percent sign.

Only one FOR..IN..DO command can be used on a line, and it cannot be nested. You can use other batch sub-commands with FOR..IN..DO.

Messages: **Syntax error.** You have not used the command in the correct format. Check your command with the format and variable definitions. Make sure you entered two percent signs before *variable* and enclosed *set* in parentheses. Also, check your spelling.

Examples: In the following batch file, *%%variable* refers to each member of *set* (file1 file2 file3) and executes the COPY command for each one, copying the file to drive B:

The batch file is entered as follows. Press **Return** after each line:

```
copy con repeat.bat
for %%f in (FILE1 FILE2 FILE3) do copy %%f b:
^Z
```

From the DOS prompt, enter

repeat ⏎

The screen will display the following:

```
A>copy FILE1 b:
     1 File(s) copied

A>copy FILE2 b:
     1 File(s) copied

A>copy FILE3 b:
     1 File(s) copied

A>
```

GOTO

Go to label

Version 2.0 Internal

Functions: Transfers processing to the line directly following *label*.

Format: GOTO *:label*

Variables: *label* is a line in a batch file that begins with a colon (:) (e.g., :nocopy). Only the first eight characters of *label* are read by DOS. DOS makes no distinction between uppercase and lowercase letters in labels and GOTO commands.

Comments: When the GOTO command is executed, batch processing jumps to the line following the label, and execution of the batch file continues. The label is actually just a marker and is not processed. The GOTO label must be on a line by itself.

If you try to jump to a label that does not exist or if *label* is not defined, the batch file stops, displaying the **Label not found** message.

GOTO labels are never displayed while the batch file is executing. Thus, unreferenced labels can be used for comments within your batch file. If you are using labels in this manner, leave a space between the colon and the beginning of the remark; this way, comments won't be inadvertently referenced as labels. To make a greater distinction between true labels and comment lines, you can place a unique character after the colon. In the examples used later in this book, an exclamation point (!) is used to make the comments stand out.

Messages: **Label not found.** DOS couldn't find the specified label in a GOTO command. The batch file terminates and the system prompt appears. Insert the label in the batch file and try again. Also, check you spelling of *label* and make sure that there is no space between the colon and the first letter of the label.

Example: In this batch file, DOS looks for the file PROG.COM on drive A. If it exists, batch processing jumps to the GOTO label **:nocopy**. If PROG.COM does not exist on drive A, batch processing continues on the next line.

The batch file is entered as follows. Press **Return** after each line.

```
copy con jumpto.bat
if exist a:prog.com goto nocopy
copy b:prog.* a:
copy b:sg?.txt a:
copy b:font.dat a:
:nocopy
rem *** Run prog file
prog
^Z
```

At the DOS prompt, enter

jumpto ⏎

The screen will display the following:

    A>if exist a:prog.com goto nocopy

    A>rem *** Run prog file

    A>prog

IF

Conditional execution
Version 2.0 Internal

Functions: Provides the conditional execution of DOS commands.

Format: IF [NOT] *condition command*

Variables: *condition* is what is being tested.

When *condition* is true, then *command* is executed; otherwise, *command* is skipped, and processing continues on the next line.

condition may be one of the following:

ERRORLEVEL *number*

> true if the previous program had an exit code greater than or equal to *number* (expressed as a decimal value).

string1 = = *string2*

> true when *string1* and *string2* are identical (characters must match in uppercase or lowercase to be identical).

EXIST *filespec*

> true if *filespec* is found on the specified drive. *filespec* is defined as [*d:*][*path*] *filename.ext*. (Path names are not allowed in DOS 2.)

command is any valid command used in a batch file.

Options: **NOT** tests for the opposite of *condition*. This option executes *command* if *condition* is false. The command is entered as IF **NOT** *condition command*.

Comments: This command is useful for setting up conditional statements in your batch files. If *condition* is true, DOS executes *command*. If *condition* is false, the next line in the batch file is executed and batch processing continues.

275

To increase the flexibility of this command, you can use the **NOT** option to test for the opposite of *condition*. In this case, if *condition* is false, DOS executes *command*. If *condition* is true, the next line in the batch file is executed.

There are three types of *condition* you can test for:

ERRORLEVEL *number*

This conditional statement can be used to test for the error level of an exit code. Both BACKUP and RESTORE use exit codes (in DOS 3.2, FORMAT and REPLACE also use exit codes). If the exit code is greater than or equal to *number* (expressed as a decimal value), then *condition* is considered true.

string1 = = *string2*

This conditional statement can be used to compare strings of characters. The characters of *string1* must match the characters of *string2* exactly, based on the ASCII character set. Even uppercase and lowercase characters must match.

You can use parameters (%0-%9) that are passed to the batch file as *string1* to compare to *string2*. If the parameter entered (*string1*) was identical to *string2*, then *command* would be executed.

For example, a valid statement would be as follows:

IF %1 == accounts GOTO accounts

Here, %1 is actually *string1* and "accounts" (without the quotes) is *string2*. If you had entered "accounts" when you executed the batch command, then the conditional statement would be true. The GOTO command would then be executed.

If you had entered "ACCOUNTS" or "Accounts" or a similar combination of uppercase and lowercase characters, however, they would not match and the conditional statement would be false.

A simple way to remedy this problem is to include two consecutive IF commands, for example:

```
IF %1 == accounts GOTO accounts
IF %1 == ACCOUNTS GOTO accounts
```

You won't catch all the possible combinations, but most keyboard input is either all lowercase or all uppercase characters, so you'll catch the greater percentage.

If you use a replaceable parameter as *string1*, and then you run the batch file without entering any parameters, you will get a syntax error. To prevent this problem from occurring, put an extra character on each side of the equation as follows:

```
IF %1x == ACCOUNTSx GOTO accounts
```

Another solution to this problem is to look for the absence of command line parameters, for example,

```
IF "" == %1 GOTO no-parm
```

EXIST *filespec*

This conditional statement can be used to check for an existing file. *filespec* is defined as [*d:*][*path*] *filename.ext*. Path names are not allowed in DOS 2.

DOS looks for the file on the specified drive and in the directory path (DOS 3.0 and higher). If the file is found, then *command* is executed. If the file is not found, processing continues to the next line.

Wild card characters can be used in file names and extensions.

Examples: These examples are not complete batch files in themselves; they are portions of batch files that demonstrate how the IF command can be used.

To test for the error level of an exit code, you could use these lines in your batch file:

```
if errorlevel 4 goto error4
if errorlevel 3 goto error3
if errorlevel 2 goto error2
if errorlevel 1 goto error1
rem Error code must be 0
echo ^G
echo Normal backup completed
goto exit
:error1
echo ^G
echo No files were found to backup
goto exit
:error2
echo ^G
echo Some files were not backed up
echo due to file sharing conflicts
goto exit
:error3
echo ^G
echo User aborted backup - Not complete
goto exit
:error4
echo ^G
echo Aborted due to error - Backup not complete
goto exit
:exit
cd \
```

The IF command checks each line to see if the error level is greater than or equal to the exit code (4, 3, 2, or 1). If it is greater than or equal, the GOTO command is executed. Processing jumps to the correct label (:error4 through :error1), where the appropriate message is displayed with ECHO. Each message tells you what has happened.

You must check the error level in descending order because IF checks for a number greater than or equal to the exit code. For example, if 1 was the first error level checked, and the exit code was 4, the statement would still be true (4 is greater than or equal to 1).

If the error level advances past 1, and a match is still not found, then the error code must be 0. Processing simply continues to the next line.

The next batch file demonstrates how you can compare strings in batch files:

```
if %1 == accounts GOTO accounts
if %1 == ACCOUNTS GOTO accounts
if %1 == letters GOTO letters
if %1 == LETTERS GOTO letters
if %1 == programs GOTO programs
if %1 == PROGRAMS GOTO programs
:accounts
cd \%1
goto :calc
:letters
cd \%1
goto :wp
:programs
cd \%1
goto :basic
```

In these lines, IF compares the %1 parameter (*string1*) that you enter when you run the batch file to *string2*. If they match, the GOTO command transfers processing to the appropriate label.

Two lines are included for each condition to allow for comparing upper- and lowercase characters. Although the IF statements don't catch all the possible combinations of upper- and lowercase, the %1 parameter will probably be either all lowercase or all uppercase.

The next batch file checks to see if a file exists. As you will soon see, there are two different approaches to the problem. Following is the first approach:

```
if exist a:calc.exe goto nocopy
copy c:calc.* a:
copy c:wksht??.cal a:
copy c:font.dat a:
:nocopy
rem *** Run calc program
calc
```

In the first line, IF looks for the CALC.EXE file on drive A and transfers processing to the :nocopy label if the file does exist. At the :nocopy label, DOS runs the CALC program.

If the CALC.EXE file doesn't exist on drive A, processing continues to the second line, where DOS begins COPYing files from drive C to drive A. Then, the CALC program is run.

Following is a different approach to this example, using the IF **NOT** command. If you want to copy all the files from the current directory on drive C before running the CALC program on drive A, the program could be shortened as follows:

```
if not exist a:calc.exe copy c:*.* a:
rem *** Run calc program
calc
```

PAUSE

Wait for keystroke
Version 2.0 Internal

Functions: Suspends processing until a key is pressed. Optionally displays *remark*.

Format: PAUSE [*remark*]

Variables: *remark* is any message (up to 121 characters) that you want to display when processing is suspended.

Comments: You can insert PAUSE commands in batch files to display messages and more effectively control execution of batch file commands. For example, a PAUSE can let you change diskettes or give you the option to end processing at any given point.

The message **Strike a key when ready...** is always displayed with this command. You can use *remark* to add an additional explanation or comment. *remark* will not be displayed if ECHO is off. Instead of placing a remark to be displayed in the PAUSE statement, a better solution is to ECHO the remark *before* the PAUSE statement, which ensures that it will be displayed, regardless of whether ECHO is on or off.

You can press any key except **Ctrl-Break** to continue batch file execution. **Ctrl-Break** aborts the batch file processing and returns you to the system prompt.

Examples: To change diskettes, you can use PAUSE as shown in the batch file below. The batch file is entered as follows. Press **Return** after each line:

```
copy con wait.bat
pause Be sure the diskette named FILE1 is in drive B.
copy a:file1-*.doc b:
pause Remove the FILE1 diskette and insert FILE2 in drive B.
copy a:file2-*.doc b:
^Z
```

At the DOS prompt, enter

wait ⏎

The screen will respond with the following display:

```
A>pause Be sure the diskette named FILE1 is in drive B.
Strike a key when ready...

A>copy file1-*.doc b:

A:FILE1-1.DOC
A:FILE1-2.DOC
     2 File(s) copied

A>pause Remove the FILE1 diskette and insert FILE2
Strike a key when ready...

A>copy file2-*.doc b:
A:FILE2-1.DOC
A:FILE2-2.DOC
     2 File(s) copied
```

After you have inserted a diskette in drive B, pressing any key executes the COPY command that follows. You can see how the *remark* option clarifies the situation. Without *remark* in each PAUSE command, you would know that processing was suspended (by the **Strike a key when ready...** message), but you wouldn't know why or what to do before continuing.

REM

Remark

Version 2.0 Internal

Functions: Places remarks in a batch file.

Formats: REM [*remark*]

Variables: *remark* can be up to 123 characters long.

Comments: As with program listings, you can insert comments and blank lines to improve batch file readability by using REM commands.

If ECHO is on, remarks will be displayed when the file is executed.

If ECHO is off, then remarks are not displayed. If you want to be sure that remarks are not displayed, place them in a label instead (see the GOTO command).

Example: In this batch file, the remarks are not displayed because ECHO is off.

The batch file is entered as follows, with a **Return** after each line. At the DOS prompt, enter

```
copy con remarks.bat
echo off
rem This is the daily backup program
rem
backup c:\ a: /s /d:12-1-85
rem
echo Backup is complete
echo Have a nice day!
^Z
```

At the DOS prompt, enter

remarks ⏎

The screen will display the following:

```
A>echo off

Insert backup diskette 01 in drive A:

Warning! Files in the target drive
A:\root directory will be erased
Strike any key when ready

*** Backing up files to drive A: ***
Diskette Number: 01

     .
     .
     .

Backup is complete
Have a nice day!
```

SHIFT

Shift replaceable parameters
Version 2.0 Internal

Functions: Shifts parameters one position to the left, letting you use more than 10 replaceable parameters in a batch file.

Format: SHIFT

Comments: Replaceable parameters are normally %0 through %9. %0 is the variable whose initial value is the name of the batch command file; %1 is the variable whose initial value is the first parameter; %2 is the second parameter, and so on.

SHIFT lets you use parameters past %9. All parameters are shifted one position to the left each time you use SHIFT; therefore, the value that was represented by %1 becomes %0; the value represented by %2 becomes %1, and so on.

Example: In this batch file named FILE.BAT, the parameters are shifted one position to the left each time the ECHO command is executed until only one parameter is displayed.

The batch file is entered as follows, with a **Return** after each line. At the A prompt, enter

```
copy con file.bat
echo %0 %1 %2 %3
shift
echo %0 %1 %2 %3
shift
echo %0 %1 %2 %3
shift
echo %0 %1 %2 %3
^Z
```

When you run the batch file, be sure to type the parameters in uppercase for this demonstration.

At the DOS prompt, enter

`file RUN1 RUN2 RUN3` ⏎

The screen will display the following:

```
A>echo file RUN1 RUN2 RUN3
file RUN1 RUN2 RUN3

A>echo RUN1 RUN2 RUN3
RUN1 RUN2 RUN3

A>echo RUN2 RUN3
RUN2 RUN3

A>echo RUN3
RUN3
```

Notice that when the first ECHO line is displayed, %0 is actually the batch file name (you can tell because it is in lowercase), and the parameters are %1, %2, and %3 (all in uppercase).

CHAPTER 8

CONFIGURATION COMMANDS

DOS allows you to change its configuration by placing information in a file named CONFIG.SYS. During the initialization process, DOS reads this file and makes adjustments or loads options, depending on the commands you place in this file.

CONFIGURING YOUR SYSTEM WITH CONFIG.SYS

The CONFIG.SYS file must be in the root directory of the disk from which you intend to boot. You can use the EDLIN command to create this file. Each of the commands that may be included in CONFIG.SYS will be described in this chapter.

BREAK

Check for Ctrl-Break

Functions: Selects checking for Ctrl-Break at each DOS function or only at DOS input/output functions.

Formats: BREAK = [$\frac{ON}{OFF}$]

Options: **ON** Turns extended Ctrl-Break checking on so DOS will check for the Ctrl-Break being entered every time a DOS function call is made.

OFF Turns extended Ctrl-Break checking off so DOS will only check for Ctrl-Break being entered when an input or output function call is made.

Comments: The default is BREAK = OFF. There is no reason to place BREAK = OFF in the CONFIG.SYS file.

If you use programs that do long calculations or disk manipulations without displaying anything on the screen or requesting input from you, then setting BREAK ON will allow you to interrupt these programs at any time; otherwise, Ctrl-Break will not work until the program encounters input or output.

The BREAK configuration command has exactly the same effect as the BREAK command entered at the DOS prompt.

BUFFERS

Reserve memory

Functions: Reserves additional memory for temporarily holding information moving from or to the disks.

Formats: BUFFERS = *n*

Variables: *n* is the number of buffer areas that you want to reserve in memory.

Comments: Buffers are a temporary storage place for information going to or coming from your disks. As information is read from the disk, it is also placed in a buffer in case it is needed again. When all the buffers are full, the buffer that has been used least recently is reused. When DOS needs information from the disk, it looks first in the buffers to see if it can save the time required to read from the disk.

Each buffer requires a space in memory of 528 bytes. Increasing the number of buffers you use can increase your computer's throughput speed but will use up memory. You must balance your need for memory with your speed requirements.

DOS, which must work in computers with a small amount of memory, normally allocates only 2 or 3 buffers.

You can substantially speed up the operation of your computer by increasing the number of buffers. It is possible, however, to assign too many buffers. If there are too many buffers, it can take DOS longer to check all the buffers for information than it takes to read the same information from the disk.

The type of work that you do will influence the number of buffers that is optimal for you; you can only tell by experimenting. Following are some suggested starting points for different types of systems:

Diskette systems:	BUFFERS = 10
PC and XT fixed disk systems:	BUFFERS = 20
AT fixed disk systems:	BUFFERS = 50

DEVICE — Load device driver

Functions: Loads a device driver program and makes it part of DOS.

Formats: DEVICE = *filespec*

Variables: *filespec* is defined as [d:][path]filename.ext, which is the drive name, directory path, file name, and extension of the device driver program you want to use. If the file is not in the root directory of the startup disk, then the full path must be specified, including the drive specifier (if it is not the startup disk).

Comments: DOS automatically loads standard input, standard output, standard printer, diskette, fixed disk, and clock drivers. If you load a device driver for any of these, DOS will replace the standard device driver with that device.

There are up to five device driver programs supplied on your DOS diskette. Table 8.1 lists their names and the first DOS version in which they were included.

Name	First Version	Function
ANSI.SYS	2.0	Enhanced input and output control
VDISK.SYS	3.0	Virtual disk
DRIVER.SYS	3.2	Enhanced diskette driver
DISPLAY.SYS	3.3	Display driver for foreign languages
PRINTER.SYS	3.3	Printer driver for foreign languages

**Table 8.1
Device Drivers Supplied With DOS**

To use these device drivers, you must include a DEVICE command in the CONFIG.SYS file. For example, to use ANSI.SYS, place the following line in the CONFIG.SYS file:

```
DEVICE=ANSI.SYS
```

ANSI.SYS

Enhanced I/O control

Functions: Extended input and output control.

Formats: DEVICE=[*d:*][*path*]ANSI.SYS

Variables: *d:* is the drive name of the disk where ANSI.SYS is located.

path is the directory path where ANSI.SYS is located.

Comments: The ANSI.SYS device driver allows you increased control over the screen. You can control the cursor position, erase the screen, change the screen colors, and change the screen mode.

Some programs require the use of ANSI.SYS. Programs that require ANSI.SYS should should inform you of this stipulation in the documentation.

Several of the applications and utilities given in this book require the use of ANSI.SYS.

After ANSI.SYS is loaded, the following codes can be used to control the display screen. The codes can be included in a file that is displayed with TYPE or COPY or can be sent to the screen with the PROMPT command.

All of the codes start with the Escape code (shown as ^[in the table), which can be entered with EDLIN by typing **Ctrl-V** [(see Chapter 9). Many of the commands contain a variable: *x*. The variable can be replaced by a number; if you omit it, the default value is 1. The letters must be entered exactly as shown; upper- and lowercase letters are not interchangeable.

Code	Function
^[[x;xH	Moves cursor to line x, column x
^[[xA	Moves cursor up x lines
^[[xB	Moves cursor down x lines
^[[xC	Moves cursor right x columns
^[[xD	Moves cursor left x columns
^[[s	Saves cursor position
^[[u	Restores cursor position
^[[2J	Clears screen
^[[k	Erases from cursor to end of line
^[[x;...;xm	Sets character attribute

Common values used in the set character attribute code are shown in the following table. Other values are used to set the color of the displayed characters and the color of the background.

Value	Meaning
0	All attributes off (normal white on black)
1	Bold characters
4	Underline characters
5	Blinking characters
7	Reverse video (black characters on white)

VDISK.SYS

Virtual disk

Functions: Provides a **virtual disk**, which is a simulated disk in the computer's memory.

Formats: DEVICE = [*d*:][*path*]VDISK.SYS [*bbb*] [*sss*] [*ddd*] [/E[:*m*]]

Variables: *d:* is the drive name of the disk where VDISK.SYS is located.

path is the directory path where VDISK.SYS is located.

bbb specifies the storage capacity of the virtual disk in kilobytes. The default is 64K. This value can range from 1K to the entire amount of available memory. DOS may adjust the value to ensure that there is 64KB of memory available for programs after the virtual disk is created.

sss specifies the sector size in bytes. The default is 128. You can use values of 128, 256, or 512. Larger values speed disk action but waste more memory space with unfilled sectors at the ends of files.

ddd specifies the maximum number of directory entries. The default is 64. You can use a value from 2 to 512. VDISK uses one directory entry for its label and may adjust the number that you enter to fill a complete sector or, if the directory is too big, to fit in the virtual disk.

Options: /E:*m* tells VDISK to use extended memory, which is beyond 1MB. Extended memory is only available on the AT. The value of *m* is the maximum number of sectors of information that are read from the virtual disk at one time. The default is 8. Allowable values for *m* are 1 through 8.

Comments: The VDISK provides a very fast virtual disk drive but has two problems: it uses up memory that you may need for your programs, and all the information on it is lost when you turn off or restart you computer.

Be sure that you copy any information that you want to keep from your virtual disk to a real disk before restarting or turning off your computer.

The virtual disk is good for running programs that use overlays. This kind of program must keep accessing the disk to get pieces of the program. If you copy these programs to the virtual disk and then run them, the virtual disk can speed them up dramatically, and you don't have to worry about losing power or other accidents because you still have a copy of the program on a real disk.

Virtual disks are also good for storing batch files that you use often. They execute very quickly from a virtual disk.

NOTE: If you find problems running programs that use a lot of interrupts, such as high-speed communication programs, then try using the programs without VDISK loaded. If this solves the problem, then reduce the value of *m* until the problem is gone.

Examples: The following command will create a virtual disk of 128KB, using 512-byte sectors with 64 directory entries. The VDISK command can contain "comments" of any normal character except the slash and digits, so the command can be self-documenting.

```
DEVICE = VDISK.SYS disk size=128 sector size=512
directory entries=64
```

If you'd rather not type that much, here's the short form of the same command (which uses the default value of 64 directory entries):

```
DEVICE = VDISK.SYS 128 512
```

DRIVER.SYS   Enhanced diskette driver

Functions: Provides support for an external diskette drive or assigns a second drive letter to a disk.

Formats: DEVICE = [d:][path]DRIVER.SYS /D:ddd [/T:ttt] [/S:ss] [/H:hh] [/C] [/N] [/F:f]

Variables: *d:* is the drive name of the disk where DRIVER.SYS is located.

path is the directory path where DRIVER.SYS is located.

Options: **/D:***ddd*

Specifies the real drive number. Diskette drives are numbered starting at 0. Fixed disk drives are numbered starting at 128.

/T:*ttt*

Specifies the number of tracks per side (from 1-999). The default is 80 tracks per side.

/S:*ss*

Specifies the number of sectors per track (from 1-99). The default is 9 sectors per track.

/H:*hh*

Specifies the number of read-write heads (1-99). The default is 2 heads.

/C   Specifies changeline support, which only works on machines that support diskette changeline, such as the AT.

/N   Specifies a nonremovable disk. Fixed disks have nonremovable media.

/F:*f* specifies the device type, or form factor. The default is 2, and the options are as follows:

Value	Drive type
0	Single-sided drives (160/180KB)
0	Double-sided drives (320/360KB)
1	High-capacity drives (1.2MB)
2	720KB 3-1/2" drives
7	1.44MB 3-1/2" drives

Comments: Diskette drives are numbered starting at 0. The internal diskette drives A and B are numbered 0 and 1. Drive B is always considered an internal drive, even if you only have one diskette drive. The first external diskette drive is drive 2, and the second drive is 3.

Fixed disks are numbered starting with 128. The value 129 specifies the second fixed disk.

The default values for all the options but /D (which has no default) are the values required for the 3-1/2" diskette. Drives A and B are always internal diskette drives. From there on, drive letters are assigned according to the order in which DOS encounters them. DOS first looks for internal physical drives, and then the CONFIG.SYS file is checked for device drivers.

If you have more than one disk device driver in your CONFIG.SYS file, DOS will assign drive letters in the order in which they are listed in the file.

You can assign a second drive letter to a physical drive by putting an extra device driver for the drive in the CONFIG.SYS file (see the examples).

The proper variable values for various drives are shown next. Put the proper physical drive number in the /D option.

Single-sided drive (160/180KB):

`DEVICE=DRIVER.SYS /D:n /T:40 /S:9 /H:1 /F:0`

Double-sided drive (320/360KB):

`DEVICE=DRIVER.SYS /D:n /T:40 /S:9 /H:2 /F:0`

High-capacity drive (1.2MB):

`DEVICE=DRIVER.SYS /D:n /T:80 /S:15 /H:2 /C /F:1`

720KB 3-1/2" drive:

`DEVICE=DRIVER.SYS /D:2`

Examples: To provide support for an external 720 KB 3-1/2" diskette drive, put the following command in your CONFIG.SYS file:

`DEVICE=DRIVER.SYS /D:2`

If you have one or two internal diskettes and a fixed disk, the 3-1/2" drive will be assigned drive letter D. If you don't have a fixed disk, it will be assigned drive letter C.

Since all the other option default values are correct for this drive, only the physical drive number needs to be specified.

To allow you to copy files from one diskette to another in the same external 3-1/2" drive, the drive must have two drive letters assigned to it. Use these two lines in your CONFIG.SYS file.

`DEVICE=DRIVER.SYS /D:2`
`DEVICE=DRIVER.SYS /D:2`

If you have one or two internal diskettes and a fixed disk, the 3-1/2" drive will be assigned drive letters D and E. If you don't have a fixed disk, the drive will be assigned drive letters C and D.

You can assign a second drive letter to your internal high-capacity (1.2MB) diskette drive A with the following command in your CONFIG.SYS file:

```
DEVICE=DRIVER.SYS  /D:0  /T:80  /S:15  /H:2  /C  /F:1
```

If you have one or two internal diskettes and a fixed disk, the high-capacity drive will be assigned drive letter D, but it will still be assigned drive letter A.

FCBS

File control blocks

Functions: Specifies the number of file control blocks that DOS uses at one time.

Formats: FCBS = *m,n*

Variables: *m* specifies the total number of files opened by FCBs at one time. The default value of *m* is 4 and can range from 1 to 255.

n specifies the number of files opened by FCBs that DOS must not close automatically if a program requests that more than *m* files be opened at once. The first *n* files opened are protected from being closed. The default value of *n* is 0 and can range from 0 to 255. The value of *n* must not be greater than *m*.

Comments: FCBs are an old way of opening files that was used before DOS 2. Some programs that use this system are still being operated, so instead of dropping support altogether, DOS makes it optional.

Don't use the FCBS command unless you need it. It uses up memory space for the FCBs that you are reserving.

If you have a program that you have used successfully in the past but that fails to work with DOS 3, then try putting the FCBS command in your CONFIG.SYS file. To start, use a number of 12 for both *m* and *n*, unless you know that the program uses more than 12 files.

Examples: To allow 12 files to be used with FCBs without DOS automatically closing any of them, put the following command in you CONFIG.SYS file:

FCBS = 12,12

FILES
Open files

Functions: Allows more than eight files to be opened at once.

Formats: FILES = *n*

Variables: *n* specifies the number of file handles to reserve space for in memory. The default value of *n* is 8 and can range from 8 to 255.

Comments: **File handles** are tools to open files and were introduced in DOS 2.

While the default value of 8 file handles is sufficient for many programs, data base and similar programs often use more than 8 files at a time.

It is recommended that you allow for 20 files to be open at a time.

Examples: To provide for 20 files to be opened at once, put the following line in your CONFIG.SYS file:

FILES = 20

LASTDRIVE

Specify highest drive

Functions: Specifies the highest drive letter you want to use.

Formats: LASTDRIVE = x

Variables: x specifies the last drive letter you want to use. The default value of x is E and can range from A through Z.

Comments: You cannot set x to a value that indicates less drives than you physically have on your computer; if you do, the command will be ignored.

Examples: To set the number of drives equal to 14, place the following line in your CONFIG.SYS file:

LASTDRIVE = N

SHELL — Alternate command interpreter

Functions: To load an alternate command interpreter.

Format: SHELL = *filespec* [/E:*xxxxx*] [/P]

Variables: *filespec* is defined as [*d:*][*path*]*filename.ext*, which specifies the drive name, directory path, file name, and extension of the command interpreter that you want loaded.

Options: The following options are only effective if the command processor is COMMAND.COM:

/E:*xxxxx*

specifies the amount of space reserved for the environment. The value *xxxxx* is an integer that specifies the number of bytes of space to reserve for the environment, and it can range from 160 to 32768. The default is 160.

/P specifies that the AUTOEXEC.BAT file is to be executed when COMMAND.COM is loaded.

Comments: Creating a command processor to replace COMMAND.COM is not a minor task, so this command is only useful in specialized applications, except for one unique use, which is explained below.

The **environment** is an area of memory that stores information DOS uses and that DOS passes on to programs that can use it. The path and prompt, among other things, are stored in the environment.

Some programs look in the environment for special information. For example, some compilers look in the environment for the path to some of the files they need. In many cases, the default environment space is not large enough to hold all the information needed, and the **Out of environment space** error message is given. The SHELL command provides a way to expand the environment and solve this problem.

Examples: To create an environment of 512 characters, place the following line in you CONFIG.SYS file:

SHELL = \command.com /E:512 /P

SECTION III

SUPPLEMENTAL PROGRAMS

CHAPTER 9

DOS' WORD PROCESSOR: EDLIN

In addition to the commands described in Section II, PC-DOS includes a few more programs. Most of these programs are specialized for programmers and are rarely touched by typical DOS users. These programs are DEBUG, LINK, and EXE2BIN, and their use is beyond the scope of this book. There is one more program, however, that *will* be of interest to many DOS users: **EDLIN** (which means "Line Editor").

EDLIN is not a state-of-the-art word processing program by any stretch of the imagination; in fact, it is rather crude by today's standards. It does not offer wordwrap or formatting of any kind. You can only edit one line at a time; you cannot use the cursor keys to move up and down between lines.

Despite its shortcomings, which are many, it is quick, easy to learn, and free. It also allows you to place control characters in files, which cannot be done with some other text editors and word processors. All in all, it is a good little editor for creating and editing batch files, which is what Section IV of this book is all about.

STARTING EDLIN

EDLIN can be used to create a new file or to edit an existing file. In either case, the command format for starting EDLIN is as follows:

EDLIN [*d:*][*path*]*filename.ext*

If the file you name does not already exist (or if DOS cannot find it in the directory you specify), then EDLIN answers **New file** and displays the EDLIN prompt, which is an asterisk (*). The EDLIN prompt serves the same purpose as the DOS system prompt; it is a signal to you that EDLIN is ready to accept input.

If the file you name does exist, EDLIN reads the file, displays **End of input file**, and then displays the asterisk prompt (*).

To create a new batch file named COLOR in your BAT subdirectory, enter

```
edlin \dos\bat\color.bat ⏎
```

The screen will display the following:

```
New file
*
```

You can only enter EDLIN commands at the prompt; you cannot enter text. To begin entering text, at the prompt type I (for Insert) and press **Return**; a new type of prompt is then displayed.

Enter

```
i ⏎
```

The screen will display the following:

```
    1:*
```

You can enter text at the line number prompt.

The above prompt consists of a line number. Next to the line number, in this case, is an asterisk, which is the current line indicator; that is, when the "1:*" is displayed, you are working on line 1. The importance of the current line will be more apparent when you use the display and edit commands.

ENTERING EDLIN COMMANDS

Within EDLIN, there are several commands that can be entered at the asterisk prompt. Most of these commands, which are summarized in Table 9.1, consist of a single letter, which can be typed as an upper- or lowercase letter.

Command	Format
Insert lines	[*line*]I
List lines	[*line*][,*line*]L
Page through file	[*line*][,*line*]P
Edit line	[*line*]
Delete lines	[*line*][,*line*]D
Copy lines	[*line*],[*line*],*line*[,*count*]C
Move lines	[*line*],[*line*],*line*M
Replace text	[*line*][,*line*][?]R[*string*][^Z*string*]
Search for text	[*line*][,*line*][?]S[*string*]
Merge file	[*line*]T[*d:*]*filename.ext*
Append from file	[*n*]A
Write lines to file	[*n*]W
End EDLIN and save	E
Quit without saving	Q

**Table 9.1
EDLIN command summary**

Most of the commands include one or more optional *line* variables. Usually, you will place a line number here. EDLIN consecutively numbers each line in the file, starting with line 1. One note of caution: whenever you add or delete lines in a file, EDLIN renumbers all the lines, so you must make sure which lines you are really referring to. The display commands show you the lines and their corresponding numbers.

Some special symbols can be used for *line* instead of line numbers. If you enter a pound sign (#), you are referring to the line *after* the last line in the file, which allows you to insert lines (with the **I** command) at the end of the file. Entering a line number greater than the number of lines in the file has the same effect.

You can also enter a period (.) for *line*, which specifies the current line—the location of the most recent change to the file. When you display the file, the current line is marked with an asterisk next to the line number.

Line number references may be made relative to the current line. Use a minus sign (-) followed by a number to refer to a line before the current line and a plus sign (+) followed by a number to refer to a line after the current line. For instance, to refer to the line that is 4 lines after the current line, enter +4 in place of *line*.

Like DOS commands, EDLIN commands may be typed in either upper- or lowercase letters and are executed when you press the **Return** key. For clarity, you may want to separate commands and parameters with a delimiter character (a space or a comma). The only place a delimiter is *required* is to separate line numbers in a command line.

DOS editing keys, which are described in Chapter 5, can be used to edit lines of text. Their functions are summarized in Table 9.2. When you enter a line number at the EDLIN prompt (to edit that line), the line is placed in the line buffer so you can use the editing keys, just as you would on a DOS command at the DOS prompt.

Key	Function
F1	Copies one character from buffer to command line.
F2*x*	Copies all characters up to first occurrence of *x*.
F3	Copies all characters from cursor to end of line.
F4*x*	Skips characters up to first occurrence of *x*.
F5	Saves current line in buffer without entering.
Ins	Starts insert mode.
Del	Deletes one character from the buffer.
Ctrl-Break	Ends insert mode.

**Table 9.2
DOS editing keys**

ENTERING CONTROL CHARACTERS

One of EDLIN's unique characteristics is the ability to enter control characters—those with ASCII codes less than 32. These characters are often used to control special features of your printer and your display monitor. Some of them perform special functions; Ctrl-G, for example, sounds the computer's bell, which can be used as a warning signal in batch files. Table 9.3 shows some of the control codes, their functions, and how to obtain them with EDLIN.

ASCII code	Displayed as	Function	Press these keys
0	^@	Null character	F7
7	^G	Sound bell	Ctrl-G
8	^H	Backspace	Ctrl-V H
12	^L	Form feed	Ctrl-V L
15	^O		Ctrl-O
18	^R		Ctrl-R
27	^[	Escape code	Ctrl-V [

Table 9.3
Control characters used in this book

Table 9.3 shows only control codes used in the example programs in this book. Any control code can be entered with EDLIN by first pressing Ctrl-V and then pressing the letter of the control character. For example, to place a Ctrl-C character in a file, press and hold the **Ctrl** key, press the **V** key, release both keys, and press **C**. When you enter the character in a line of text, it will be displayed exactly as you typed it: ^VC (the carat symbol (^) means "Ctrl"); however, if you enter the line and then display it, the actual character placed in the file will be displayed. In this case, ^C would be displayed.

DISPLAYING TEXT

EDLIN has two commands that can be used to display the file you are editing. The L (for List lines) command will display a specified range of lines; the P (for Page) command displays a range of lines and changes the current line number.

L Command

The L command displays a range of lines on the screen. The format of the command is as follows:

[*line*][,*line*]L

To display line numbers 1 through 5, at the EDLIN prompt (*), enter

1,5l ⏎

The first five lines of the file will be displayed:

```
       1:*echo off
       2: date
       3: time
       4: cls
       5: path a:\;c:\
*
```

Notice the asterisk on line 1, which indicates that it is the current line.

You can also use the L command without any parameters. If you enter L at the prompt, EDLIN will display 23 lines: eleven lines before the current line, the current line, and eleven lines after the current line. If there are not eleven lines before the current line, extra lines are displayed after the current line, for a total of 23.

If you specify a starting line number but not an ending line number (e.g., 8l), a total of 23 lines are displayed, starting with the specified line number.

You can specify an ending line without specifying a starting line. To do so, precede the line number with a comma; this way, EDLIN will know you are entering the second parameter instead of the first. EDLIN displays all the lines starting eleven lines before the current line up to the specified line number. For example, if you enter

,24l ⏎

The screen might respond with the following:

```
11: Bernt, Carl            344-8637
12: Berntsen, Geo          993-0168
13: Bernuy, Paulita        205-1172
14: Bernuy, Raul           385-3088
15: Berny Silver Mfg Co    231-1215
16: Berohn, William        226-2006
17: Beroma Co              973-5018
18: Beron, Edward A        481-7730
19: Berookhim, Albert      678-5274
20: Beroza, Janet          258-8718
21: Berquist, Richard      938-3107
22:*Berrard, Sydney        393-9120
23: Berrens, Fred          665-7102
24: Berreondo, E           356-9647
*
```

P Command

The P (for Page) command is similar to the L command in that it is used to display lines of the file on the screen. The primary difference between the commands is that L never changes the current line; the P command does. The format of the P command is as follows:

[*line*][,*line*]P

This command can be used to page through a file by simply entering P at the prompt. If you do not specify the first *line*, EDLIN will start the display at the line after the current line. If the second *line* is not specified, 23 lines will be displayed.

The last line displayed becomes the new current line, which is marked by an asterisk.

EDITING TEXT

EDLIN has five commands used for editing files: I (for Insert), D (for Delete), M (for Move), C (for Copy), and the edit line command.

I Command

The I (for Insert) command is used to add lines of text to a file. The format for the command is as follows:

[*line*]I

When you use the command, you will be able to enter new lines of text before the specified *line* number. If you do not specify *line*, then lines will be inserted before the current line. To return to the EDLIN prompt after entering the new lines, press **Ctrl-Break** (hold the **Ctrl** key and press the **ScrollLock/Break** key).

Following is an example of text entered at each of the numbered prompts (a line number, colon, and asterisk). First, from the EDLIN prompt, enter

4i ⏎

Then, enter text until the screen appears as follows. Press **Return** after you complete each line (do not type the *line number:** prompts):

```
         4:*This is the first new line.
         5:*Each time you press Enter
         6:*a new line number is displayed.
         7:*At that moment, it is the current
         8:*line, so an asterisk is displayed
         9:*next to the line number.
        10:*After you enter the last line,
        11:*press Ctrl-Break, which displays
        12:*as "^C". It will return you to
        13:*the EDLIN prompt.
        14:*^C
*
```

WORD PROCESSOR: EDLIN

315

Edit Line Command

If you want to edit a line that already exists in the file, merely enter the line number at the EDLIN prompt, which will cause the line to be displayed, followed by a blank line. You can then retype the line or use the DOS editing keys to modify the existing line.

If you decide not to change the line, press **Ctrl-Break** or the **Escape** key. The original line will remain unchanged.

This example shows how to edit line 9. At the * prompt, type

9 ⏎

The screen will display line nine:

    9:*This line has not been edited.
    9:*

You could change the text to "That line has not been edited" by pressing **F1** twice, typing "at" (without the quotes), pressing **F3** and then pressing the **Return** key. This process changes the line and returns you to the asterisk prompt.

D Command

The D command (for Delete lines) can be used to delete one or more lines from the file. The format of the command is as follows:

[*line*][,*line*]D

The first *line* parameter is the number of the first line you want deleted; the second *line* parameter is the number of the last line you want deleted. All lines in between those two lines will also be deleted. The line following the deleted range becomes the new current line.

If you don't specify starting or ending line numbers (and just enter D), only the current line will be deleted.

If you specify only a starting line number, only that line will be deleted. If you don't specify a starting line number, EDLIN deletes all lines from the current line to the line specified by the second parameter. To omit the first parameter, you must precede the second line number with a comma, for example,

,24d

In this example, if the current line was 18, lines 18 through 24 would be deleted. The remaining lines will be renumbered, and the line after the deleted lines (which was line 25 but is line 18 after renumbering) becomes the new current line.

M Command

EDLIN allows you to change the order of lines in a file with the M (for Move) command. The format of the command is as follows:

[*line*],[*line*],*line*M

The first two *line* parameters specify the starting and ending numbers of the lines you want to move. If either one is omitted when you enter the command, the current line is the default value.

The third *line* parameter specifies the location where you want to move the lines. They will be inserted before the line number you specify here. For example, to move the current line and six lines after the current line and insert them before line 45, enter

,+6,45m ⏎

C Command

Occasionally, you will want to repeat a section of a file. Instead of retyping it, you can use the EDLIN C (for Copy) command. The format is as follows:

[*line*],[*line*],*line*[,*count*]C

Like the M command, the first two *line* parameters specify the range of lines you want to copy. If either parameter is omitted, the current line is the default. The third *line* parameter is the place where you want the lines copied to. The lines will be inserted before the specified line number.

The block of lines is copied the number of times specified by *count*. If you don't enter a value for *count*, the block is copied one time.

In this example, the current line will be copied 25 times and placed before line 10. Enter

,,10,25c ⏎

The first of the copied lines becomes the new current line. In the previous example, line 10 would be the current line after the command just shown is entered.

AUTOMATIC SEARCH AND REPLACE

Although EDLIN can't claim many of the features of newer text editing programs, it does have two commands that make quick editing possible. The S (for Search) command looks through your file to find a particular text string. The R (for Replace) command not only finds the string you are looking for, but replaces it with another string.

S Command

The S (for Search) command searches through a specified range of lines to find a particular text string. The format for the command is as follows:

[*line*][,*line*][?]S[*string*]

The *line* parameters specify the range of lines to be searched. If you omit the first parameter, EDLIN will start searching in the line after the current line. If you omit the second parameter, EDLIN defaults to the last line in memory. If you do not specify either parameter, EDLIN searches from the line after the current line to the end of the file.

string is the character string you are looking for. The S command looks for strings that match *exactly*, including case. If you do not enter a string, EDLIN will use the same one used in the last S or R command.

The first line that contains the specified string is displayed and the search ends. The line containing the string becomes the current line.

If you include the ? parameter, EDLIN pauses after it finds the string, displays the line, and prompts you with the message **O.K.?** If you press **Y** or the **Return** key, then that line becomes the current line and the search ends. If you enter any other character in response to the prompt, EDLIN will continue its search until it finds the next occurrence of *string*; it will again stop and ask if that is the line you are looking for.

This example command looks through the entire file for the word "and," pausing at each line. Enter

1?sand ⏎

The screen responds with

```
        6: reactor meltdown and explosion caused
O.K.?
```

Enter

n ⏎

The screen responds with

```
        7: untold death and suffering and raised
O.K.?
```

Enter

n ⏎

The screen responds with

>   8: the prospect of long-term health and
> O.K.?

Enter

n. ⏎

The screen displays the following:

> Not found
> *

R Command

While the S command can be used to search for a string, the R (for Replace) command not only finds the string but replaces each occurrence with a second string. The format for the command is as follows:

[*line*][,*line*][?]R[*string*][^Z*string*]

The *line* parameters specify the range of lines to be searched. If you omit the first parameter, EDLIN will start searching in the line after the current line. If you omit the second parameter, EDLIN defaults to the last line in memory. If you do not specify either parameter, EDLIN searches from the line after the current line to the end of the file.

Unlike the S command, R does not stop after it finds and replaces the first occurrence of the specified string. It will replace *all* occurrences of the string (even multiple occurrences on the same line) within the specified range of lines.

You can use the ? parameter to ensure that EDLIN doesn't replace some lines you didn't really intend to change. If you use ?, then each time the search string is found, the line will be displayed (with the replacement made) and you will be prompted with **O.K.?** If you enter **Y** or **Return**, then the replacement will be made in the file; if you enter any other key, the line will remain as it was before the replacement. In either case, EDLIN continues its search for the next occurrence of *string*.

The first *string* is the character string you are looking for. The R command looks for strings that match *exactly*, including case. If you do not enter a string, EDLIN will use the same search string used in the last S or R command.

The second *string* is the string with which you want to replace the existing string; it must be preceded by a Ctrl-Z character, which you can get by pressing the **F6** function key. If you do not enter a string, then EDLIN will use the same replace string used in the last R command.

This example will replace all occurrences of "ECHO ^G" with "BEEP," starting with line 5 and continuing to the end of the file. Each line is displayed as it is changed. At the EDLIN prompt, enter

5rECHO ^G^ZBEEP ⏎

The screen will display the replacements:

    5: BEEP
  11: BEEP
  24: BEEP
*

ENDING AN EDLIN SESSION

After editing a file with EDLIN, there are two ways to exit the program and return to DOS. Normally, you will use the E (for End edit) command. If you don't want to save the changes you've made, use the Q (for Quit) command.

E Command

Usually when you edit a file with EDLIN, you will use the E (for End edit) command to return to DOS. Just enter E at the EDLIN prompt. The edited file will be saved, using the same drive, directory, and file name that you used when you started EDLIN.

If you were editing an existing file (as opposed to creating a new file) with EDLIN, the old file will also be retained on the disk. It is renamed; however, its extension is changed to .BAK.

Before you start editing a file, be sure that there is enough room on the disk for the original file *and* the edited version. If there is not enough room for both files when you use the E command, some of the changes you made will be lost. If this happens, the old file is not renamed. EDLIN saves as much of the new file as there is room for on the disk and discards the rest. The new (partial) file is given a file extension of .$$$.

Q Command

Occasionally, you may make a mistake in editing. Rather than trying to correct the mistake, it may be easier to quit and start over with the original file again. The Q (for Quit) command allows you to quit the editing session without saving any of the changes you have made.

To use the command, just type Q at the EDLIN prompt. To make sure that you really want to quit without saving your changes, EDLIN prompts you with **Abort edit (Y/N)?** If you enter **Y**, then you will return to the DOS prompt. No .BAK file will be created, and any changes you made with EDLIN are lost.

Enter any other key in response to the **Abort edit (Y/N)?** message if you want to continue with your EDLIN session.

OTHER FEATURES

EDLIN has two commands (A for Append and W for Write) that can be used to edit very large files (larger than will fit in memory). In addition, there is a command (T for Transfer file) that allows you to merge additional files into the one you are currently editing.

The purpose of introducing EDLIN in this book is to give you an easy way to enter and edit the batch files in Section IV, which should not require the use of the A, W, and T commands. If your work requires the use of features like these, EDLIN is probably not the editor for you anyway; there are other commercially available programs more suited to working quickly and easily with large files.

With the 11 commands discussed in this chapter, you should have no trouble creating and using the useful batch programs in the next section of this book.

EDLIN MESSAGES

Abort edit(Y/N)? When you use the Q command to quit EDLIN, all of your changes are lost. This message is shown to protect you in case you accidentally pressed the **Q** key. If you do want to quit EDLIN without saving your changes, press **Y** to return to DOS; to continue the EDLIN session, type **N**.

Cannot edit .BAK file — rename file. You started EDLIN and specified a file with the extension .BAK, which causes a conflict within EDLIN, since at the end of the editing session it would save the edited file with the original file name and extension and the old file with the extension .BAK. If you really want to edit the file you named, use the RENAME command to give it a different extension before you start EDLIN.

Disk full. Edits lost. When you use the E command to end your EDLIN session, the old file is renamed with the extension changed to .BAK, and the edited file is also saved. If there is not room on the disk for both files, you will receive this error message. At this point, your work is lost; you must copy the old file onto a disk with more free space and start over. The ideal solution is to make sure you have enough free space (use the DIR command) *before* you start EDLIN.

Entry Error. You made a syntax error in a command entered at the EDLIN prompt. Check the command format in this chapter and re-enter the command.

File is READ-ONLY. The file you named when you started EDLIN is marked as read-only, which means it is protected against any modification. If you really want to edit that file, then you must change the read-only attribute with the ATTRIB command.

File name must be specified. You tried to start EDLIN without naming a file to be edited. Whether you are creating a new file or editing an existing file, you must specify its name when you start EDLIN.

Line too long. The R command has attempted to make a replacement that extends one line beyond the 253-character limit, which terminates the R command, possibly before it has made all the necessary replacements. To get around this problem, break the offending line into smaller lines and use the R command again.

Must specify destination line number. The M (Move) and C (Copy) commands require that you specify a location where the range of lines is to be moved. This location is the third parameter on the command line; if you are not specifying a range of lines, then the destination line number must be preceded by two commas so that EDLIN will recognize it as the third parameter.

No room in directory for file. This is another message you don't want to see, for it means that all of your changes are lost. This problem is caused when the directory is full (each disk has a maximum number of directory entries, depending on the type of disk and device driver). The solution is to copy the file to be edited to another disk and start over.

Not found. This message indicates that the search string specified in an S or R command can't be found in the specified range of lines. It also occurs in the S command when you use the ? prompt parameter, answer N, and no more occurrences of the string are in the file. If you think the string really is in the file, make sure that you specified the range of lines correctly, and that you entered the search string in upper- and lowercase letters, exactly as it appears in the file.

Read error in:
x:\xxxxxx\xxxxxx. An error occurred while reading the file (where *x:\xxxxxx\xxxxxx* is the drive, path, and file name) into memory. Try copying the file to another disk, and start EDLIN again.

Too many files open. EDLIN was unable to open the file you named. Increase the value of the FILES command in your CONFIG.SYS file.

SECTION IV

APPLICATIONS

CHAPTER 10

SETTING UP A DISKETTE SYSTEM

In this chapter, you will learn how to set up and maintain a useful, flexible, diskette-based system. You will learn how to organize the files on your diskettes to keep the maximum amount of information on the fewest possible diskettes.

You will develop a three-disk system. The first disk is the **startup diskette**. This disk is only used when you start your computer. The second disk is a **program disk**; it contains one of the programs that you use with your computer. You should make a program disk for each of the programs that you use. The third disk is the **data disk**. This disk holds the files that you create with your programs. As you work with your computer, you will use many data diskettes.

CREATING A STARTUP DISKETTE

The first step is to create a startup diskette. This diskette will contain all the programs that you only need once each time you start your computer. To create your startup disk, put your DOS diskette in drive A, and a new, blank diskette in drive B. Start your computer and format the disk in drive B by entering

format b: /s /v ⏎

The screen will display the following:

    Insert new diskette for drive B:
    and strike ENTER when ready

    Format complete
    System transferred

    Volume label (11 characters, ENTER for none)?

Enter

startup ⏎

The screen will display the following:

```
362496 bytes total disk space
 69632 bytes used by system
292864 bytes available on disk
```

Format another (Y/N)?

Enter

n ⏎

This procedure produces a diskette with DOS on it. Now, add some of the external commands and other files that you will need to get your computer running the way you want it. Start by copying some of the necessary files to the new startup diskette in drive B. From the A prompt, type the following lines, pressing the **Return** key at the end of each line (each time you press **Return**, the screen will display the **1 File(s) copied** message):

copy vdisk.sys b:

copy ansi.sys b:

copy mode.com b:

copy graphics.com b:

copy graftabl.com b:

copy edlin.com b:

copy more.com b:

copy find.exe b:

copy sort.exe b:

The commands you just entered are the external commands you will need on your startup disk. If you have a monochrome display adapter, you don't need GRAFTABL.COM or GRAPHICS.COM since these commands both work with the color graphics adapter. In special cases, the following commands may be necessary on a startup diskette: SHARE, ASSIGN, JOIN, or SUBST.

The startup diskette should also contain any memory-resident programs that you use, such as SideKick. These programs are loaded into memory, and then don't need to be on a disk in the computer while they are running; however, some of the programs, such as SideKick, have a file containing Help screens that must be kept in the computer if you want to use their Help facilities. SideKick calls this file SK.HLP, and you will see that it is on both the startup and the program disk.

If you are going to use a memory-resident program like SideKick, copy it onto your startup disk now. SideKick will be used as an example as you continue. Place the disk with the program in drive A and copy the program files to the startup disk in drive B. Enter

copy sk.com b: ⏎

Enter

copy sk.hlp b: ⏎

Configuring Your Startup Disk

You now must create two very important files: AUTOEXEC.BAT and CONFIG.SYS. These files tell DOS what options you want to use when you start your computer.

The CONFIG.SYS file provides a way to tell DOS what configuration options you want to include when you start DOS. Start EDLIN to create a CONFIG.SYS file on drive B as follows. Enter

```
edlin b:config.sys ⏎
```

Refer to Chapter 9 if you need help with EDLIN. The file should contain the following:

```
device=vdisk.sys 16 128 16
device=ansi.sys
buffers=20
files=20
```

This CONFIG.SYS file creates a small (16K bytes) VDISK and loads the ANSI device driver. The VDISK is an electronic disk (or RAM drive) and is used to hold small batch files that you use throughout the day. ANSI tells DOS how to interpret special control codes for the display. These control codes are used in the prompt that will be shown in the next example.

Next, create an AUTOEXEC.BAT file, again on drive B, that looks like the following. Use EDLIN, and remember to press **Return** at the end of each line:

```
@echo off
date
time
cls
path a:\;c:\
prompt $e[s$e[1;H$e[K $e[7m $d $t$h$h$h$h$h$h $p $e[0m$e[u$n$g
sk
copy more.com c:
copy find.exe c:
copy sort.exe c:
copy startup.cmd c:startup.bat
startup
```

First, this file requests the date and time. DOS records the current date and time whenever a file is created or changed. These dates and times are shown in the disk directory. If you don't enter the correct date and time when you start your computer, there is no way to tell which version of a file is the most recent.

After the date and time are entered, the screen is cleared, and a path is set up. This PATH command includes the root directory of diskette drive A and the VDISK (drive C). Since drive B is usually used for data, DOS will automatically find most programs (except those in a subdirectory). Drive B is not in the path because it is sometimes empty, and DOS will produce an error if it looks on that drive for a program and there is no disk.

The next command is the PROMPT command. This prompt provides the date, time, and current directory in a banner at the top of your screen and then provides the normal prompt at the left of the screen. Figure 10.1 shows how this prompt command works.

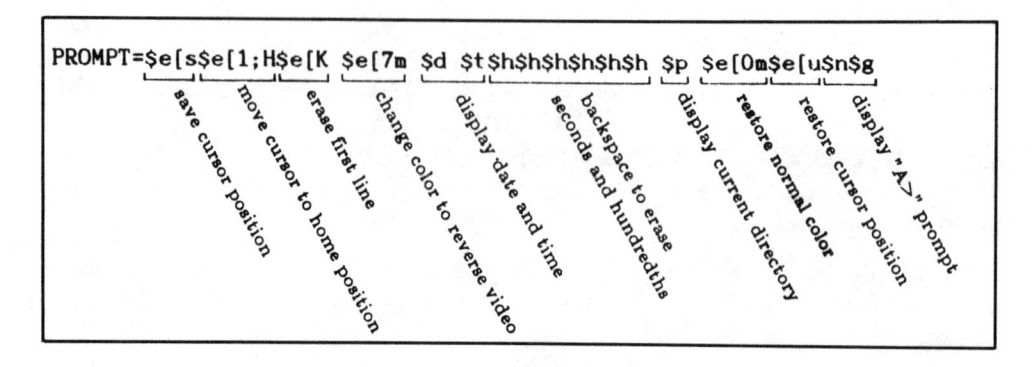

```
PROMPT=$e[s$e[1;H$e[K  $e[7m  $d  $t$h$h$h$h$h$h  $p  $e[0m$e[u$n$g
```
- save cursor position
- move cursor to home position
- erase first line
- change color to reverse video
- display date and time
- backspace to erase seconds and hundredths
- display current directory
- restore normal color
- restore cursor position
- display "A>" prompt

Figure 10.1 The PROMPT Command

The next line of the AUTOEXEC.BAT file starts the SideKick program. If you use a different memory-resident program, this line must change.

Three COPY commands move three DOS utilities to drive C, where they will always be available.

The next two lines work together. First, a batch file is copied to drive C, then the STARTUP command calls the batch file. The workings of this batch file will be discussed next.

The STARTUP.BAT File

This batch file displays a message telling you to change the program and data diskettes and then automatically starts your program.

This file will be stored on the startup disk, but it will be copied to the VDISK before it is used. You must be sure that DOS can't find it on the startup diskette, or you will get an error message when you change the disks. It is easy to "hide" this file from DOS on the startup disk; all you have to do is use a file name extension that is *not* .BAT, so name this file STARTUP.CMD on the startup disk. The COPY command in AUTOEXEC.BAT renames it to STARTUP.BAT when it copies it to drive C so DOS can find it there (DOS will be looking for a file that you have already removed). Use EDLIN to create a file called STARTUP.CMD on drive B that resembles the following. Remember to press **Return** at the end of each line.

```
:! STARTUP.BAT -- Reminder to change disks
echo off
cls
echo Place program disk in drive A,
echo and data disk in drive B
pause
cls
start
```

This batch file displays a message telling you to change diskettes, and, when you have confirmed that the diskettes have been changed, it automatically starts the program on your program disk; you just create a batch file on each of your program diskettes called START.BAT that contains the proper command to start the program on that disk. The last line in every START.BAT file should be

startup

This line will start the STARTUP command again, so the next program you use also will start automatically. A typical START.BAT file to run the Microsoft Word program would look like this:

word
startup

Checking the Startup Disk

Your startup disk should now be ready. Check that you have all the files you need by using the DIR command as follows:

dir b: ⏎

The screen should resemble the following:

```
 Volume in drive B is STARTUP
 Directory of   B:\

COMMAND     COM     23791    12-30-85    12:00p
VDISK       SYS      3307    12-30-85    12:00p
ANSI        SYS      1651    12-30-85    12:00p
MODE        COM      6864    12-30-85    12:00p
EDLIN       COM      7508    12-30-85    12:00p
GRAPHICS    COM      3220    12-30-85    12:00p
GRAFTABL    COM      1169    12-30-85    12:00p
MORE        COM       295    12-30-85    12:00p
FIND        EXE      6416    12-30-85    12:00p
SORT        EXE      1911    12-30-85    12:00p
SK          COM     39117     5-03-85     2:00p
SK          HLP     53632     5-03-85     2:00p
CONFIG      SYS        68     4-23-86     4:24p
AUTOEXEC    BAT       205     4-23-86     4:42p
STARTUP     CMD       147     4-23-86      :58p
      15 File(s)     157696 bytes free
```

Don't be concerned if the files on your disk are not in the same order as shown above, but do be sure that they are all there. If the size of any of the three files that you created (CONFIG.SYS, AUTOEXEC.BAT, and STARTUP.CMD) is not the same as shown above, you should proofread your work; you may have made a typing mistake.

When everything checks out, put the new startup diskette in drive A and restart your computer by simultaneously pressing **Ctrl-Alt-Del**. After you have entered the date and time again, your screen should display the following:

```
Place program disk in drive A,
and data disk in drive B
Strike a key when ready . . .
```

Press a key. You will get the **Bad command or file name** message for a moment because there is no START.BAT on the startup diskette. This message is not a problem.

You will see the new prompt, which should resemble the following:

    Wed   4-23-1986 17:12 A:\
    A>

CREATING A PROGRAM DISKETTE

Now you can create a program diskette. The program disk will have everything you need to run your program, but it won't be able to properly start the computer. It will contain the DOS commands you are most likely to need during normal operations.

The program disk that you create here will have everything on it you need except one thing—the application program. You will have to look at your application program's manual to see how to copy the program on this disk. It is recommended that you make one of these program disks for each of your major application programs. You may also want to make one or two program disks with utility programs on them.

To create a program disk, start by putting your DOS disk in drive A and a blank disk in drive B. Do not restart DOS. The following procedure formats the disk and places some DOS command files on it. Enter

format b: /s /v ⏎

The screen displays the following:

        Insert new diskette for drive B:
        and strike ENTER when ready

        Format complete
        System transferred

        Volume label (11 characters, ENTER for none)?

Enter

program ⏎

The screen displays the following:

```
362496 bytes total disk space
 69632 bytes used by system
292864 bytes available on disk
```

Format another (Y/N)?

Enter

n ⏎

And then enter

copy format.com b: ⏎
copy chkdsk.com b: ⏎
copy diskcopy.com b: ⏎

When you press the **Return** key after each line, the screen displays the following:

1 File(s) copied

Now place your SideKick disk in drive A. The startup disk loads SideKick into memory, so you don't need the SideKick program on this disk, but you do need SideKick's Help file (called SK.HLP). When you press SideKick's Help key, the program must look at this file to display the on-screen help, so this file must be on the disk that is normally in drive A. If your program disk is almost full, you can remove this file. SideKick will operate normally, except that on-screen help will not be available. Put the SK.HLP file on your program disk with the following command:

copy sk.hlp b: ⏎

The next step is to create an AUTOEXEC.BAT file. This disk is not meant to be used to start the computer, so this file will just contain a warning to that effect. Use COPY to create this file as follows. Press the **Return** key at the end of each line:

```
copy con b:autoexec.bat
echo off
echo ^G                      (Use the Ctrl-G keys)
echo This is not a startup diskette.
echo Put your startup diskette in drive A,
echo and press Ctrl-Alt-Del.
^Z                           (^Z is obtained by pressing the F6 key)
```

As you can see, this file just provides a warning to use the proper startup disk.

You have just one more file to create—the START.BAT file. The file created here will be a "dummy" file. You will need to create a different START.BAT file for each of your program disks. This process will be explained later in this chapter. For now, just create the file with the following commands. Press the **Return** key where indicated:

```
copy con b:start.bat ⏎
echo off ⏎
cls ⏎
a: ⏎
echo Put the command to start your program in this batch file. ⏎
echo Press Ctrl-Break to stop this loop. ⏎
pause   Then eliminate this line and the two echo statements above. ⏎
startup ⏎
^Z ⏎                         (Use the F6 key)
```

Checking your Disk

You should first check your disk by looking at the directory. Enter

dir b: ⏎

The screen should resemble the following:

```
Volume in drive B is PROGRAM
Directory of  B:\

COMMAND   COM      23791    12-30-85    2:00p
FORMAT    COM      11135    12-30-85   12:00p
CHKDSK    COM       9832    12-30-85   12:00p
DISKCOPY  COM       6224    12-30-85   12:00p
SK        HLP      53632     5-03-85    2:09p
AUTOEXEC  BAT        130     4-24-86    3:02p
START     BAT        204     4-24-86    4:57p
     7 File(s)    207872 bytes free
```

Check this directory to be sure that you have all the files. The DOS and Sidekick files may be different sizes, depending on which version you have. If either of the two files you created is a different size than shown above, you should check it; there may be a typing error. You can use EDLIN to change the file without retyping all its contents.

If the directory looks correct, you can move on to the next step. Remove the DOS disk, and put the new program disk into drive A. Enter

start ⏎

Your START.BAT file will display the following message:

```
Put the command to start your program in this batch file.
Press Ctrl-Break to stop this loop.
Strike a key when ready . . .
```

Now press a key (*except* **Ctrl-Break**), and the message will change to the following:

```
Place program disk in drive A,
and data disk in drive B
Strike a key when ready . . .
```

You should recognize this message; it is from your STARTUP.BAT file that the startup disk put on the VDISK. These two messages will alternate until you press **Ctrl-Break**. Your automatic startup system is working; it just doesn't have a program to start yet.

The last test to make is to restart the computer with the program disk in drive A. Perform this task by pressing **Ctrl-Alt-Del**, and you should see the following message:

```
A>echo off

This is not a startup diskette.
Put your startup diskette in drive A,
and press Ctrl-Alt-Del.

A>
```

This message gives you some good advice. Follow it.

MODIFYING START.BAT

The START.BAT file will be different on each one of your program disks. The file must be modified to start the program on each particular disk. For example, a program disk that has the Microsoft Word program on it would have a START.BAT file that resembles the following:

```
a:
word
startup
```

This file just makes sure that drive A is the default drive and starts Word. When you finish using Word, the last line of the file calls the STARTUP command on the VDISK so the next program disk you use will also start automatically. Notice that in this file the first two lines of the original START.BAT have been removed. These two lines ("echo off" and "cls") just clear the screen. Since Word clears the screen when it starts, these two lines aren't necessary.

Some programs are copy-protected, so you can't copy them onto your own program disk. Most copy-protected programs do, however, allow you to put more files on the disk. If this is the case, just put a START.BAT file on the program disk.

Some programs start automatically if you start the computer when they are in drive A. This procedure is usually done with the program's own AUTOEXEC.BAT file. If programs have an AUTOEXEC.BAT file, it probably contains the commands you need in your START.BAT file. Use the TYPE command to look at the AUTOEXEC.BAT file supplied with your program.

If the program doesn't have an AUTOEXEC.BAT file, you can put the previously shown AUTOEXEC.BAT file on the disk to remind you to start with your startup disk.

CREATING DATA DISKS

Creating data disks is easy. Since they are supposed to hold the information you use with your application programs, they start out with no files on them.

With your program disk in drive A, put a blank disk in drive B, and follow this procedure. Enter

format b: /v ⏎

The screen displays the following:

```
Insert new diskette for drive B:
and strike ENTER when ready

Format complete

Volume label (11 characters, ENTER for none)?
```

Enter

data ⏎

The screen displays the following:

```
362496 bytes total disk space
362496 bytes available on disk

Format another (Y/N)?n
```

You now have a working data diskette. You may want to be more creative in labeling your data diskettes. You will have many of them, so you will probably want to use labels that indicate the type of information they contain.

ORGANIZING YOUR FILES

Diskettes are relatively inexpensive, and you should not try to crowd too much information on any one working data diskette. It is much easier to keep track of where things are if you allocate one diskette to each project (or even to parts of a project, such as chapters in a book). You will always have working room on the diskettes, and the directories won't become too cumbersome.

When you finish a project, you can combine the files that are on the working data diskettes onto fewer diskettes for storage. Be careful if you have files of the same name on different diskettes. You may need to create a subdirectory on the storage diskettes for each of the working diskettes.

PROTECTING YOUR DATA

Diskettes are vulnerable to a myriad of hazards. They are delicate items that can succumb to any number of not-too-unusual occurrences. Sooner or later, you will find out how important it is to make backup copies of your important information. Following are several hints to make backing up as painless as possible.

There are basically two ways to make copies of the files that are on your diskettes: you can copy the entire diskette, or you can copy the individual files. It is recommend that you try both methods.

Use CHKDSK to see how full your working disk is. If it is less than half full (and most of them should be), use COPY to copy the files to a backup diskette. If the diskette is more than half full, use DISKCOPY to copy the entire disk. Remember that DISKCOPY destroys (by overwriting) any information that is on the disk to which you are copying.

If you want to conserve archive diskettes, you can fill them with more information than is on your working diskettes. Create a subdirectory on the archive diskette for each working diskette you want to archive. You can use the working diskette's disk label as the directory name.

CHAPTER 11

SETTING UP A FIXED DISK SYSTEM

In this chapter, you'll learn the steps required to get a fixed disk up and running. Then, you'll learn some recommendations for setting up the directory structure and some hints for making your computer's operation more effective.

STARTING OUT WITH A NEW FIXED DISK

The following steps are required to get a new, blank, fixed disk running. These steps must be performed in the proper order or the disk won't work properly.

NOTE: These steps completely erase everything from the fixed disk; do not follow this procedure if you have information or programs on your fixed disk that you want to keep. If you don't want to erase your fixed disk, skip ahead to the section titled "Creating a Directory Structure."

Creating a DOS Partition

In an IBM PC or compatible, you can use the fixed disk to store information for more than one operating system. PC-DOS is by far the most widely used operating system, but it isn't the only one. The first thing you must do with your fixed disk is determine how much space on it you are going to reserve for PC-DOS. Most users allocate the entire fixed disk to PC-DOS since other operating systems are used on very few computers, and that approach will be taken in this book.

The FDISK command is used to tell DOS how much room it can use on the fixed disk. Place your DOS diskette in drive A and start your computer. DOS will ask you for the date and time. Enter that information. The current date and time are recorded on the fixed disk when you format it (no one will believe that you formatted your fixed disk after the New Year's Eve party in the early hours of 1980).

The first message you will see on the screen is as follows:

```
Current date is Tue  1-01-1980
Enter new date (mm-dd-yy):
```

Type today's date, using hyphens to separate the month, day, and year. For example, to enter July 4, 1986, you would type 7-4-86. Press **Return** after you have typed the date. DOS will request the time as follows:

```
Current time is 0:00:47.01
Enter new time:
```

Type the current time using the 24-hour system, and use colons to separate the hours, minutes, and seconds. You don't have to enter seconds if you don't want to. For example, to enter 3:45 p.m., type 15:45. Press **Return** after entering the time.

DOS now indicates that it is ready to work by displaying the copyright and version messages. DOS then displays the following prompt:

```
A>
```

Now, enter the FDISK command as follows:

fdisk ⏎

The screen displays the following:

```
IBM Personal Computer
Fixed Disk Setup Program Version 3.10
(C) Copyright IBM Corp. 1983, 1984

FDISK Options

Choose one of the following:

       1.   Create DOS partition
       2.   Change Active Partition
       3.   Delete DOS Partition
       4.   Display Partition Data

   Enter choice: [1]

   Press Esc to return to DOS
```

Select item 1 by pressing **Return**. If the fixed disk has already been set up, the response will be as follows:

```
DOS partition already created
```

The command will end and return you to the prompt; otherwise, FDISK will ask you some more questions, such as the following:

```
Create DOS Partition

Current Fixed Disk Drive: 1


Do you wish to use the entire fixed disk
for DOS (Y/N) .....................?  [Y]
```

Press **Return** to answer yes. The command will finish its work and then display the following:

```
System will now restart
Insert DOS diskette in drive A:
Press any key when ready . . .
```

Since the DOS diskette is already in drive A, you can just press a key. The computer will restart and again ask you for the date and time. Enter them again.

Formatting the Fixed Disk

The next step is to format the fixed disk. Formatting removes all the information currently on the fixed disk and creates a new, blank directory. You must format a new fixed disk to make it function properly, but if you format a fixed disk that already has information on it, you will lose all that information.

NOTE: The following warning is not displayed by some earlier versions of DOS. In fact, versions earlier than 2.1 do not give you any warning at all but start right in erasing the disk. Be sure that you want to format your fixed disk before you proceed any further.

To format the fixed disk, enter the format command as follows:

format c: /s /v ⏎

If the fixed disk has previously been formatted, the computer will ask you to enter the current volume label. Then, DOS will respond with a message such as the following, warning you that you will lose all the information on your fixed disk:

```
Enter current Volume Label for Drive C:
     (Press ENTER for none):
WARNING, ALL DATA ON NON-REMOVABLE DISK
DRIVE C: WILL BE LOST!
Proceed with Format (Y/N)?
```

Press **Y** followed by **Return** to proceed.

It takes a while to format the fixed disk. Spend this time thinking up an 11-character (maximum) name for your disk. The format command will stop and ask you to enter a volume label when it is done. This label is displayed every time you use the DIR command, so you will want to use something catchy but not so trendy that you will get tired of it. Having a label on your fixed disk also adds another level of protection to the FORMAT command as shown above. When FORMAT is ready for you to enter a label, it will display:

```
Formatting . . . Format Complete
System Transferred

Volume label (11 characters, ENTER for none)?
```

Enter your label and press **Return**. You can use all the characters that are allowed in file names, plus spaces. FORMAT will now tell you the results of your efforts in the following format:

```
10592256  bytes total disk space
   62464  bytes used by system
   12288  bytes in bad sectors
10517504  bytes available on disk
```

FIXED DISK SYSTEM SETUP

You have now formatted your fixed disk. Test your work by restarting the computer to see if it will start from the fixed disk. Open the diskette drive door on drive A so the computer will start from the fixed disk. DOS attempts to start from drive A before it starts from the fixed disk; the drive A door must be open. Next, restart the computer from the keyboard by pressing **Ctrl-Alt-Del**. The computer should beep, the drives will whir, and finally, DOS will request the date and time once again.

If the computer doesn't start from the fixed disk, try restarting it again. If it still doesn't work, return to the beginning of this chapter and repeat the procedure.

Loading DOS Onto the Fixed Disk

The next step is to copy the rest of the DOS programs onto the fixed disk. Before you actually copy the files, you will create a subdirectory on the fixed disk to hold them, which keeps your main or root directory free of miscellaneous files. As you set up your fixed disk, you will create several more subdirectories to keep all your information organized.

To create a subdirectory to hold the rest of the DOS files, use the MKDIR (make directory) command. At the C> prompt, enter

mkdir dos ⏎

Now, make the new directory your current directory with the CHDIR (change directory) command by entering

chdir dos ⏎

Remember that these commands have short forms; MD for MKDIR and CD for CHDIR. From now on, the short form of these commands will be used.

Use CD to check that you are in the correct current directory. Type CD and press **Return**. Your screen should resemble the following:

    C:\DOS

If the screen does not respond, go back a few steps and try again.

You are now ready to copy all your DOS files into this directory. Close the door on the A drive with the DOS diskette in it. Use the COPY command to copy all the files on the diskette to the DOS directory as follows:

`copy a:*.* c:` ⏎

COPY will list the files as it copies them. When this process is done, COPY will tell you how many files it copied.

If you are using DOS 3.3 with 5-1/4" diskettes, repeat the copying procedure for the second diskette. If you are using an earlier version of DOS, you need only copy the files from the DOS diskette; you won't need any of the files from the supplemental diskette.

Several files are included with DOS 3 that you probably won't need. These files, which are concerned primarily with setting up your system for use with foreign languages, can be deleted to save disk space (if you ever need them, you still have your original DOS diskette).

It is recommended that you delete the following files to leave more room for useful information on your disk. Follow the format of this example for each name in the list that follows. From the C> prompt, enter

`del basic.com` ⏎

Then, delete the following other files if appropriate:

BASIC.COM	Basica.com has more features.
BASIC*.PIF	Useful only if you use BASIC and TopView or Windows.
COMMAND.COM	You already have a copy of COMMAND in the root directory.
COUNTRY.SYS	Used for foreign languages (DOS 3.3 only).
DISPLAY.SYS	Used for foreign languages (DOS 3.3 only).
KEYB*.COM	Used for foreign languages.
KEYBOARD.SYS	Used for foreign languages (DOS 3.3 only).
NLSFUNC.EXE	Used for foreign languages (DOS 3.3 only).
PRINTER.SYS	Used for foreign languages (DOS 3.3 only).
SELECT.COM	Used for foreign languages.
*.CPI	Used for foreign languages (DOS 3.3 only).

If you receive the message **File not found**, don't worry. The file is not included in your version of DOS.

As you use DOS, you may find that there are other DOS commands you never use because you have no need for a particular command or because you have purchased a commercial utility program that does the job better. Norton Utilities, for example, effectively replaces the ATTRIB, LABEL, RECOVER, and TREE commands. Fastback, from Fifth Generation Systems, functionally replaces the BACKUP and RESTORE commands with improved versions. In such cases, you may want to delete the unnecessary DOS commands from your hard disk.

CREATING AN ORGANIZED FILE STRUCTURE

Now it is time to set up your file structure. DOS allows you to create as many subdirectories as you like, which allows you to organize the storage of your files in any way you want.

Over-organizing your fixed disk can be counter-productive. The directory structure presented here is a workable system that keeps your files organized without becoming unwieldy.

This system includes two kinds of subdirectories: those that are kept small (so that it is easy to find any file in them) and those that are allowed to grow (with many files in them). The small subdirectories are the project directories that contain the files you need to locate from day to day.

The other directories are directories containing the programs and commands you use but are automatically located for you by the path you define. The DOS subdirectory is one of these large directories; you never need to look at any of the files in it as long as they are there when you need them.

The suggested starting directory structure is shown in Figure 11.1. It is the same file structure described in Chapter 3 and will be used in some of the applications presented in this chapter.

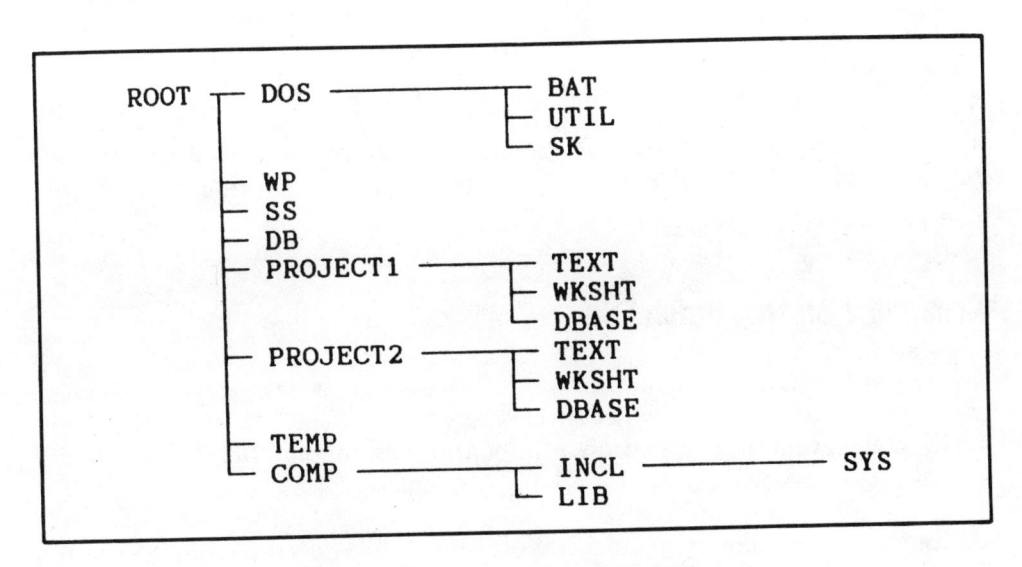

```
ROOT ─┬─ DOS ──────────┬─ BAT
      │                ├─ UTIL
      │                └─ SK
      ├─ WP
      ├─ SS
      ├─ DB
      ├─ PROJECT1 ─────┬─ TEXT
      │                ├─ WKSHT
      │                └─ DBASE
      ├─ PROJECT2 ─────┬─ TEXT
      │                ├─ WKSHT
      │                └─ DBASE
      ├─ TEMP
      └─ COMP ─────────┬─ INCL ──────── SYS
                       └─ LIB
```

Figure 11.1 The directory structure

Naming your Directories

You are free, of course, to name your directories anything you like, but you are encouraged to name your utility directories (DOS and its subdirectories) as outlined in this book. In the next few chapters, you will learn many ways to streamline your operations, and these examples will be much clearer if you don't have to think about changing the names.

To set up the directory structure, type the following lines at the C> prompt, pressing **Return** after each line:

cd \dos

md bat

md util

md sk

cd \

md wp

md ss

md db

md temp

These lines set up the the basic directory structure. You will begin placing data in those directories as you proceed through the rest of this chapter.

Creating a Startup Batch File

Every time you start your computer, there are a few steps you must take. If there is a file called AUTOEXEC.BAT in the root directory, DOS will automatically execute the commands in that file as part of its initialization process.

Among the first steps you must take every time you start your computer is to enter the correct date and time. DOS uses the current date and time to time-stamp files as they are created or changed. On a fixed disk that may have hundreds of files, it is very important to know when those files were last modified.

Many newer computers have a built-in battery-operated clock/calendar, so you don't need to enter the date and time when you start your computer. Also, many multi-function memory boards include a battery-operated clock/calendar. You may find that this feature is a great asset to your computer. You may still need a command in your AUTOEXEC.BAT file to tell DOS to look at the clock/calendar.

Some other commands you will want in your startup batch file include the PATH command and the PROMPT command. If there are any memory-resident programs you use frequently, they too can be started by the AUTOEXEC.BAT file.

Use EDLIN (described in Chapter 9) to create the AUTOEXEC.BAT file for the fixed disk. Press **Return** at the end of each line:

```
@echo off
cls
date
time
path c:\dos;c:\dos\bat;c:\dos\util;c:\wp;c:\ss;c:\db
FASTOPEN C:=100
PROMPT=$e[s$e[1;H$e[K $e[7m $d $t$h$h$h$h$h$h $p $e[0m$e[u$n$g
cd \dos\sk
sk
cd \
cls
menu
```

The first four lines of the file are pretty simple; they clear the screen and request the date and time. The PATH command sets up a path to all the directories that will have programs in them. For example, your batch files, which are in \DOS\BAT, can be used from any directory, as can all external DOS commands, your utility programs, and your major programs.

The FASTOPEN command reserves an area of memory to save part of the disk directory in, which should speed up disk access. This feature is not available in DOS versions before 3.3.

The PROMPT command is obscure, but it produces a very useful display. It gives some useful information in reverse video on the top line of the screen and then puts the usual C prompt, as expected, at the left edge of the screen. Figure 11.2 shows what each part of the PROMPT command does.

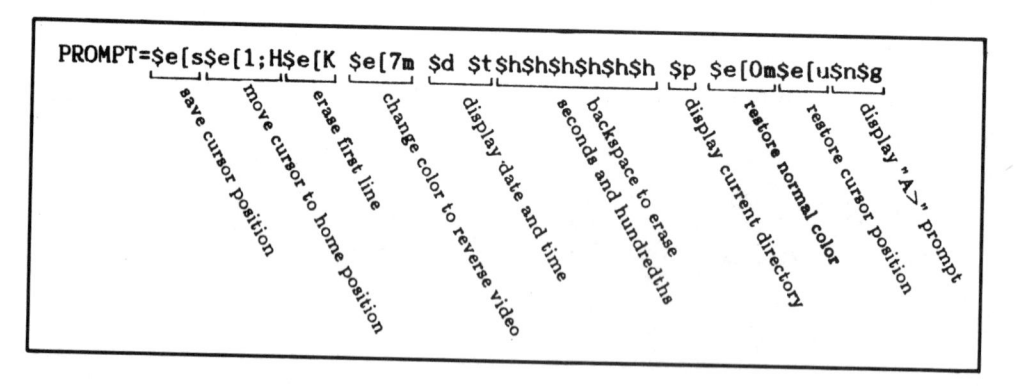

```
PROMPT=$e[s$e[1;H$e[K  $e[7m  $d  $t$h$h$h$h$h$h  $p  $e[0m$e[u$n$g
       │    │    │     │      │  │                │  │    │    │
       │    │    │     │      │  │                │  │    │    display "A>" prompt
       │    │    │     │      │  │                │  │    restore cursor position
       │    │    │     │      │  │                │  restore normal color
       │    │    │     │      │  │                display current directory
       │    │    │     │      │  backspace to erase seconds and hundredths
       │    │    │     │      display date and time
       │    │    │     change color to reverse video
       │    │    erase first line
       │    move cursor to home position
       save cursor position
```

Figure 11.2 The PROMPT Command

The next three lines start the SideKick program. You must be in SideKick's directory when you start the program so DOS can find its Help file. Change directories to \DOS\SK, start SideKick (with the "sk" command), and return to the root directory.

NOTE: If you don't have the SideKick program, leave these three lines out of your AUTOEXEC.BAT file. If you have a different memory-resident program, you can substitute the proper commands in your AUTOEXEC.BAT file.

Finally, the screen is cleared and the menu is displayed. You will see how to create a simple menu system later in this chapter.

Making a Configuration File

There is one more file that you need in the root directory of your fixed disk. This file configures DOS the way you want it. The configuration file must be named CONFIG.SYS. DOS reads this file as part of the initialization process and executes the special commands found there.

Use EDLIN to create the CONFIG.SYS file for the fixed disk system you are building as follows. Press the **Return** key at the end of each line:

```
device=\dos\ansi.sys
device=\dos\vdisk.sys
files=20
buffers=25
```

The two DEVICE commands load the ANSI and VDISK device drivers. Device drivers are optional parts of DOS. If you include them in your CONFIG.SYS file, they are loaded and remain a part of DOS. The ANSI device driver tells DOS how to recognize ANSI control sequences used to control the screen. There are several ANSI control sequences in the PROMPT command in the AUTOEXEC.BAT file just shown.

The VDISK device driver creates a virtual disk in the memory of your computer. This disk has a drive designator one letter beyond the last physical disk drive in your computer. The virtual disk works just like a real disk drive and is very fast, but it disappears when you restart or turn off your computer, and it takes up memory that may be required to run other programs. If you use the virtual disk to store files, make sure that you have copies of those files on a real disk before you end your session at the computer.

The FILES command instructs DOS that you may need to use up to 20 files at once. DOS reserves space in an internal table for the number of files specified in the command. The FILES command doesn't use up much space for each file, so you can be liberal with this number. Programs that require many files will probably tell you in their installation instructions what number should be in the FILES command.

The BUFFERS command tells DOS to reserve space in memory (called **buffers**) for temporarily storing the information it reads from the disk. Saving the information that DOS reads from the disk can speed up your work because information that DOS needs repeatedly, such as the disk directory, will probably already be in memory, saving the time to read it from the disk. The BUFFERS command uses a significant amount of memory (each buffer is 512 bytes), and if you use too many buffers, it can take longer to look through all the buffers than it would to read the disk. There is no set optimal number of buffers; it depends on what programs you use and how you use them. The number used in this book — 25 — is slightly higher than average.

The basics of your fixed disk are now set up. Restart your computer by pressing **Ctrl-Alt-Del**, and all you have done will take effect.

NOTE: At this point, you should expect several error messages when the AUTOEXEC.BAT file executes. Neither the SideKick program nor the MENU batch file are on your disk. DOS will give the **Bad command or filename** message because these files don't exist. Don't worry about these messages at this point.

A MENU SYSTEM

Batch files provide a convenient way to create a menu system. By using batch files, you can easily make changes to your menu system, making it easy to keep the system up to date as you add applications to your fixed disk.

The following menu system is simple. In fact, it hardly exists at all. The heart of the menu system is a file named MENU.TXT that is displayed to show what choices are available. The choices are simply the names of batch files that start the various programs.

First, move to the \DOS\BAT subdirectory and use EDLIN to create the file MENU.TXT that resembles the following:

```
************************************************************
              ^[[7m M A S T E R    M E N U ^[[0m
************************************************************
                    WP = Word Processing

                    SS = Spread Sheet

                    DB = Data Base
        Any of the above can be followed by a project
        directory name and a file name to automatically
        move to the right subdirectory and open the file.
        If you don't include a file name the program will
        start in the right subdirectory but with no file
        loaded. If you don't include a project directory
        name you will be put in the \TEMP directory

************************************************************
```

Again, ANSI command sequences are being used to control the display. Remember to insert an Escape code when you are using EDLIN; press **Ctrl-V** followed by [. This procedure is somewhat confusing when you use ANSI command sequences because the Escape codes are always followed by a [, which means you must press **Ctrl-V** [[to get an Escape code followed by a [.

When you are done creating this file, display it with the following command:

type menu.txt ⏎

You will see that part of the menu is in reverse video. Instead of using EDLIN, use the "COPY con" shortcut to create a MENU.BAT file as follows. Press **Return** at the end of each line:

```
copy con menu.bat
type \dos\bat\menu.txt
^Z                            (use the F6 key)
```

Now, try to call up your menu with the following command:

menu ⏎

The menu should display on your screen with the C prompt below it. Next, use EDLIN to create batch files for each of the choices you have on the menu. Following are the batch files. Press **Return** at the end of each line:

WP.BAT File

```
:! WP.BAT
@echo off
cls
if x==%1x goto temp
cd \%1\text
goto execute
:temp
cd \temp
:execute
word %2 %3 %4
menu
```

SS.BAT File

```
:! SS.BAT
@echo off
cls
if x==%1x goto temp
cd \%1\wksht
goto execute
:temp
cd \temp
:execute
sc4 %2 %3 %4
menu
```

DB.BAT File

```
:! DB.BAT
@echo off
cls
if x==%1x goto temp
cd \%1\dbase
goto execute
:temp
cd \temp
:execute
dbase %2 %3 %4
menu
```

All three of these batch files are similar. To use them, you can enter up to four parameters. The first parameter is the name of the project directory that you want to work on. The appropriate project subdirectory becomes the current directory. If no parameters are entered, the \TEMP directory becomes the current directory.

The second, third, and fourth parameters are passed to the program that you want to start. Typically, the second parameter is the name of the file you want to work on, and the third and fourth parameters are the program's command-line options.

The batch files start by clearing the screen and then checking if any parameters have been entered on the command line. If no parameters have been entered, they branch to the label "temp," which changes the current directory to \TEMP. If a parameter has been entered, it is used as the name of a project directory. The subdirectory for the appropriate program is added to the project directory name to create the correct name for the current directory.

Then, the appropriate program is run with the second, third, and fourth parameters passed on to it. Finally, when you are done using your application program, the menu batch file is executed to display the menu again.

NOTE: The example batch files run the Microsoft Word word processing program, the SuperCalc4 spreadsheet program, and the dBASE data base program. If your programs are different, you must change your batch files accordingly.

You can see that it is simple to change the menu that is displayed and the batch files that are used and to add or change applications. The simplicity of changing this menu system is one of a batch file's most useful features.

STARTING A NEW PROJECT

When you start a new project, you must create four new directories. Creating them isn't a great strain, but it is simpler if the computer can do it for you. This batch file does just that; it creates the four directories (the project directory in the root directory plus three subdirectories) required for a new project.

Change directories (CD) to your \DOS\BAT directory and use EDLIN to create this batch file named MAKEDIR.BAT. Press **Return** at the end of each line:

```
:! MAKEDIR.BAT
@echo off
cls
if ""=="%1" goto error
cd \
mkdir %1
cd %1
for %%A in (text wksht dbase) do mkdir %%A
cd \
echo ^@
dir %1
goto end
:error
echo ^G
echo ^@
echo ^@
echo MAKEDIR must be followed by a directory name
:end
```

When you use this command, you must follow the command name, MAKEDIR, with a project name. The batch file uses this project name to create a new project directory in the root and then creates the three required subdirectories in that directory. If you forget to enter the project name, the batch file branches to the "error" label and reminds you how to use it. If you use a project name that is more than eight characters long, only the first eight characters are used for the project directory name.

You now have a working fixed disk system. In the next chapter, you will learn more fixed disk tricks to make you a "power user."

CHAPTER 12

APPLICATIONS FOR FIXED DISK USERS

In this chapter, you will learn about more DOS applications that can streamline your work with the fixed disk. You will learn how to keep track of what you have on the disk and to protect your important information from loss or damage.

Some batch files in this chapter rely on your disk having the directory structure described in the last chapter. If your disk is set up differently, you must modify some of the files.

All applications in this chapter use batch files. Use EDLIN to create these batch files because some of them contain special characters that are hard to create with other programs. There are three of these special characters: the **null** character, the **bell** character, and the **escape** character. Table 12.1 shows how the special characters you will use are created with EDLIN.

Character	Shown as	Press these keys
Null	^@	[F7]
Bell	^G	Ctrl-V G
Escape	^[	Ctrl-V [

**Table 12.1
Control codes created with EDLIN**

The Escape character is used in ANSI control sequences to control the display and is always followed by the "[" character, which means that you must press the **Ctrl-V** combination and then the "[" key twice (once to create the escape and once for the "[" character). When EDLIN displays this entry, it appears as ^[[.

MOVING FILES BETWEEN DIRECTORIES

It is often necessary to move a file from one directory to another. Following is a batch file that works just like the COPY command but also removes the file from the source directory. Instead of making an additional copy of a file, it simply moves the file. This command will work between directories on the same disk or between directories on different disks. Use the MOVE command just like the COPY command to move single files, several files using wild card symbols, or whole directories.

Since many things can go wrong while using the COPY command (such as a disk filling up or a write error), the following batch file instructs the COPY command to show you a directory of the target disk after the copy is made. You must confirm that the file or files were actually copied before the original files are deleted.

```
:! MOVE.BAT
copy %1 %2 /v
@echo off
cls
echo Check that all the files that you want
echo to move are in the following list:
echo ^G
echo ^@
dir %2 | more
echo ^@
echo If any files are missing, press Ctrl-Break
echo to cancel this command. Otherwise
pause
echo on
del %1
```

This batch file passes the command line parameters to the COPY command. Notice that the COPY command includes the /V parameter, which makes the COPY command check its work. Since you will erase the original file, you must be sure that the copy is good.

FIXED DISK APPLICATIONS

After COPY is done, the target directory is displayed. This directory can be a directory of one file, a group of files, or an entire directory, depending on the target parameter that you enter. The message tells you to check for the files that you want, and the PAUSE command gives you an opportunity to quit before the original files are erased.

MAKING A DIRECTORY OF YOUR ENTIRE DISK

Keeping track of all files on a fixed disk can be quite a chore. DIRALL.BAT is a batch file that creates a system directory for you. The directory is stored in a file called SORTED.DIR in the root directory.

The DIRALL command accepts up to two parameters. One parameter is the drive designator for the drive for which you want to create a directory. The other parameter is the option /O, which stands for "old." If you use the /O option, this command will not create a new directory file but will only display the current directory file. If you don't enter any parameters, a directory file is created for the default drive. Following is the batch file for the DIRALL command.

```
:! DIRALL.BAT -- directory of entire disk
@echo off
cls
if "%1"=="/o" goto show
if "%1"=="/O" goto show
if "%2"=="/o" goto show
if "%2"=="/O" goto show
:create
echo ^G              (use Ctrl-VG key combination)
echo About to create a directory of the entire disk. This can
echo take a minute or more to complete. To view an existing
echo disk directory, use the /O option like this:
echo DIRALL A: /O
echo ^@              (use F7 key)
echo Press Ctrl-Break to stop now, or
pause
echo ^@
```

continued...

...from previous page

```
echo Creating the Directory
chkdsk %1 /v >dir.dir
echo         Complete Disk Directory >%1\sorted.dir
echo ^@ >>%1\sorted.dir
echo         List of Directories >>%1\sorted.dir
echo ^@ >>%1\sorted.dir
echo ^@
echo Listing the Directories
type dir.dir ¦ find "Directory" ¦ sort >>%1\sorted.dir
echo ^@ >>%1\sorted.dir
echo         List of Files by Directory >>%1\sorted.dir
echo ^@ >>%1\sorted.dir
echo ^@
echo Listing the Files
type dir.dir ¦ find "\" >>%1\sorted.dir
del dir.dir
:show
if "%1"=="/o" shift
if "%1"=="/O" shift
if not exist %1\sorted.dir goto error
more <%1\sorted.dir
goto end
:error
echo ^@
echo ^@
echo Directory file not found, you must create it.
goto create
:end
```

The DIRALL.BAT batch file starts out by checking both parameters (%1 and %2) for a /O. Notice that you must check for both an upper- and lowercase letter. If the /O parameter is found, the command goes directly to the "show" label and displays the current file.

Next, a message is displayed warning you that it takes some time to create a directory for an entire disk. The proper usage of the command is also shown. The PAUSE command gives you a way out if you want to stop at this point.

The CHKDSK command with the **/V** option is used to create the directory. The output of the CHKDSK command is redirected to the file DIR.DIR for temporary storage.

Some ECHO commands are redirected to put headings into the output file, SORTED.DIR. Notice that the directory file is put into the root directory of whatever disk the command is working on so that you always know where to look for the directory file.

The FIND and SORT filters are used to extract and then alphabetize all the directory names from the temporary file (DIR.DIR). They are added to the SORTED.DIR file.

Another heading is added to the directory file, and then the FIND command is used to add all the directory and file names to the directory file. By looking for a backslash, the command eliminates all the other messages that CHKDSK puts out, and you receive only the file and directory names. This action completes the directory file, so the temporary file (DIR.DIR) can be deleted.

Now you have reached the "show" label, and you must be sure that the first parameter is not a /O. The two IF statements take care of this condition; they just shift the second parameter up 1 if the first parameter is a /O, which ensures that the file name in the IF NOT EXIST command is reasonable. If the file doesn't exist, a message is displayed, and you go back to the top of the file to create a file.

Finally, the SORTED.DIR file is displayed, using MORE to keep it from scrolling off the screen too quickly.

The DIRALL command is great for fixed disks, and the file it creates is used for the next command that you will create, which is used for locating files on the fixed disk. This command will also create a directory file of a floppy disk and is especially useful if you use subdirectories on your floppy disks.

LOCATING FILES ON A FIXED DISK

Sometimes, you need to know which directory a file is in on the fixed disk, or you may need to see if you have duplicate copies of a file on your fixed disk. The LOCATE command will find files on the fixed disk and report the directory in which they are located. Following is the batch file that creates the LOCATE command.

```
:! LOCATE.BAT -- locate a file on a fixed disk
@echo off
if ""=="%1" goto error1
if not exist \sorted.dir goto error2
find "%1" \sorted.dir ¦ more
goto end
:error1
echo ^@
echo ^@
echo You must give the name of the file that you are
echo trying to find, in all CAPS, like this:
echo    LOCATE FILENAME
:error2
echo ^@
echo ^@
echo The disk directory file does not exist. After
echo creating it with DIRALL, use the LOCATE command again.
pause
dirall
:end
```

The LOCATE command must be followed by a file name (or partial file name) in uppercase letters. The batch file starts by checking that there is a parameter. If there is no parameter, it branches to the "error1" label, and you are shown the proper way to use the command.

The next step is to confirm that the \SORTED.DIR file exists. If it is missing, another message is displayed, and the DIRALL command is used to build a new file.

Now you are to the point where all the work is being done. The FIND filter looks through the directory file and displays all occurrences of the parameter you entered. FIND isn't a real sophisticated program, so all occurrences of the entered parameter are displayed, even if they are part of a longer file name (similar to having default wild card characters).

FIXED DISK APPLICATIONS

BACKING UP YOUR FIXED DISK

Making backup copies of the information on a fixed disk is a chore that no one looks forward to. It's like buying life insurance; you're betting against yourself that something is going to go wrong.

This chapter will show you how to keep your fixed disk fully backed up with a minimum expenditure of time.

The approach in this book is to make a periodic, full backup of your fixed disk, and then make a daily backup of only the files that have changed since the last backup. There is no prescribed schedule for making a full backup; this system will indicate when you need to make another full backup.

To operate this system, there are two batch files: BACKALL.BAT and BACKDAY.BAT. BACKALL.BAT performs a complete backup of the fixed disk. BACKDAY.BAT backs up all the files that have changed since the last full backup.

The DOS BACKUP command has several options, and this system uses the option that looks at a file's date to determine if it should be backed up or not.

BACKDAY.BAT uses the file date instead of the archive flag, so all the files that have changed since the last full backup are backed up every day, which means that some files are backed up every day, even though they don't change every day. It also means, however, that restoring your fixed disk after a loss is very simple.

This system requires two complete sets of diskettes for your full backups and two sets of daily backup diskettes. The full backups can require a lot of diskettes—about 20 for a full 10-megabyte fixed disk. For daily backups, you should only need two or three diskettes. You will know it's time to do another complete backup when your daily backup uses up more than one or two diskettes. Depending on the type of work you do, this time span can range from one to three months.

NOTE: If you are using a version of DOS before 3.3, all disks to be used for backup must be formatted before they can be used. Be sure that you have enough blank, formatted disks on hand before you begin your backup procedure.

Limitations of this Backup System

This backup system has one glaring inadequacy: if you copy a file onto your fixed disk and that file has a file date earlier than your last complete backup, it won't be backed up during the daily backups.

Take another look at this situation. If you copy a file onto your fixed disk, you already have a backup of it on the diskette that you copied it from. In most cases, the files that you copy onto your fixed disk and don't change are programs. You always have the original copies of the programs to return to in case of a problem.

Another limitation of the system is that it counts on you to enter the correct date (unless your computer has a battery-operated clock/calendar). If you fail to enter a date, all the files created or changed that day will not be backed up because the date on those files will be January 1, 1980.

Making Full Backups

This batch file creates complete backups of your entire fixed disk. You don't need to enter any parameters when you enter the BACKALL command.

```
:! BACKALL.BAT -- Full backup
@echo off
verify on
backup c:\ a: /s
if errorlevel 4 goto error4
if errorlevel 3 goto error3
:normal
echo Full backup complete.
echo Be sure to put today's date in BACKUP.BAT file.
goto exit
```

continued...

FIXED DISK APPLICATIONS

...from previous page

```
:error3
echo ^G
echo Backup not complete -- User abort
goto exit
:error4
echo ^G
echo Backup not complete -- Aborted due to error
goto exit
:exit
```

This batch file is quite simple. It turns VERIFY ON, so that DOS will check what it has written, and then uses the BACKUP command do a full disk backup. From there on, the rest of the file performs error-checking. BACKUP is one of the few DOS commands that returns an error code. Making a full disk backup is important enough that you should spend time being sure that everything works correctly. Notice that the IF ERRORLEVEL commands start with 4 and work down because the ERRORLEVEL command finds the errors with numbers equal to or greater than the specified number.

When this command is successfully completed, it reminds you to put the current date in the BACKDAY.BAT files. This is the date that the daily backups depend on, and this system doesn't work if you don't change the date in BACKDAY.BAT each time that you use BACK-ALL.BAT.

Daily Backups

The daily backup batch file is a little more complicated than the full backup batch file. It uses a small file to tell which set of backup disks should be used. This file is named one of two names that correspond to the two sets of disks.

Before you can use this system, you must create this small file. The contents of the file are not important; the key to its use in the BACK-DAY command is its name. To create the file, enter the following commands, pressing **Return** at the end of each line:

```
copy con \dos\bat\d2
File for BACKDAY.BAT
Don't erase me!
^Z              (Use the F6 key)
```

The screen will display the following:

```
1 File(s) copied
```

Following is the batch file that creates the BACKDAY.BAT command.

```
:! BACKDAY.BAT -- Daily backups
@echo off
if exist c:\dos\bat\d1 goto d1
echo Use Daily Backup Set #1
goto backup
:d1
echo Use Daily Backup Set #2
:backup
verify on
backup c:\ a: /s /d:6-17-86
if errorlevel 4 goto error4
if errorlevel 3 goto error3
if errorlevel 1 goto error1
:normal
echo Daily backup complete
if exist c:\dos\bat\d2 goto d2
ren c:\dos\bat\d1 d2
goto exit
:d2
ren c:\dos\bat\d2 d1
goto exit
:error1
echo ^G
echo No files found to back up
echo so check date in BACKUP.BAT file
goto exit
:error3
echo ^G
echo Backup not complete -- User abort
goto exit
```

continued...

FIXED DISK APPLICATIONS

373

...from previous page

```
:error4
echo ^G
echo Backup not complete -- Aborted due to error
goto exit
:exit
```

BACKDAY.BAT starts by looking for a file named D1 in the \DOS\BAT directory. The name of this file is used to determine which set of backup disks should be used. An appropriate message is displayed, and the backup is begun.

The key to proper execution of this system is the date entered on the line with the BACKUP command. This date must be the date of the last full backup.

If the backup is completed successfully, the name of the file is changed from D1 to D2, or vice versa. If BACKUP exits with an error, the appropriate message is displayed, and the file name is not changed.

DUPLICATING DISKETTES

Sometimes it's a bit of a trick to make a copy of a diskette on a computer with a fixed disk and only one diskette drive. You can always use the DISKCOPY command, but that copies the entire diskette, even if you only have a few files to copy, and it doesn't help the organization of the diskette like COPY does. The command DISKDUP makes a copy of a diskette by using the COPY command, and then uses the fixed disk to temporarily hold the files from the source diskette. The DISKDUP command requires no parameters; it uses drive A for both source and destination. Following is the batch file for the DISKDUP command.

```
:! DISKDUP.BAT -- Duplicates floppy disks using the fixed
disk
echo off
cls
echo Y >c:\yesresp
md c:\temp$$$
```

continued...

...from previous page

```
echo Diskette Duplicator
echo ^@                        (use the F7 key)
echo Insert the source diskette into drive A
pause
echo ^@
echo Copying files to fixed disk
copy a:\ c:\temp$$$ > nul
echo ^@
echo The target diskette will now be formatted.
if exist c:\temp$$$\command.com format a: /s
if not exist c:\temp$$$\command.com format a:
echo ^@
echo ^@
echo Copying files to diskette
copy c:\temp$$$ a: > nul
del c:\temp$$$ <c:\yesresp > nul
del c:\yesresp
rd c:\temp$$$
echo Duplication completed
```

This batch file creates a temporary directory on the fixed disk, copies all the diskette files to it, asks you to insert the target diskette, formats it, and then the files are copied to it. Finally, the temporary directory is removed.

This batch file will copy only files from the root directory of the diskette; any subdirectories will be ignored. DOS 3.2 users can overcome this shortcoming by using the XCOPY /S command instead of COPY.

This batch file has a few tricks in it. At the beginning, it creates a file called YESRESP that only contains the letter "Y." This letter is used near the end of the batch file as the response to the query from DEL when the temporary directory is erased.

If the source diskette has COMMAND.COM on it, the target diskette is formatted with the /S option to make it a system diskette. The IF EXIST and the IF NOT EXIST commands make this decision.

After all the files are copied to the target diskette, all the files in the temporary directory are erased using the YESRESP file to make DEL continue, and then YESRESP and the temporary directory are removed.

RETURNING TO A PREVIOUS DIRECTORY

Sometimes you must change directories for a few minutes and then return to the previous directory. Following is a pair of files that allow you to do just that. The first file, CDSAVE.BAT, not only changes directories using CD but remembers what directory you were in when it was called. When you are ready to return, use the CDBACK command to return to the first directory. The CDSAVE command uses the same parameters as the CD command.

Following is the batch file for the CDSAVE.BAT command.

```
:! CDSAVE.BAT -- Save a directory name for future return
@echo off
copy \dos\bat\cdsave.cmd \dos\bat\cdback.bat > nul
cd >> \dos\bat\cdback.bat
cd %1
```

The above batch file actually creates the CDBACK.BAT file, combining the CDSAVE.CMD file with the output of the CD command (which is the current directory). The CDSAVE.CMD command is created using the COPY CON shortcut as follows. Enter the following, pressing **Return** at the end of each line:

```
cd \dos\bat
copy con cdsave.cmd
cd ^Z            (Use the F6 key)
```

Be sure to put one space after the "cd" in the last line, and then press the **F6** key on the same line. Press **Return** to close the file.

The screen displays the following:

    1 File(s) copied

These two commands are useful in their own right, but they are especially useful in other batch files. Instead of putting CDSAVE in another batch file, put the two lines that do the work in the batch file. Then make CDBACK the last line of the batch file to return to the directory from which you started.

CHAPTER 13

USEFUL DOS APPLICATIONS

Most people think of DOS as a "necessary evil." You must have it to make the computer run, but it doesn't do anything constructive. In this chapter, you will learn how to use DOS to get some real work done. You will learn applications that use the power of DOS to help you with your work.

IMPORTANT: Because the batch files are longer in this chapter, they will be shown differently than in the previous chapters. Batch files in this chapter will be shown as they look in EDLIN (with line numbers). You can refer to the line numbers as the function of the batch files are described. Remember, however, that you should *not* type the line numbers when you are creating the batch files.

A TIME LOG

Anyone using a computer for business purposes at home is faced with keeping track of computer use for tax reasons. DOS has all the tools required to keep a time log for you. It just takes one batch file that creates a simple data file.

How to Use the Time Log

The name of the time log command is LOG. Using it is easy; when you start a project, just enter

```
log in Title of project ⏎
```

The current time and date and the project name that you enter are put into a temporary holding file. The project name can contain up to eight words.

When you are done working on that activity and want to record the quitting time, just enter

```
log out ⏎
```

The time and date are again saved, and the entire entry is moved to the permanent time log file named TIMELOG.DAT.

The LOG command has two other functions. To display the contents of the time log file, enter

`log display⏎`

A typical time log file might resemble the following:

```
Logged in to: Developing timelog.bat
Current date is Wed   5-28-1986
Current time is 19:21:53.64
Logged off
Current date is Wed   5-28-1986
Current time is 19:32:15.88

Logged in to: Testing timelog
Current date is Wed   5-28-1986
Current time is 19:32:29.33
Logged off
Current date is Wed   5-28-1986
Current time is 19:36:53.77
```

To print the contents of the time log file, enter

`log print⏎`

If you enter the LOG command with no parameters, it will display a message showing the correct usage as follows. Enter

`log⏎`

The screen displays the following:

```
LOG must be followed by IN, OUT, DISPLAY or PRINT
```

If you enter a parameter that LOG does not recognize, it will display a message to that effect. Enter

`log xx⏎`

and the screen will display the following:

    Label not found

Retype the command with one of the parameters that LOG recognizes, and it will work.

On a fixed disk, LOG.BAT keeps all its files in the \DOS\BAT directory. On a diskette system, the LOG.BAT file and the TIMELOG.TMP files are on the VDISK (drive C), and the TIMELOG.DAT file is on drive B.

The LOG program requires the use of two external DOS commands: FIND and MORE. Before you use this program, make sure that FIND.EXE and MORE.EXE are available to you. These two files should either be in the current directory of the default drive or in a directory named in the PATH command in your AUTOEXEC.BAT program.

The LOG.BAT File

LOG.BAT is the batch file that creates the LOG command. Use EDLIN to enter it. Remember that you do not type the numbers or the colons at the beginning of the lines; they are furnished by EDLIN. Since there are some differences in the way that files are called between diskette and fixed disk systems, both versions of the LOG.BAT file are shown.

This is the fixed-disk version of LOG.BAT. Put this file in the \DOS\BAT directory.

```
 1: :! LOG.BAT -- Tax log, fixed disk version
 2: @echo off
 3: if ""=="%1" goto prompt
 4: goto %1
 5: :prompt
 6: echo ^@                    (Use the F7 key)
 7: echo ^@
 8: echo LOG must be followed by IN, OUT, DISPLAY or PRINT
 9: goto end
10: :in
11: :on
12: echo Logged in to: %2 %3 %4 %5 %6 %7 %8 %9 >\dos\bat\timelog.tmp
13: date >>\dos\bat\timelog.tmp <\dos\bat\cr
14: time >>\dos\bat\timelog.tmp <\dos\bat\cr
15: echo Logged in to: %2 %3 %4 %5 %6 %7 %8 %9
16: goto end
17: :out
18: :off
19: echo Logged off >>\dos\bat\timelog.tmp
20: date >>\dos\bat\timelog.tmp <\dos\bat\cr
21: time >>\dos\bat\timelog.tmp <\dos\bat\cr
22: echo ^@ >>\dos\bat\timelog.tmp
23: type \dos\bat\timelog.tmp ¦ find /v "Enter new" >> \dos\bat\timelog.dat
24: echo Logged Off
25: goto end
26: :print
27: copy \dos\bat\timelog.dat prn
28: echo ^L >prn              (Use the Ctrl-L keys)
29: goto end
30: :display
31: more <\dos\bat\timelog.dat
32: :end
```

Next is the diskette version of LOG.BAT. Put this file on your startup diskette.

```
 1: :! LOG.BAT -- Tax log, diskette version
 2: @echo off
 3: if ""=="%1" goto prompt
 4: goto %1
 5: :prompt
 6: echo ^@                    (use the F7 key)
 7: echo ^@
 8: echo LOG must be followed by IN, OUT, DISPLAY or PRINT
 9: goto end
10: :in
11: :on
12: echo Logged in to: %2 %3 %4 %5 %6 %7 %8 %9 >c:timelog.tmp
13: date >>c:timelog.tmp <:cr
14: time >>c:timelog.tmp <:cr
15: echo Logged in to: %2 %3 %4 %5 %6 %7 %8 %9
16: goto end
17: :out
18: :off
19: echo Logged off >>c:timelog.tmp
20: date >>c:timelog.tmp <:cr
21: time >>c:timelog.tmp <:cr
22: echo ^@ >>c:timelog.tmp
23: type c:timelog.tmp | find /v "Enter new" >> b:timelog.dat
24: echo Logged Off
25: goto end
26: :print
27: copy b:timelog.dat prn
28: echo ^L >prn                (Use the Ctrl-L keys)
29: goto end
30: :display
31: more <b:timelog.dat
32: :end
```

How LOG.BAT Works

The LOG.BAT file contains some interesting tricks; the file will be covered one step at a time so that you can understand each of them. The first line is just a title and a reminder of what this command does. The second line turns ECHO off to keep the screen from getting cluttered (only DOS 3.3 users should include the @ sign).

Line 3 checks to make sure that there is at least one parameter on the entry line. If there is no parameter, the command goes to the "prompt" label at line 5. Lines 6 and 7 just print blank lines on the screen. At line 8, a message is displayed telling the user how to use the command. Line 9 then jumps to the end of the file.

If line 3 finds a parameter, it lets you drop through to line 4. Line 4 uses an easy way to branch to several locations in a batch file. The command line parameter is used as the label to which to branch; if the first parameter is "in," then the file branches to the label "in."

There is one drawback to this system of control. If you enter an incorrect parameter, the file doesn't know where to branch, and the **Label not found** message is displayed, which is not very helpful to someone trying to remember what the correct parameters are.

At lines 10 and 11, there are two labels in a row. You see the "in" label that you expect in line 10, and the label "on" follows it. The "on" label is used just to prevent an obvious error—entering "log on" instead of "log in." Both terms are commonly used, so one extra label has been added to catch this error. Labels don't waste much time in batch files, so it is all right to use a few extras here and there.

Line 12 actually starts the work of the batch file. The ECHO statement is redirected to the file TIMELOG.TMP, so the phrase "Logged in to:" and the activity name are written to this file. Since a single angle bracket (>) is used, the current contents of the file are destroyed, which prevents you from logging in to two projects at once.

Lines 13 and 14 write the time and the date to the TIMELOG.BAT file. Since double angle brackets (>>) are used, this information is added to the file. Notice that the TIME and DATE commands have their input redirected from the file CR. The CR file contains nothing but a carriage return, and you create it as follows. Enter

copy con cr⏎
⏎
^Z (Use the F6 key)⏎

The screen dispalys the following:

   1 File(s) copied

The CR file must be in the \DOS\BAT directory of a fixed disk and on the startup disk of a diskette system.

Line 15 displays a message on the screen, reporting the successful completion of the job, and line 16 sends you to the end of the file.

Lines 17 and 18 contain two labels, again to minimize errors. This section of the file takes over when you are done with your activity. Line 19 adds the phrase "Logged off" to the temporary file, and then lines 20 and 21 add the time and date. Again, the CR file is used to answer the query of the TIME and DATE commands. Finally, line 22 adds a blank line to the temporary file. This blank line puts a space between the entries in the permanent file when they are transferred there.

Line 23 transfers the information from the temporary file to the permanent file. The output of the TYPE command is piped to the FIND filter, which uses the /V option to find all the lines that *don't* contain the phrase "Enter new." ("Enter new ..." is in the second line down from the DATE and TIME commands.) The lines that pass through the filter are added to the permanent TIMELOG.DAT file.

Line 24 displays a message noting successful completion, and line 25 sends you to the end of the file.

Lines 26 through 29 are the print routine. Line 27 copies the permanent TIMELOG.DAT file to the printer, and then line 28 sends a form feed (Ctrl-L) to advance the paper to the start of the next page.

Lines 30 and 31 provide the display option. The MORE filter in line 31 displays the time log file one screen at a time.

For Diskette Users

On a diskette system, the following two lines must be inserted into your AUTOEXEC.BAT file on your startup diskette. Place these two lines just *before* the last line of the file.

```
copy cr c:
copy log.bat c:
```

A BATCH FILE DATA BASE

Obviously, dBASE III cannot be created with batch files, but this little data base batch file *will* keep a list of phone numbers and addresses and let you find them quickly. You can add names and addresses, find any particular name, find groups of names, or sort and list the entire directory.

How to Use The Phone List

The name of the phone list command is PHONE. Parameters that you add to the command line tell the PHONE command what to do. The simplest thing to do is to display the entire phone list. To display the entire list, just type the command without any parameters as follows. Enter

phone ⏎

A phone list might resemble the following:

PHONE DATA FILE

```
barb     818-555-3136   Barbara Wood
carl     818-555-6655   Carl Siechert
chris    818-555-3136   Chris Wood
eric     213-555-2034   Eric Wood
jim      818-555-8765   Jim Law
paula    213-555-1212   Paula Kausch
```

If you haven't created a phone list, you will get a message telling you how to create an empty phone list file. You can create an empty phone list file, or remove an existing phone list, by entering

phone erase⏎

This command creates an empty file. To add names to the phone list file, just type "phone" followed by the complete entry as follows:

phone_joe 805-555-3465 Joe Johnson 432 Maple St Anytown 90056⏎

The first part of the entry is the **keyword** (joe). The keyword is entered in lowercase so you don't have to worry about capitalization when you do a quick search. The phone number is next, followed by the full name and address. You can include up to nine words on the entry line, including the keyword and phone number. Anything beyond nine words will be ignored.

Now you can create a data base, add things to it, and list it. The PHONE command can do three more things. To see what else it can do, enter

phone help⏎

The screen displays the following:

```
To add to the file, type "phone", and then a 7 character
(max) keyword, followed by a phone number (000-000-0000),
and then a name or any other information that you want.
You can use up to 8 words after the phone number.

To see the whole file, just type "phone" alone.

To find an entry, type "phone keyword" where keyword is the
keyword, or any other part, of one of the entries.

To sort the phone.DAT file, type "phone SORT"

To erase the phone.DAT file, type "phone ERASE"

To see this again, type "phone HELP".
```

Just like expensive programs, PHONE provides on-screen help. As you can see, to view a particular entry, just type the command followed by the keyword as follows:

phone joe ↵

The screen displays the following:

```
---------- phone.dat
joe 805-555-3465 Joe Johnson
     432 Maple St Anytown 90056
```

Note that the name "joe" was not capitalized, like the entry. The word that you type must match exactly, including capitalization, for PHONE to find the entry.

Your search is not limited to keywords, however. PHONE looks through the entire data base for matches, so to find all entries in the 213 area code, you can just as easily enter the following:

phone 213- ⏎

The screen displays the following:

```
---------- phone.dat
eric      213-555-2034   Eric Wood
paula     213-555-1212   Paula Kausch
```

If you want your list organized, PHONE will sort it for you if you enter

phone sort ⏎
phone ⏎

The screen displays the following:

```
PHONE DATA FILE

barb      818-555-3136   Barbara Wood
carl      818-555-6655   Carl Siechert
chris     818-555-3136   Chris Wood
eric      213-555-2034   Eric Wood
jim       818-555-8765   Jim Law
joe       805-555-3465   Joe Johnson  432 Maple St Anytown 90056
paula     213-555-1212   Paula Kausch
```

PHONE sorts by the keyword, so the entries won't be sorted by last name unless you use the last name as the keyword.

PHONE keeps its data file, called PHONE.DAT, in the \DOS\BAT directory on a fixed disk. On a diskette system, the data file is on drive B, and the batch file itself is on the VDISK (drive C).

PHONE also has one other unique feature. If you want to keep more than one phone list, just make another copy of PHONE.BAT using another name, such as FRIENDS.BAT. PHONE will create another data file, using the same name and the .DAT extension. For example, enter

copy phone.bat phone2.bat ⏎

The PHONE2 command will create and use a data file called PHONE2.DAT. To use the first list, use the PHONE command. To use the second list, use the PHONE2 command. Notice that the file labels and help screens automatically use the correct file name.

The PHONE.BAT File

Two versions of the PHONE.BAT file are provided. The first is for use on a fixed disk, where PHONE.BAT and PHONE.DAT are both in the \DOS\BAT directory. The second version of the file is for use on a diskette system. PHONE.BAT is put on the VDISK (drive C), and the PHONE.DAT file is put on drive B.

The PHONE program requires the use of three external commands: FIND, MORE, and SORT. Before you use this program, make sure that FIND.EXE, MORE.EXE, and SORT.EXE are available to you. These three files should either be in the current directory of the default drive or in a directory named in the PATH command in your AUTOEXEC.BAT program.

On a diskette system, the following line must be added to your AUTOEXEC.BAT file on the startup diskette. Place this line just *before* the last line of the file:

copy phone.bat c:

Here is the fixed disk version of PHONE.BAT. Place this file in the \DOS\BAT directory.

```
 1: :! PHONE.BAT -- Batch file database, fixed disk version
 2: @echo off
 3: if erase==%1 goto killit
 4: if ERASE==%1 goto killit
 5: if help==%1 goto help
 6: if HELP==%1 goto help
 7: if sort==%1 goto sortit
 8: if SORT==%1 goto sortit
 9: if ""=="%1" goto showit
10: if ""=="%2" goto lookup
11: echo %1     %2      %3 %4 %5 %6 %7 %8 %9
    >>\dos\bat\%0.dat          (Use Tab key between %1, %2, %3)
12: goto end
13: :showit
14: cls
15: if not exist \dos\bat\%0.dat goto error
16: more <\dos\bat\%0.dat
17: echo ^@                    (Use the F7 key)
18: echo For help type "%0 HELP"
19: goto end
20: :lookup
21: find "%1" \dos\bat\%0.dat
22: goto end
23: :sortit
24: if exist \dos\bat\%0.bak del \dos\bat\%0.bak
25: rename \dos\bat\%0.dat %0.bak
26: sort <\dos\bat\%0.bak >\dos\bat\%0.dat
27: goto end
28: :killit
29: if not ""=="%2" goto end
30: if exist \dos\bat\%0.bak del \dos\bat\%0.bak
31: if exist \dos\bat\%0.dat rename \dos\bat\%0.dat %0.bak
32: echo >\dos\bat\%0.dat
33: echo >>\dos\bat\%0.dat
34: echo              %0 DATA FILE >>\dos\bat\%0.dat
35: echo >>\dos\bat\%0.dat
36: goto end
37: :help
38: cls
39: goto help1
40: :error
41: echo ^@
```

continued...

...from previous page

```
42: echo ^G The %0.DAT file is empty      (Use the Ctrl-G keys)
43: echo To initialize the file, type "%0 ERASE".
44: :help1
45: echo ^@
46: echo To add to the file, type "%0", then a 7 character
(max) keyword,
47: echo followed by a phone number (000-000-0000), and
then a name or any
48: echo other information that you want. You can use up to
8 words after
49: echo the phone number.
50: echo ^@
51: echo To see the whole file, just type "%0" alone.
52: echo ^@
53: echo To find an entry, type "%0 keyword" where keyword
is the
54: echo keyword, or any other part, of one of the entries.
55: echo ^@
56: echo To sort the %0.DAT file, type "%0 SORT"
57: echo ^@
58: echo To erase the %0.DAT file, type "%0 ERASE"
59: echo ^@
60: echo To see this again, type "%0 HELP".
61: :end
```

This is the diskette version of the PHONE.BAT file. Put this file on your startup diskette.

```
 1: :! PHONE.BAT -- Batch file database, diskette version
 2: @echo off
 3: if erase==%1 goto killit
 4: if ERASE==%1 goto killit
 5: if help==%1 goto help
 6: if HELP==%1 goto help
 7: if sort==%1 goto sortit
 8: if SORT==%1 goto sortit
 9: if ""==%1" goto showit
10: if ""==%2" goto lookup
11: echo %1     %2     %3 %4 %5 %6 %7 %8 %9 >>c:%0.dat
          (Use Tab key between %1, %2, %3)
12: goto end
13: :showit
```

continued...

...from previous page

```
14: cls
15: if not exist c:%0.dat goto error
16: more <c:%0.dat
17: echo ^@
18: echo For help type "%0 HELP"
19: goto end
20: :lookup
21: find "%1" c:%0.dat
22: goto end
23: :sortit
24: if exist c:%0.bak del c:%0.bak
25: rename c:%0.dat %0.bak
26: sort <c:%0.bak >c:%0.dat
27: goto end
28: :killit
29: if not ""=="%2" goto end
30: if exist c:%0.bak del c:%0.bak
31: if exist c:%0.dat rename c:%0.dat %0.bak
32: echo >c:%0.dat
33: echo >>c:%0.dat
34: echo                      %0 DATA FILE >>c:%0.dat
35: echo >>c:%0.dat
36: goto end
37: :help
38: cls
39: goto help1
40: :error
41: echo ^@                                (Use the F7 key)
42: echo ^L The %0.DAT file is empty      (Use the Ctrl-G keys)
43: echo To initialize the file, type "%0 ERASE".
44: :help1
45: echo ^@
46: echo To add to the file, type "%0", then a 7 character (max) keyword,
47: echo followed by a phone number (000-000-0000), and then a name or any
48: echo other information that you want. You can use up to 8 words after
49: echo the phone number.
50: echo ^@
51: echo To see the whole file, just type "%0" alone.
52: echo ^@
```

continued...

...from previous page

```
53: echo To find an entry, type "%0 keyword" where keyword is the
54: echo keyword, or any other part, of one of the entries.
55: echo ^@
56: echo To sort the %0.DAT file, type "%0 SORT"
57: echo ^@
58: echo To erase the %0.DAT file, type "%0 ERASE"
59: echo ^@
60: echo To see this again, type "%0 HELP".
61: :end
```

How PHONE.BAT Works

The first line of the file is a comment line, giving the name of the file and a brief description of what it does. The second line turns ECHO off to keep the screen from getting cluttered (if you are using a version of DOS earlier than 3.3, omit the @ sign).

Lines 3 through 8 control branches to the various routines, depending on the parameter entered. Note that all the keywords are given both in lowercase and uppercase so that the words can be typed either way on the command line.

If line 9 doesn't find any parameters on the command line, it branches to the "showit" label, which displays the entire file. Line 10 looks for a second parameter. If there is none, the file goes to the "lookup" label to look for an entry in the file.

If none of the lines above has directed the action somewhere else, then it must be a new entry, so line 11 writes the entry to the data file. There are tab characters between %1, %2, and %3 so that the fields all stay in alignment in the file. Notice the name of the file that you are writing to (%0). %0 is the name of the command that is currently being executed (it is the first entry on the command line, which is the name of the file on which you are working). Remember, you learned that if you rename this batch file, it will automatically create a new data file of the same name. If you refer to the file as %0, it will always be the same name as the batch file.

Adding a new record to the data base is easy; it only takes one line, so line 12 sends you to the end of the batch file.

Line 13 starts the "showit" routine. This routine starts by clearing the screen (line 14) and then checks if the file exists in line 15. If there is no file, you go to "error" and are told how to create a file.

Line 16 displays the file using the MORE filter so that it doesn't just scroll off the screen. Lines 17 and 18 provide a little reminder about the Help capabilities, and then line 19 sends you to the end of the program.

The "lookup" routine is in lines 20-22. The FIND filter does the whole job, looking for %1 (the first parameter) in the PHONE.DAT file (called %0.DAT in the batch file).

The SORT routine is called "sortit" and starts in line 23. The SORT filter can't have the same file for both source and destination, so you must create a second file for one or the other. In this case, creating a second file serves two purposes; it is used as a source for SORT, and it will provide a backup file for the data file. The file will have the extension .BAK, which is a standard extension for backup files.

Line 24 erases the current backup file, if one exists. Then, line 25 renames the PHONE.DAT file to PHONE.BAK. The SORT filter in line 26 sorts the contents of PHONE.BAK into PHONE.DAT, creating a new data file.

The "killit" routine in lines 28 to 36 is used to empty an old file or to create a new one. The same procedure is used as in the sort routine to rename the current file to a backup (.BAK) file. Note that the RENAME command in line 31 is only used if a data file already exists. You would receive an error message if you tried to rename a file that doesn't exist. Lines 32 through 35 write the file name and some blank lines into the new data file.

The rest of the batch file contains help and error messages. Note that throughout the Help messages, %0 is used as the file name. Even in an ECHO message, the %0 is replaced with the file name.

A SIMPLE NOTE FILER

How many times do you pick up a pencil and paper to jot down a quick note to yourself while you are working at your computer? This note filer will keep your short notes for you.

How to Use the Note Filer

The note filer automatically adds your notes to the NOTE.DAT file. Just type NOTE followed by the sentence that you want to add to the note file. You can type up to a line and a half. DOS will stop accepting characters and beep at you if you go too far. There are a few characters that you can't use in your notes. DOS will remove commas, semicolons, equal signs, and tabs, and you can't use the piping and redirection symbols. Following is an example of how NOTE works.

Enter

note This is a test of the note filer from the book by Siechert & Wood.⏎

You can get help with the note filer by typing NOTE alone, as follows:

note ⏎

The screen displays the following:

    NOTE keeps your notes in a file called NOTE.DAT

    NOTE followed by the notes that you want to save adds to the file.

    NOTE SHOW displays your notes

    NOTE PRINT prints your notes

    NOTE ERASE clears the note file.

The Help screen shows you the other commands. SHOW displays the notes on your screen. Enter

note show ⏎

The screen responds with the following:

```
This is a test of the note filer from
the book by Siechert & Wood.
```

As you can see, the note filer splits your lines into fairly short lines. The lines are a maximum of nine words long, and you'll see why when you learn how this batch file works.

You can print the entire note file by entering

note print ⏎

and you can erase the note file by entering

note erase ⏎

Like any good program, the note filer doesn't really delete the note file. It just renames it to NOTE.BAK so that if you erase it by mistake, you can just change the name back to recover it. Only the most recent file is kept, so don't make this mistake too frequently.

On a diskette system, you must add the following line to the AUTOEXEC.BAT file on your startup diskette:

copy note.bat c:

Make sure that the line comes before the STARTUP command in the file.

The NOTE program requires the use of an external DOS command: MORE. Before you use this program, make sure that MORE.EXE is available to you. This file should either be in the current directory of the default drive or in a directory named in the PATH command in your AUTOEXEC.BAT program.

The NOTE.BAT File

This batch file is the fixed disk version of the NOTE.BAT file. Place this file in the \DOS\BAT directory:

```
 1: :! NOTE.BAT -- For keeping quick notes, fixed disk version
 2: @echo off
 3: if ""=="%1" goto help
 4: if not ""=="%2" goto write
 5: if show==%1 goto show
 6: if SHOW==%1 goto show
 7: if print==%1 goto print
 8: if PRINT==%1 goto print
 9: if ERASE==%1 goto erase
10: if erase==%1 goto erase
11: :write
12: echo %1 %2 %3 %4 %5 %6 %7 %8 %9 >>\dos\bat\note.dat
13: shift
14: shift
15: shift
16: shift
17: shift
18: shift
19: shift
20: shift
21: shift
22: if not ""=="%1" goto write
23: goto end
24: :help
25: cls
26: echo ^@                    (Use the F7 key)
27: echo ^@
28: echo NOTE keeps your notes in a file called NOTE.DAT
29: echo ^@
30: echo NOTE followed by the notes that you want to save adds to the file.
31: echo ^@
32: echo NOTE SHOW displays your notes
33: echo ^@
34: echo NOTE PRINT prints your notes
35: echo ^@
36: echo NOTE ERASE clears the note file.
37: echo ^@
```

continued...

...from previous page

```
38: goto end
39: :show
40: more <\dos\bat\note.dat
41: goto end
42: :print
43: copy \dos\bat\note.dat prn >nul
44: echo ^L >prn              (Use the Ctrl-L keys)
45: goto end
46: :erase
47: if exist \dos\bat\note.bak del \dos\bat\note.bak
48: rename \dos\bat\note.dat note.bak
49: :end
```

This next batch file is the diskette version of NOTE.BAT. Place this file on your startup diskette:

```
 1: :! NOTE.BAT -- For keeping quick notes, diskette version
 2: @echo off
 3: if ""=="%1" goto help
 4: if not ""=="%2" goto write
 5: if show==%1 goto show
 6: if SHOW==%1 goto show
 7: if print==%1 goto print
 8: if PRINT==%1 goto print
 9: if ERASE==%1 goto erase
10: if erase==%1 goto erase
11: :write
12: echo %1 %2 %3 %4 %5 %6 %7 %8 %9 >>b:note.dat
13: shift
14: shift
15: shift
16: shift
17: shift
18: shift
19: shift
20: shift
21: shift
22: if not ""=="%1" goto write
23: goto end
24: :help
25: cls
26: echo ^@                    (Use the F7 key)
27: echo ^@
```

continued...

...from previous page

```
28: echo NOTE keeps your notes in a file called NOTE.DAT
29: echo ^@
30: echo NOTE followed by the notes that you want to save
adds to the file.
31: echo ^@
32: echo NOTE SHOW displays your notes
33: echo ^@
34: echo NOTE PRINT prints your notes
35: echo ^@
36: echo NOTE ERASE clears the note file.
37: echo ^@
38: goto end
39: :show
40: more <b:note.dat
41: goto end
42: :print
43: copy b:note.dat prn >nul
44: echo ^L >prn                    (Use the Ctrl-L keys)
45: goto end
46: :erase
47: if exist b:note.bak del b:note.bak
48: rename b:note.dat note.bak
49: :end
```

How NOTE.BAT Works

The NOTE.BAT file starts out with a comment line that gives the name and a description of its function. The second line turns ECHO off to keep the screen from becoming cluttered. Line 3 checks to see if you have entered any parameters on the command line. If there are no parameters, then you need help with the command, so you go to the "help" label.

Line 4 checks for a second parameter. If there are two parameters, then you are not entering one of the special commands, which allows you to start a note phrase with one of the keywords of the command. For example, if you enter the following:

note show the report to bill

the progam will go into the note file instead of displaying the NOTE.DAT file on the screen.

Lines 5 through 10 check for the three keywords, in both upper- and lowercase letters. If none of the commands are recognized, then the file proceeds to the "write" command.

Line 12 is the heart of this batch file. It writes the first nine parameters (words) to the file NOTE.BAT, which is why all your notes are split up into nine-word lines. DOS only has nine replaceable parameters.

Once the first nine words have been written, lines 13 through 21 shift the command line parameters nine times. Then, line 22 checks to see if there is still at least one parameter left. If there is one, you go back to "write" and do it again. Line 22 keeps sending you back to "write" until all the parameters (words) have been written to the file. When the work is all done, you go to "end."

The Help screen comes next in lines 24 through 38. This screen consists of a series of ECHO commands that display the help messages on the screen.

The "show" routine is in lines 39 to 41. The MORE filter is used to keep the notes from scrolling off the screen before you can read them.

The "print" routine is in lines 42 to 45. COPY sends the file to the printer. The output of the copy command is redirected to the NUL device so that you don't receive the message **1 File(s) copied.** After the file is printed, line 44 sends a form-feed character to the printer to advance the paper to the top of the next page.

Lines 46 through 48 make up the "erase" routine. The NOTE.DAT file isn't really erased; it is just renamed to NOTE.BAK. First, line 47 checks to see if there is already a NOTE.BAK file, and, if there is, it erases it. Then, line 48 renames the file NOTE.DAT to NOTE.BAK.

A PRINTER SETUP COMMAND

Changing the way your printer prints from DOS has always been a problem. Following is a command that solves that problem. This command will change your printer from Letter-Quality to Draft and back again in addition to performing eight other functions.

How to Use the PRINTER Command

The printer command is easy to use. Just follow the command name with the options that you want. For example, to print in letter-quality elite, you would enter

`printer lq elite`⏎

The supported options are as follows:

RESET   Clears Expanded (Wide), Condensed, Bold and Elite, thus returning the printer to normal Pica printing. It sets the left margin to zero. RESET does not affect LQ or Draft and does not set the top of form.

LQ   Selects Letter-Quality printing.

DRAFT   Selects Draft-style printing.

BOLD   Selects double-strike printing.

PICA   Selects 10 character-per-inch character pitch.

ELITE   Selects 12 character-per-inch character pitch.

COND   Selects condensed printing.

WIDE   Selects expanded printing.

FF (Form Feed)

      Advances the paper to the top of the next page.

LF (Line Feed)

      Advances the paper one line.

MARGIN   Sets a left margin of 8 character spaces.

You can use multiple options with this command, but enter them in the order in which they are shown here. The commands are sent to the printer in the order in which you enter them, and if you mix them up, the results may not be what you expect. For example, the PICA option clears WIDE and COND, so if you want Wide Pica characters, you must enter PICA WIDE to get them.

NOTE: The following batch file is set up for Epson printers. If you have a different brand of printer, you may have to change some of the printer commands.

The PRINTER.BAT File

Following is the PRINTER.BAT file. Use EDLIN to create this file. It has several characters that are hard to create in other editing programs. Press **Return** at the end of each line:

```
 1: :! PRINTER.BAT -- Sets printer modes
 2: @echo off
 3: if ""=="%1" goto help
 4: goto %1
 5: :reset
 6: rem Esc W 0 Ctrl-R Esc H Esc P Esc 1 ^@
 7: echo ^[W0^R^[H^[P^[1^@ >prn   (Esc = Ctrl-V[)
                                  (^R  = Ctrl-R)
                                  (^@  = F7 )
 8: goto end
 9: :bold
10: rem Esc G
11: echo ^[G >prn
12: goto end
13: :LQ
14: rem Esc x 1
15: echo ^[x1 >prn
16: goto end
17: :draft
18: rem Esc x 0
19: echo ^[x0 >prn
20: goto end
21: :pica
22: rem Esc P Ctrl-R Esc W 0    (^R = Ctrl-R keys)
23: echo ^[P^R^[W0 >prn
```

continued...

...from previous page

```
24: goto end
25: :elite
26: rem Esc M Ctrl-R Esc W 0
27: echo ^[M^R^[W0 >prn
28: goto end
29: :cond
30: rem Ctrl-O
31: echo ^O >prn              (Use the Ctrl-O keys)
32: goto end
33: :wide
34: rem Esc W 1
35: echo ^[W1 >prn
36: goto end
37: :ff
38: rem Ctrl-L
39: echo ^L >prn              (Use Ctrl-L keys)
40: goto end
41: :lf
42: rem Ctrl-@
43: echo ^@ >prn              (Use the F7 key)
44: goto end
45: :margin
46: rem Esc 1 Ctrl-H
47: echo ^[1^H >prn           (^H = Ctrl-V Shift-H)
48: goto end
49: :help
50: echo ^@
51: echo ^@
52: echo PRINTER offers the following options:
53: echo ^@
54: echo RESET, LQ, DRAFT, BOLD, PICA, ELITE,
55: echo COND, WIDE, FF, LF, and MARGIN.
56: echo ^@
57: echo You can use more than one option at a time,
58: echo if you enter them in the order shown above.
59: echo ^@
60: echo For example:
61: echo      PRINTER DRAFT BOLD PICA
62: :end
63: shift
64: if not ""=="%1" goto %1
```

How the PRINTER.BAT File Works

This batch file is very simple, but it has many of options, and the printer codes that it contains look confusing. Examine this file in two phases: how the batch file works, and what the printer control codes are.

The logic of the batch file is quite easy. Line 3 checks to see if there are no parameters. If there are none, then you need help, so that is where you are sent. Line 4 controls all the branching throughout the file. The line sends you to the label of the option that you entered (%1). Note that it even works if you enter "HELP."

Each option only takes four lines. The first line is the label, the second line is a comment line that shows what printer codes are being sent, and the third line is an ECHO command that is redirected to the printer to send the control codes. Finally, the fourth line sends you to "end."

Once the particular option is completed and you arrive at "end," line 49 shifts the parameters by one, and then line 50 checks to see if there are any more options. If there are more options, then that is where you go; otherwise, you exit.

Now examine the printer commands. The commands in this file are for Epson printers, but they will work with many Epson-compatible printers. The comment lines in each option show you the codes that have been included for the option. Note that some options send more than one command to the printer. For example, the PICA option not only sets Pica width but clears Expanded and Condensed print as well. If you need to change any of the commands, look in your printer manual to find the correct codes. Remember the tricks of using EDLIN for entering control codes.

TURNING YOUR PRINTER INTO A COPIER

This command, called MPRINT for Multi-Print, can produce up to 20 copies of a file on your printer. You may even be able to save yourself a trip to a copy store.

How to Use MPRINT

To use MPRINT, follow the command name with the number of copies you want and the name of the file you want to print. For example, to print eight copies of the file NWSLTR.DOC, you would enter

```
mprint 8 nwsltr.doc⏎
```

The screen displays the following:

```
    8 copies of file nwsltr.doc printed.
```

If you enter less than two parameters, the MPRINT command will give you some help, such as the following. Enter

```
mprint⏎
```

The screen displays the following:

```
    To print multiple copies of a file, enter
        MPRINT followed by the quantity and then the filename.

    For example:
        MPRINT 14 TEXT.FIL

    will print 14 copies of the file TEXT.FIL.

    You can make up to 20 copies.
```

The MPRINT.BAT File

Following is the MPRINT.BAT file. It is fairly long, but a quick inspection will show you how simple it really is.

```
1: :! MPRINT.BAT -- Print multiple copies of a file
2: @echo off
3: if exist %2 goto %1
4: echo ^@
```

continued...

...from previous page

```
 5: echo ^@
 6: echo To print multiple copies of a file, enter
 7: echo MPRINT followed by the quantity and then the
filename.
 8: echo ^@
 9: echo For example:
10: echo         MPRINT 14 TEXT.FIL
11: echo ^@
12: echo will print 14 copies of the file TEXT.FIL.
13: echo ^@
14: echo You can make up to 20 copies.
15: goto end
16: :20
17: copy %2 prn >nul
18: :19
19: copy %2 prn >nul
20: :18
21: copy %2 prn >nul
22: :17
23: copy %2 prn >nul
24: :16
25: copy %2 prn >nul
26: :15
27: copy %2 prn >nul
28: :14
29: copy %2 prn >nul
30: :13
31: copy %2 prn >nul
32: :12
33: copy %2 prn >nul
34: :11
35: copy %2 prn >nul
36: :10
37: copy %2 prn >nul
38: :9
39: copy %2 prn >nul
40: :8
41: copy %2 prn >nul
42: :7
43: copy %2 prn >nul
44: :6
45: copy %2 prn >nul
46: :5
```

continued...

...from previous page

```
47: copy %2 prn >nul
48: :4
49: copy %2 prn >nul
50: :3
51: copy %2 prn >nul
52: :2
53: copy %2 prn >nul
54: :1
55: copy %2 prn >nul
56: echo %1 copies of file %2 printed.
57: :end
```

How the MPRINT.BAT File Works

This batch file starts by making sure that there are two parameters. If there are two parameters, then the first parameter is used as a label to branch to; otherwise, the Help screen is displayed. All the options to this command are the same; they each print the file one time. The second parameter is used as the file name. Since none of the options ends in a GOTO command, all the options that are below the one that was entered are also executed, which is why the options are in descending order. If you enter 14 for the first parameter, then you branch to option 14, and it prints the file once. Then, option 13 prints the file again, and so on through option 1.

Finally, line 56 reports how many copies have been made.

CHAPTER 14

DOS UTILITIES

Utilities are often thought of as commands that don't really do anything constructive; they just make life easier. In this chapter, you will learn about some useful utilities that display sorted directories, automatically delete backup files, and provide a wild card capability to the TYPE command. You will also learn a few tricks to help take some of the worry out of using your computer. You will be shown how to prevent accidental formatting of your fixed disk and how to "hide" files that you don't want other people to see.

THE SORTED DIRECTORY COMMAND

The DIR command provided by DOS is quite flexible, but there is one useful function that it won't perform—sorting the directory before it is displayed. The command presented here, called DIRSORT, will sort your directory four different ways.

The DIRSORT command can sort your directory by name, extension, size, and date. The keywords for each of these options are as follows:

NAME   Sorts by file name.
EXT   Sorts by file name extension.
SIZE   Sorts by file size.
DATE   Sorts by the date the file was created or changed.

To use the DIRSORT command, follow the command name by the keyword for the sort that you want. You can also add a directory name or file specification, just as you would with the DIR command.

For example, to display a directory listing of the root directory sorted by the file name extension, enter

`dirsort ext \`⏎

The screen will display a directory similar to the following:

```
\ DIRECTORY SORTED BY ext

AUTOEXEC  BAT      205     4-29-86    3:49p
STARTUP   CMD      147     4-23-86    5:13p
MORE      COM      295    12-30-85   12:00p
GRAFTABL  COM     1169    12-30-85   12:00p
GRAPHICS  COM     3220    12-30-85   12:00p
MODE      COM     6864    12-30-85   12:00p
EDLIN     COM     7508    12-30-85   12:00p
COMMAND   COM    23791    12-30-85   12:00p
SK        COM    39117     4-23-86    4:53p
SORT      EXE     1911    12-30-85   12:00p
FIND      EXE     6416    12-30-85   12:00p
SK        HLP    53632     5-03-85    2:09p
CONFIG    SYS       68     4-26-86    1:25p
ANSI      SYS     1651    12-30-85   12:00p
VDISK     SYS     3307    12-30-85   12:00p
```

The DIRSORT.BAT File

This batch file displays sorted directories. The file uses three external DOS commands: FIND, MORE, and SORT. When you use DIRSORT, the FIND.EXE, MORE.EXE, and SORT.EXE programs must be available to you. They must be in the current directory of the default drive or in a directory specified in the PATH statement of your AUTOEXEC.BAT file. Following is the DIRSORT.BAT file:

```
 1: :! DIRSORT.BAT -- Displays sorted directory
 2: @echo off
 3: cls
 4: echo ^@
 5: echo ^@
 6: echo              %2 DIRECTORY SORTED BY: %1
 7: if name==%1 goto name
 8: if NAME==%1 goto NAME
 9: if ext==%1 goto ext
10: if EXT==%1 goto EXT
11: if size==%1 goto size
12: if SIZE==%1 goto SIZE
13: if date==%1 goto date
```

continued...

...from previous page

```
14: if DATE==%1 goto DATE
15: :help
16: echo ^@
17: echo DIRSORT must be followed by NAME, EXT, SIZE, or DATE
18: echo which can optionally be followed by a path and/or filespec.
19: goto end
20: :name
21: dir %2 ¦ find /v "bytes" ¦ sort ¦ more
22: goto end
23: :ext
24: dir %2 ¦ find /v "e" ¦ sort /+10 ¦ more
25: goto end
26: :size
27: dir %2 ¦ find /v "e" ¦ find /v "<DIR>" ¦ sort /+16 ¦ more
28: goto end
29: :date
30: dir %2 ¦ find /v "e" ¦ find /v "." ¦ sort /+25 ¦ more
31: :end
```

How DIRSORT.BAT Works

The DIRSORT batch file starts off by clearing the screen and displaying a message telling you what kind of a directory you are going to see. Then, in lines 7 through 14, the keyword is checked and you proceed to the proper routine. If the keyword isn't recognized, you end up in the "help" routine (lines 15 through 19), which displays a reminder of how to use DIRSORT.

Next come the routines for the different types of sorts. All of these routines are the same except for two areas. The first difference is the number after the SORT filter that determines the first column that the SORT filter looks at.

The second difference is in the FIND filters used. A normal directory includes several lines of information that are not file names. If you sort a complete directory listing, these lines become mixed into the middle of the directory. The FIND filter is used to remove the lines that become mixed up in the display. The /V option to the FIND filter receives everything except lines containing the strings specified, so lines with the letter "e" in them are eliminated in several of the routines. The file names in the directory listing are all in uppercase letters, so this action won't remove any file names.

The output of the DIR command is piped through one or two FIND filters and then through the SORT filter. Finally, the output is displayed by the MORE filter so it doesn't scroll off your screen.

AUTOMATICALLY DELETING BACKUP FILES

Many programs create backup files with a .BAK extension, allowing you to recover the last version of the file in case you make a serious error. These files tend to accumulate on your disk, however, and once you are sure that you no longer need the previous version, they aren't of much use. The next command, called DELBAK, will help you remove these .BAK files.

How to Use DELBAK

The DELBAK command will delete the backup files from all the directories that you request. Enter the command name followed by one or more directory names (you can enter as many as nine directories). DELBAK will show you what files will be deleted, and, if you approve, it will then delete them. If you enter DELBAK with no parameters, it will display a reminder of the proper usage.

To delete the files with the .BAK extension from the \PROJECT1\TEXT and the \PROJECT1\WKSHT directories, enter

```
delbak \project1\text \project1\wksht
```

The screen responds with the following:

    Processing, please wait

    The following files will be deleted:

```
   Directory of   A:\PROJECT1\TEXT

  CHAP2    BAK        16   6-06-86   3:02p
  CHAP5    BAK        16   6-06-86   3:02p
  CHAP7    BAK        16   6-06-86   3:02p

   Directory of   A:\PROJECT1\WKSHT

  CHAP1    BAK        16   6-06-86   3:02p
  CHAP4    BAK        16   6-06-86   3:02p
  CHAP6    BAK        16   6-06-86   3:02p
  CHAP8    BAK        16   6-06-86   3:02p
```

    Press Ctrl-Break if you want to keep any of these files, otherwise
    Strike a key when ready . . .

To delete the backup files in the current directory, just use a period (.) for the directory name. DOS uses the period as the name of the current directory.

The DELBAK.BAT File

This batch file creates the DELBAK command. It uses two external DOS commands: FIND and MORE. When you use DELBAK, the FIND.EXE and MORE.EXE programs must be available to you. They must be in the current directory of the default drive or in a directory specified in the PATH statement of your AUTOEXEC.BAT file. Following is the DEKBAK.BAT file.

```
1:  :! DELBAK.BAT -- Deletes .BAK files
2:  @echo off
3:  if ""=="%1" goto error
4:  cls
5:  echo Processing, please wait
6:  echo The following files will be deleted: >temp$$.dat
```
   continued...

...from previous page

```
 7: for %%a in (%1 %2 %3 %4 %5 %6 %7 %8 %9) do dir %%a\*.bak >>temp$$.dat
 8: echo ^@ >>temp$$.dat          (Use the F7 key)
 9: echo Press Ctrl-Break if you want to keep any of these files, otherwise >>temp$$.dat
10: type temp$$.dat | find /v "Volume" | find /v "File" | more
11: del temp$$.dat
12: pause
13: for %%a in (%1 %2 %3 %4 %5 %6 %7 %8 %9) do del %%a\*.bak
14: goto end
15: :error
16: echo ^G                       (Use the Ctrl-G keys)
17: echo DELBAK must be followed by one or more directory names.
18: :end
```

How DELBAK.BAT Works

The first two lines identify the file and turn ECHO off. The third line checks to see that you have entered at least one parameter on the command line. If there are no parameters, a short help message is displayed by the "help" routine in lines 16 and 17; otherwise, the screen is cleared in line 4, and a message is displayed by line 5, informing you that something is happening. The **Processing, please wait** message is displayed because lines 6 through 10 can take a while to work if you are deleting files from a number of directories.

Lines 6 through 9 create a file called TEMP$$.DAT containing a list of all the files that are going to be deleted, a message at the beginning, and another message at the end. The messages are put in this file because the timing of the display looks better than if you just use ECHO commands. They are also under the control of the MORE filter when they are in the file, so they don't scroll off the screen before you can read them.

After using the FIND filter twice to remove some extraneous lines from the list, line 10 displays the list of files to be deleted. The MORE filter prevents the list from scrolling off the screen too quickly. When the entire file has been viewed, line 11 deletes the temporary file.

The PAUSE in line 12 gives you a chance to save these files. Finally, line 13 actually deletes the backup files. The rest of the file is the Help routine.

ADDING WILD CARD CAPABILITIES TO TYPE

The TYPE command provides a quick way to look at a file, but it has one limitation—it won't accept wild cards. The TYP command presented here overcomes that problem and allows you to display multiple files with one command.

Using the TYP Command

The TYP command is used just like the TYPE command. Just follow the file name with the filespec of the file or files that you want to see. The TYP command uses the MORE filter so the files won't scroll off your screen before you can read them.

To display all the files that have a .BAT extension in the current directory, enter

typ *.BAT ⏎

The screen displays the following:

    Filename:MOVE.BAT

    Ctrl-Break to skip, or
    Strike a key when ready . . .

The TYP command pauses before it displays each file and waits for you to press a key. You can press **Ctrl-Break** to skip to the next file.

The TYP.BAT and TY.BAT Files

The TYP command consists of two files. Both are necessary for it to operate. In addition, MORE.EXE must be in the current directory of the default drive or in a directory named in the PATH command of your AUTOEXEC.BAT file. Following are the TYP.BAT and TY.BAT files.

```
1: :! TYP.BAT -- TYPE command with wildcards
2: @echo off
3: for %%f in (%1) do \command /c ty %%f
```

```
1: :! TY.BAT -- This does the work for TYP.BAT
2: echo off
3: echo ^@
4: echo           Filename: %1
5: echo ^@
6: echo Ctrl-Break to skip, or
7: pause
8: more <%1
```

One line does all the hard work in the TYP.BAT file. Line 3 uses the COMMAND command to call the TY command for each file that is to be displayed.

The TY command is only slightly longer. Everything down to line 7 provides you with messages about what's happening. Then, line 8 actually displays the file, using the MORE filter.

Two files are required because of a limitation of the MORE filter, which presents a problem: if you use the name of a batch file as a command in another batch file, control will pass to the called batch file but won't return to the calling batch file. Further commands in the calling batch file are ignored.

The way around this limitation is to use the COMMAND command, which can execute a batch file and then return to the calling batch file. The FOR command in TYP.BAT executes the COMMAND command, which in turn executes the TY command for each file that you want displayed.

NOTE: The COMMAND command was not documented by IBM before DOS version 3, but it does work in version 2; however, COMMAND.COM must be in a directory named in the PATH command of your AUTOEXEC.BAT file in version 2; you can't just put the backslash in front of it as previously shown.

PREVENTING ACCIDENTAL FORMATTING

Accidentally formatting your fixed disk can be a major tragedy. Before DOS version 3, there wasn't much to prevent inexperienced users from accidentally formatting the fixed disk. FORMAT would just start to work on the default drive, which is usually the fixed disk.

The solution to this problem is simple. Rename the FORMAT command to XFORMAT.COM, and create a small batch file that supplies drive A as the default. Enter

```
cd \dos

ren format.com xformat.com

copy con format.bat
xformat a: %1 %2
^Z                        (Use the F6 key)
```

Now when you use FORMAT, it will automatically work on drive A. You can still use the options with FORMAT, but you don't need to enter a drive designator.

If you ever need to format a disk in a different drive, you can still use the original FORMAT command by calling it XFORMAT.

A LOW-COST SECURITY SYSTEM

If several people are using your computer, you may have some files that you would rather not share with other users. The following trick will prevent most people from seeing or using your files.

The whole basis of this security system is to create a directory name that no one else can enter. The method is simple—just use a character that can't be seen on the end of the directory name of your directory. Then, when people type what looks like the name of your directory, DOS refuses to accept it as a valid directory name.

This trick is easier to do than it is to explain. Start to create a directory as shown below, but stop before you press **Return**:

md test

Now, hold down the **Alt** key and press the digits 2, 5, and 5 on the numeric keypad. Release the **Alt** key and press **Return**.

You have just created a secret directory. Try to change to it by typing

cd test ⏎

The screen responds with the following:

    Invalid directory

What good is a secret directory if you can't access it? Actually, you can access it, but no one else will be able figure it out (very easily).

Start to change to the directory again, but stop before you press **Return**. Enter

cd test

Now, as before, hold the **Alt** key while you press the keys 2, 5, and 5 on the numeric keypad. Press **Return**. You are now in the "secret" directory.

The trick to this security system is that you are simply adding a special space character to the end of the file name. No one can see it, but *you* know it is there. Whenever you refer to the directory (including when it is specified as part of the path to a file), you must add the special space to the directory name by using the **Alt** key and the numeric keypad.

NOTE: Don't count on this method for absolute security. There are any number of ways to defeat this system (including reading this book). It is just intended to keep busybodies out of your files.

USING A SERIAL PRINTER

The IBM PC expects the printer to be connected to the parallel port; however, many people don't live up to their computer's expectations and have serial printers. If you have a serial printer, the following section shows you how to use it with a minimum of difficulty.

Even though DOS expects the printer to be connected to the parallel port, it is easy to tell DOS that the printer is actually connected to a serial port. From then on, DOS behaves nicely and sends everything to the proper place.

All you must do is add two lines to your AUTOEXEC.BAT file. Diskette users should make sure to add it to the file on the startup diskette. Following are the two lines:

```
mode com1:1200,N,8,2,P
mode lpt1:=com1:
```

These lines set the asynchronous communications port up for 1200 baud, 8 data bits with no parity, and 2 stop bits. This configuration is very common for serial printers, but you should check your printer manual to be sure that it is right for your printer.

If, by chance, you have both serial and parallel printers, you can stop sending the printer output to the serial port with the following command line:

```
mode lpt1:
```

You can put this command in a batch file called PARALLEL.BAT and put the two previous commands in a file called SERIAL.BAT so you can switch back and forth.

MODE is an external DOS command, so MODE.COM must be in the current directory or in a directory named in a PATH command before you can use it.

USING PROGRAMS THAT DON'T UNDERSTAND PATHS

Some old programs still don't understand the paths and transferred tree-structured directories introduced with DOS version 2. Most notable among these programs is WordStar, although WordStar Version 4, released in 1987, corrects this shortcoming. These programs have a difficult time working on a hard disk; they are generally designed for the program to be on one disk and data files on another disk. If you have one fixed disk and one diskette drive, this design presents a problem.

Since these programs don't recognize directories, you have several choices. You can place a copy of the program in every directory that contains files for which you need the program. You can put the program on a diskette in drive A. Or you can use one of the following solutions that use the power of the more recent DOS versions.

If you have DOS version 3, you can use the SUBST command to create an "imaginary" diskette for the program. Change to the directory that contains the files you want to use, and then enter the following commands:

```
subst b: c:\wp
b:ws
```

You have started WordStar on what the program thinks is drive B so that you can use the files that are on drive C. WordStar doesn't understand that you are actually in a subdirectory, but DOS will take care of you.

You can put these commands in your WP.BAT file so they are carried out automatically when you start your word processor. Add the following four lines to the WP.BAT file.

```
subst b: c:\wp
b:
ws
subst b: /d
```

The last line removes the substitution when you are done with it. When you start WordStar, at the first menu, you can "log in" to drive C.

Using Old Programs with DOS Version 2

If you don't have version 3 of DOS, you can't use the SUBST command, but you can set up a virtual disk like VDISK (there are many available, including the source listing of one in the DOS 2.0 manual). Place the three required WordStar files on the virtual disk (the files are WS.COM, WSOVLY1.OVR, and WSMSGS.OVR) and use them there. For example, if your virtual disk is drive D, you could add the following lines to your WP.BAT file just before the MENU command:

```
copy \wp\ws*.* d:
d:
ws
c:
```

Make sure that your WP.BAT file assigns you to the directory that contains the files on which you want to work. Once you start WordStar, you must "log in" to drive C to access your files.

INDEX

* wild card character 61
.. (two periods) 35
/ (slash character) 56
< redirection character 43
> redirection character 43
>> redirection character 43
? wild card character 61
[] (square brackets) 56
\ (backslash character) 29, 35
| piping character 48

A

ANSI.SYS 292, 331, 355, 357
APPEND command 72
Appending files 44
Archive file 78
ASCII codes 311
ASSIGN command 76
Asterisk 61
Asynchronous 20
Asynchronous adaptor 179, 181
ATTRIB 78
AUTOEXEC.BAT 37, 261, 303, 330, 337, 352, 420
AUX 20

B

BACKALL.BAT 370
BACKDAY.BAT 370
Backing up files 370
Backspace key 58
BACKUP command 79, 82
Backup files 216
    deleting 413
Bad sector 207
BAT file extension 258
Batch commands 258
Batch file subcommands 261
Brackets ([]), square 56
BREAK command 90, 289
BUFFERS command 290, 355

C

CALL command 266
CD command 34, 92
CDBACK.BAT 376
CDSAVE.BAT 376
Change directory 34, 92
Changing the default drive 21
CHDIR command 34, 92
CHDSK command 16
Check disk 16, 97
CHKDSK command 97
Clear screen 104
CLS command 104
Codes, exit 57, 85, 160, 212, 218
Color/graphics adaptor 184
COM1 20
COM2 20
COM3 20
COM4 20
Combining files 114
COMMAND command 105
Command format 54
Command processor 105
    environment 226
Command, APPEND 72
   ASSIGN 76
   ATTRIB 78
   BACKUP 79, 82
   batch 258
   Batch file 261
   BREAK 90, 289
   BUFFERS 290
   CALL 266
   CD 34, 92
   CHDIR 92
   CHDSK 16
   CHKDSK 97
   CLS 104
   COMMAND 105
   COMP 45, 110
   COPY 114
   CTTY 119
   DATE 121
   DEL 123

DEVICE 291
DIR 26, 34, 127
DISKCOMP 130
DISKCOPY 138
ECHO 264, 268
entering 58
ERASE 146
external 54
FASTOPEN 147
FCBS 300
FDISK 344
FILES 301
FIND 149
FOR 271
FORMAT 15, 154
format of 55
GOTO 273
GRAFTBL 167
GRAPHICS 169
IF 275
internal 54
JOIN 171
LABEL 173
LASTDRIVE 302
MD 176
MKDIR 176
MODE 179, 181, 184, 187
MORE 48, 190
PATH 36, 55, 192
PAUSE 281
PRINT 195
PROMPT 202
RECOVER 207
REM 283
RENAME 209
REPLACE 211
RESTORE 216
RMDIR 224
SET 226
SHARE 228
SHELL 303
SHIFT 285
SORT 230
SUBST 235

    SYS 238
    TIME 241
    TREE 37, 48, 243
    TYPE 245
    VER 247
    VERIFY 248
    VOL 250
    XCOPY 79, 251
COMMAND.COM 238, 265
COMP command 45, 110
Comparing diskettes 130
Comparing files 110
COMSPEC 265
CON 20
Concatenate 114
CONFIG.SYS 288, 330, 355
Connecting directories 171
Console 119
Control codes 311, 364
COPY command 114, 365
COPY con 357
Copying directories 251
Copying disks 138, 374
Copying files 114, 251
Creating directories 32
Creating subdirectories 176
Ctrl-Break keys 90, 289
CTTY command 119
Current directory 34

D

Damaged directory 207
Data base 385
Data disks 340
Data, protecting 341
DATE command 121
DB.BAT 359
Default drive 21, 34
DEL command 123
DELBAK.BAT 414
Delete files command 123
Delete key 60
Device 19
DEVICE command 291

Device drivers 291
    ANSI.SYS 292
    DRIVER.SYS 296
    VDISK.SYS 294
DIR 34
DIR command 26, 127
DIRALL.BAT 366
Directories 350
    copying 251
    moving files 365
Directory 26
    changing 34, 92
    connecting between drives 171
    creating 32
    damaged 207
    entries 28
    errors 97
    files 127
    management 26
    of entire disk 366
    parent 35
    removing 38, 224
    root 27
    search path 192
    sorted 410
    structure 37, 351
    subdirectories 27, 176
    tree 243
    tree-structured 26
DIRSORT.BAT 411
Disk buffers 290
Disk drives, checking 97
    connecting directories 171
    default 21, 34
    double-sided 15
    fixed 20
    high-capacity 15
    single-sided 15
Disk operating system 4
Disk, capacity 13
Disk, virtual 294
DISKCOMP command 130
DISKCOPY command 138
DISKDUP.BAT 374

Diskette drive 20
Diskette drive, external 296
Diskette system 328
Diskettes 12
    comparisons 130
    copying 138, 374
    erasing 154
    formatting 154
Disks, labeling 173
Display options 184
Display screen 42
Displaying directory structures 37
    files 245
    text 312
DOS 4
    editing keys 58
    loading on fixed disk 348
    start 34
    transferring 238
    version number 247
Double-sided drive 15
Drive letter 302
DRIVER.SYS 296
Duplicating diskettes 374

E

ECHO command 264, 268
Editing text 315
Editing, DOS keys 58
EDLIN Editor 308
    displaying text 312
    editing text 315
    search and replace 318
    commands 309
Entering commands 58
Environment 105, 226, 265, 303
ERASE command 146, 154
Erasure 18
Error messages 57, 62
Error, standard 47
ERRORLEVEL 57, 275
Escape key 58
EXIST 275, 277
Exit codes 57, 85, 160, 212, 218

Extended memory 294
Extension, file name 22
External command 54
External diskette drive 296

F

FASTOPEN command 147
FCBS command 300
FDISK command 344
File allocation table 97
    control blocks 300
    handles 301
    name 22
    sharing 228
    specification 56
    specifications, wild cards 60
    structure 350
FILES command 301, 355
Files, backup 216
    combining 114
    comparisons 110
    concatenating 114
    copy 114
    copying 251
    deleting 123
    directory 127
    naming 22, 209
    organizing 341
    printing 195
    recovering 207
    replacing on disk 211
    restoring 216
    sorting 230
    text search 149
Filespec 56
Filter 48
    FIND 149
    MORE 190
    SORT 230
FIND command 48, 149

Fixed disk 20
    backing up 370
    erasing 154
    formatting 154, 346
    labeling 173
    loading DOS 348
    locating files 368
    new 344
    partition 344
FOR command 271
Format 12, 18
FORMAT command 15, 55, 154
FORMAT.BAT 418
Formatting disks 154
Formatting fixed disk 346

G

GOTO command 273
GRAFTBL command 167
Graphics characters 167
GRAPHICS command 169

H

High-capacity drive 15

I

IF command 275
Initializing, disks 154
Input, redirection 43, 45
    standard 42
Insert key 60
Internal command 54
Italic 55

J

JOIN command 171

K

KB 14
Keyboard 42
Kilobyte 14

L

LABEL command 173
Label, disk 173, 250
LASTDRIVE command 302
Line editor 308
LOCATE.BAT 369
Locating files 368
LOG.BAT 380
LPT1 20
LPT2 20
LPT3 20

M

Make directory 32
MAKEDIR.BAT 360
Managing directories 26
MB (megabyte) 14
MD command 32, 176
Megabyte 14
Memory-resident programs 330
Menu system 356
MENU.BAT 357
Messages 57, 62
Meta-string 202
MKDIR command 32, 176, 360
MODE command 179, 181, 184, 187
Monitor, switching 184
Monochrome display 184
MORE command 190, 48
MOVE.BAT 365
Moving files 365
MPRINT.BAT 405
MS-DOS 5

N

Naming files 22, 209
New project 360
NOT 275, 280
Note files 395
NOTE.BAT 397
NUL 20

O

One-drive systems 21
Options 56
Organizing files 341
Output, redirection 43, 179
    standard 42

P

Parallel 187
Parallel printer 20
Parameter, replaceable 265, 285
Parent directory 35
Partition, fixed disk 344
Path 35
PATH command 36, 55, 192, 332, 353
Path, search 36
    specifications 56
    substitute drive 235
PAUSE command 281
PC-DOS 5
Phone directory 385
PHONE.BAT 385, 389
Piping 48
Preparing disks 18
Preventing erasure 18
PRINT command 195
Printer 404, 20
    graphics 169
    options 187
    sending files 195
    serial 420
    setup 400
PRINTER.BAT 402
PRN 20
Program disk 335
Project, new 360
Prompt 8, 58, 202
PROMPT command 202, 332, 354
Protecting data 341
Protocol, communications 181

Q

Question mark (?) 61

R

RD 38
Re-boot 8
Read-only 78
RECOVER command 207
Redirecting input 45
    output 179
        Redirection 42
REM command 283
Remarks 283
Removing directories 38, 224
RENAME command 209
REPLACE command 211
Replaceable parameter 265, 285
RESTORE command 216
RMDIR command 38, 224
Root directories 27

S

Search and replace 318
Search path 36
Searching text 149
Security system 418
Serial 20, 179, 181
Serial printer 420
SET command 226
Setting printer options 187
SHARE command 228
SHELL command 303
SHIFT command 285
SideKick 330, 354
Single-drive systems 21
Single-sided drive 15
Slash 56
SORT command 48, 230
SORTED.DIR 368
Sorting files 230
Spooling, to printer 195
Square brackets ([]) 56
SS.BAT 358
Standard error 47
    input 42
        output 42

Start DOS 34
START.BAT 337, 339
    startup disk 328, 330
STARTUP.BAT 332
Subdirectories 27
    creating 176
SUBST command 235
Substitute drive for path 235
Switches 56
Switching modes 184
Syntax 55
SYS command 238
System date 121
System environment 226

T

TIME command 241
Time log 378
TIMELOG.DAT 380
Transferring operating system 238
TREE command 48, 37, 243
Tree-structured directories 26
TY.BAT 417
TYP.BAT 417
TYPE command 245

V

Variables 55, 56
VDISK.SYS 294, 331, 355, 422
VER command 247
VERIFY command 248
Version of DOS 54, 247
Virtual disk 294
VOL command 250
Volume label 173, 250

W

Wild card characters 60
WP.BAT 358
Write-protect notch 18

X

XCOPY command 79, 251

RELATED TITLES FROM MIS:PRESS

Hard Disk Software Management

A clear and concise explanation of how to utilize popular software applications packages on a hard disk. Includes detailed techniques of mastering DOS, installing the programs, writing the menus, managing the memory, finding the files you need and, as an added bonus, integrating the packages into a powerful management tool.

Emily Rosenthal   0-943518-67-9 $21.95

The Power Of: Lotus 1-2-3 Release 2 for Business Applications

An easy-to-use, keystroke-by-keystroke tutorial hailed for its broad repertoire of useful applications.

Robert Williams   0-943518-64-4 $19.95 (w/disk $34.95)

The Power Of: Lotus 1-2-3 Complete Reference Guide

Places the commands, functions, and macros of Lotus 1-2-3 Release 2 literally at the user's fingertips. A complete guide with alphabetically organized references, fingertip tabs, and emphasized information highlighted in red.

Robert Williams   0-943518-65-2 $19.95

Memory Resident Utilities, Interrupts, and Disk Management with MS and PC DOS

An indispensable resource for serious DOS programmers. Includes chapters on disk data storage, BIOS and DOS interrupts, utility programming, and memory resident utilities. Addresses topics of DOS and multi-tasking, subprograms and overlays, writing pop-ups, and reentrancy, and provides step-by-step exploration of the partition table, boot record, traverse paths, and more.

Michael Hyman   0-943518-73-3   22.95 (w/disk $44.95)

MS DOS Professional Developer's Handbook

The ultimate source for professional MS DOS developers has arrived. Never before has a single volume contained as much valuable information on professional program development in the MS DOS environment. Steven Mikes has developed complete, functional programs that conquer the most sophisticated programming tasks. All programming code is written in C or Assembly Language. All examples are fully explained.

Steven Mikes   0-943518-44-X $23.95 (w/disk $43.95)

dBASE II PLUS Power Tools

A detailed discussion of previously undocumented dBASE III PLUS applications. Outlines integrating data into spreadsheets and documents, accessing mainframe data, installing memory resident utilities, debugging and compiling the program, and expanding dBASE III PLUS into a comprehensive computing system.

Rob Krumm   0-943518-86-0 $21.95

The Power Of: Running PC-DOS 3.3

An essential desktop reference guide for all PC users. Easier to use and understand than the DOS manual, this book's clear organization, concise instructions, and illustrations help users make the most of their computer's operating system. Second Edition. Includes version 3.3.

Carl Siechert and Chris Wood   0-943518-47-4 $22.95

Absolutely Essential Utilities For the IBM PC

Fully documents the features and applications of popular utilities and compares different programs within a given function. Includes discussions of the Norton Utilities, Sidekick, SmartKey, Windows, Sideways, XTree, Lotus 1-2-3, and dBASE III compilers and application generators.

Emily Rosenthal   0-943518-29-6 $19.95

Available where fine books are sold.

MANAGEMENT INFORMATION SOURCE, INC.
P.O. Box 5277 • Portland, OR 97208-5277
(503) 222-2399

*C*all free
1-800-MANUALS

MIS:PRESS

MANAGEMENT INFORMATION SOURCE, INC.